T0247550

The End of Ambition

A Council on Foreign Relations Book
Oxford University Press

The Council on Foreign Relations (CFR) is an independent, nonpartisan membership organization, think tank, and publisher dedicated to being a resource for its members, government officials, business executives, journalists, educators and students, civic and religious leaders, and other interested citizens in order to help them better understand the world and the foreign policy choices facing the United States and other countries. Founded in 1921, CFR carries out its mission by maintaining a diverse membership, with special programs to promote interest and develop expertise in the next generation of foreign policy leaders; convening meetings at its headquarters in New York and in Washington, DC, and other cities where senior government officials, members of Congress, global leaders, and prominent thinkers come together with CFR members to discuss and debate major international issues; supporting a Studies Program that fosters independent research, enabling CFR scholars to produce articles, reports, and books and hold roundtables that analyze foreign policy issues and make concrete policy recommendations; publishing *Foreign Affairs*, the preeminent journal on international affairs and U.S. foreign policy; sponsoring Independent Task Forces that produce reports with both findings and policy prescriptions on the most important foreign policy topics; and providing up-to-date information and analysis about world events and American foreign policy on its website, www.cfr.org.

The Council on Foreign Relations takes no institutional positions on policy issues and has no affiliation with the U.S. government. All views expressed in its publications and on its website are the sole responsibility of the author or authors.

The End of Ambition

America's Past, Present, and Future in the Middle East

STEVEN A. COOK

A Council on Foreign Relations Book

OXFORD
UNIVERSITY PRESS

Oxford University Press is a department of the University of Oxford. It furthers
the University's objective of excellence in research, scholarship, and education
by publishing worldwide. Oxford is a registered trade mark of Oxford University
Press in the UK and certain other countries.

Published in the United States of America by Oxford University Press
198 Madison Avenue, New York, NY 10016, United States of America.

Library of Congress Cataloging-in-Publication Data
Names: Cook, Steven A., author.
Title: The end of ambition : America's past, present, and future in
the Middle East / Steven A. Cook.
Other titles: America's past, present, and future in the Middle East
Description: New York, NY : Oxford University Press, [2024] |
Includes bibliographical references and index.
Identifiers: LCCN 2023046750 | ISBN 9780197578575 (hardback) |
ISBN 9780197578599 (epub) | ISBN 9780197578605 (ebook)
Subjects: LCSH: United States—Foreign relations—Middle East. |
Middle East—Foreign relations—United States.
Classification: LCC DS63.2.U5 C667 2024 | DDC 327.73056—dc23/eng/20240131
LC record available at https://lccn.loc.gov/2023046750

DOI: 10.1093/oso/9780197578575.001.0001

Printed by Sheridan Books, Inc., United States of America

For Madelyn and Mia,
the two bravest young women in the world.

And for Tulip,
whose unbounded love has brought us so much joy.

"Moral exuberance had inspired both overinvolvement and isolationism."

—Henry Kissinger, *White House Years*

Contents

Acknowledgments   ix

1. Original Sins   1
2. Prime Directive   15
3. Unbreakable Bonds   37
4. The Great Transformation   65
5. The Aborted Revolution   88
6. Retrenching and Hedging   104
7. Back to the Future   124

Notes   157
Works Cited   171
Index   187

Acknowledgments

The End of Ambition is my fourth book. As I researched and wrote the previous three, I often felt as if I was reinventing the wheel, which presented unique intellectual and emotional challenges. This book is different. It was written during the COVID-19 pandemic that has killed more than a million Americans and more than six million people worldwide. Against the backdrop of this mind-boggling tragedy was the ongoing political instability in the United States. Given all that was swirling around my family and me during this time, I often found myself reading about advances in epidemiology or the latest threats to America's democratic institutions while I should have been writing.

Yet even with all the distractions, I was continually drawn back to the Middle East intellectually. Oddly, it was a form of solace to throw myself into researching and drafting this book, which asks big questions about the role of the United States in the region after Washington's enormous investment in the Middle East spanning of the late twentieth and early twenty-first centuries. I owe tremendous thanks to Richard Haass, the former president of the Council on Foreign Relations (CFR), for both his encouragement throughout this project and his wisdom about its central themes. Jim Lindsay, the Council's director of studies, was unsparing in his critique of my drafts. I am and will always remain grateful for Jim's sugar-free approach because it has made for a richer and more interesting book. Shannon O'Neil, CFR's deputy director of studies, offered timely and trenchant advice on the manuscript. Unlike Jim, Shannon delivered her comments with a little bit of sweetener. Thank you to the Council's president, Mike Froman, for seeing this project to the end.

Outside of the Council, David McBride from Oxford University Press continues to be a prince and a champion. I am forever grateful for Dave's interest in my work.

I drove three research associates crazy while researching and writing this book. Katharine Poppe and Francesca Eremeeva played critical roles helping it see the light of day. Christina Bouri took over where Francesca left off and added her sophisticated eye and attention to detail to the project as I revised the manuscript. I appreciate their enormous efforts. A talented crew of interns assisted Katherine, Francesca, and Christina, chasing down facts, helping refresh my memory of events, and at times going on wild-goose chases for information that, in the end, I decided I did not need. Many thanks to Sydney Scarlata, Max Lessans, Jordan Rothschild, Olivia Babski, Madelyn Haden, Sam Gang, Tima Dasouki, Julian Milan, Isabella Torre, and Janet Younan.

Since I am not a traditional academic who teaches at a college or university, I do not have any students whose careers I can follow. Instead, I have a wonderful assemblage of former research associates and interns, all of whom I am quite proud of. Of this brilliant group, two have pitched in at various times as I wrote *The End of Ambition*. The extraordinarily talented Alexander Brock, associate editor at the *Virginia Quarterly Review*, read through the entire manuscript several times. The manuscript reads better and has a sharper analytic edge for Alex's efforts. Lindsay Iversen—my very first intern—came back to the Council to help me push the first full draft of this book over the finish line when Francesca accepted a position of a lifetime, but before Christina began her tenure at the Council. Her work on the manuscript was invaluable.

I have a wonderful group of friends and colleagues who have been enormous sources of support throughout the conception, research, and writing of this book. I owe a special debt of gratitude to Brian Katulis, Hussein Ibish, Ken Pollack, Steve Galpern, Jonathan Tepperman, Catherine Herrold, Manjari Chatterjee Miller, and Evan Trager Muney, who have read all or parts of the manuscript. I also would be remiss not to mention Amy Hawthorne, Henri J. Barkey, James Goldgeier, Robert Danin, Howard Eissenstat, Nicholas Danforth, Sinan Ciddi, and Aaron Stein, who at different times have lent their expertise and advice in helping shape this project. My dear friend, Ambassador Yousef Al Otaiba, has been generous with his time, friendship, and insights. The same goes for a long list of colleagues, friends, and officials from a variety of Middle Eastern countries including Egypt, Israel, Iraq, Saudi Arabia, the United Arab Emirates, Qatar, and Bahrain who have been kind enough to share their perspectives with me. I have done everything I can to ensure their anonymity as they requested.

All my colleagues at the David Rockefeller Studies Program are terrific, but I am especially indebted to Martin Indyk, Sebastian Mallaby, Gideon Rose, and Miles Kahler, who offered extraordinarily useful comments on early drafts of Chapter 1. The anonymous reviewers who took time with both the book's proposal and the manuscript were generous with their praise, but, more important, were thorough in their constructive criticism, which undoubtedly made the book better than it would have been without their hard work.

The staff at the CFR's library are simply the best. Christian Kreznar went above and beyond in helping to put the manuscript together. Patricia Dorff, CFR's director of publications, is an unparalleled source of knowledge about everything and anything related to book publishing. She held my hand at various times from first draft to final draft.

Ravi Agrawal, Jennifer Williams, and Cameron Abadi of *Foreign Policy* magazine are wonderful editors and generous people. They not only allowed me explore ideas and themes that show up in this book, but they also made them better.

I owe a lot to Brad Rothschild, a fellow funster and the brother I never had, and he has often helped keep me focused while I was writing. The same goes for Richard Vuernick, who has put up with me and my antics since the spring of 1987. I know I can count on Adam Kaplan at any time of day or night. He will, and he has, come running. Eric Goldstein, Endy Zemenides, Kathy Gilsinan, Felicia Hendrix, Bruce Mendelsohn, Joseph Glicksberg, Michele Commercio, Nancy Lane Kaplan, Wayne Wolf, Alison Fargis, Michele Camardella, Loline Leyva, Michael Weiner, John Crosson, Sue Adams, and James Green, as well as the Segal, Kass, Myers, and Piervencenzi families, played important roles—large and small—in helping make this book possible. My yogi, Melissa Weinrieb Feldman, did her best to keep me centered. Zahraa al-Najjar has not only worked hard to keep my Arabic language skills sharp, but she is also a wealth insight and knowledge about the Middle East and her native Syria.

My mom, Iris Cook, along with my late father, are the sources of all my curiosity about the world. I would not have had the wonderful opportunity to write books without my parents' guidance, devotion, and love. When we were kids, my sister, Julie, used to know exactly what to say to set me off. She now knows how to calm me down, proven by my many calls freaking out about this book. Many thanks to my in-laws, Nancy and Richard Rossman, who have been unfailingly generous over now twenty-five years. Amy, Sam, Emily, and Talia Deich are always a fun distraction. My nephews, Seth and Justin Schuster, are wellsprings of inspiration for me.

I suspect my daughters, Madelyn and Mia, are used to the fact that I am at times not present, even when I am around, because I am driven to distraction by writing. Hopefully, with each book, I have gotten a little better at being a father and an author. Everything I do, I do for my precious children.

And my wife, Lauren . . . there are not enough words, so I will repeat what I have said in previous books: She is my everything.

The usual stipulation applies: despite all the help I received writing *The End of Ambition*, the errors contained within it are mine alone.

1

Original Sins

Bardarash Refugee Camp, December 2019

The emotional pain leveled me. We had set out from Dohuk before sunrise, making a number of stops before arriving at the gates of the Bardarash refugee camp late in the afternoon. The scene inside was right out of a movie: cold, wind-swept rain fell intermittently; ankle-deep mud; and the gaggle of small, curious children that congregated around my colleagues and me. The camp was decommissioned in 2017 only to reopen in the fall of 2019 after Syrian Kurds fled to Iraq seeking safety from Turkish airstrikes. Camp officials informed us that Bardarash had "only" ten thousand inhabitants, but it was hard to make sense of that qualifier. From where I stood—and extending in every direction for what seemed like miles—were rows and rows of white tents emblazoned with "UNHCR"—United Nations High Commissioner for Refugees—in the familiar UN blue.

I had come to Iraq a few days earlier to learn firsthand about the devastating aftershocks of US policy and the people most affected by it. By then, Iraq had become an afterthought for much of the foreign-policy community. In the months since President Trump's 2019 declaration of the "100 percent" defeat of the Islamic State, policymakers, members of Congress, analysts, editors, and journalists mostly had forgotten about Iraqis. The whirlwind of the Trump presidency presented a cascade of other issues, ranging from China and North Korea to Venezuela and Iran, that kept the folks inside the Beltway busy. Plus, the condition of Iraq and its society was not something officials and analysts cared to dwell on. The American invasion in 2003 was, after all, a calamitous mistake for which there had been no reckoning. Assigning accountability was hard because so many were complicit in the folly. Whereas Iraq once made careers in Washington, it had become an issue that was better left to an unpleasant past. Of course, there were some who continued to follow developments in the country, but they were a small handful of analysts and officials. What had once been the biggest news story of the young century now regularly failed to elicit the interest of American newspapers, much less the cable news networks that had long dispensed with any pretense of actual journalism in favor of punditry.

The willful and collective effort to move on could not obscure the fact that Iraq in late 2019 seemed to be in a state of impending collapse. There was government dysfunction at the national level, mass protests in the streets, provincial governments with few resources, a caretaker prime minister, a corrupt and venal ruling class, and nonexistent social services. Governors and small-town volunteer mayors spoke derisively of officials in Baghdad and Erbil—the capital of Iraq's Kurdish region—who left them to manage every imaginable problem with meager, if any, resources. As a result, millions of Iraqis fended for themselves.

At times, the only evidence of the Iraqi state's existence was the ubiquitous presence of security forces, but even that was misleading. To the uninitiated, the personnel manning checkpoints all appeared to be on the same team, but upon closer inspection, they were not. The military stood guard at some, military police at others; what are called Popular Mobilization Units had their own, as did Kurdish forces known as *peshmerga*. At some locations, checkpoints were combined, but in others they were not. In Baghdad, there were two different security stations within sight of each other that required "papers" before entering the Green Zone. It was not at all clear to me whom the well-armed men at each of these checkpoints represented.

Many Iraqis remained unbowed and even defiant of their circumstances after decades suffering under Saddam Hussein's cruelty, war with Iran (1980–1988), war with the United States and an international coalition (1991), international sanctions, the American invasion (2003), the American occupation, and extremist violence. It was also Iraq's misfortune that calamities in other parts of the region added to its tribulations. In one tent at the refugee camp, a man in his late twenties told the story of his family's perilous flight from the predominantly Kurdish region of Syria's northeast. In one of those odd twists, complications, and contradictions in American foreign policy in the Middle East, the United States supported a fighting force against the Islamic State that Washington's NATO ally Turkey called a terrorist organization. The People's Protection Units (known by the Turkish acronym YPG) formed the core of the Syrian Democratic Forces, which worked closely with American special forces to "degrade and defeat" the caliphate that Abu Bakr al-Baghdadi had declared in the summer of 2014. The YPG was also directly linked to a Turkish Kurdish militant group that had been waging an on-again, off-again war on Turkey since 1984. Not surprisingly, Turks took great offense to the American military relationship with the YPG, which they believed would lead to the emergence of a Kurdish state in the region that would pose a threat to Turkey. So, the Turkish government marshaled its own Syrian allies and its fearsome airpower against the YPG and, as is always the case, civilians were caught in the crossfire.

The young man I met in his tent had managed to outrun Turkish attacks with his wife, small children, mother, his two siblings—both of whom had mental and physical challenges—and an elderly neighbor in tow. After bribing his way across the Syrian-Iraqi frontier, he led his desperate charges to Bardarash. Now that they'd arrived, they were stuck. As the head of his "household," he made of his situation what he could. Through Iraqi locals, he was able to secure a supply of candy, packaged cookies, chewing gum, soda, and potato chips—ironically, most of it made in Turkey—that he in turn sold to other camp inhabitants. He spoke hopefully about earning back the money he had spent getting across the border and maybe transferring his family to a camp near Erbil, where there was a cousin and access to medication his sister needed. Bardarash was officially a "temporary camp," and thousands of people had cycled through it, but given the vagaries of Iraq's bureaucracy and the extensive security screening required to leave, none of the people who sought refuge there knew when they would be able to move on.

The afternoon was a gut-wrenching moment during a tour that revealed, layer by layer, the compounding tragedies of the previous decades. As I stood among the sea of UNHCR tents in the cold rain, a pang of responsibility welled up in me over the collective foolishness of American foreign policy during the preceding decades. I did a quick survey as my Land Cruiser pulled out of Bardarash's front gate. My Syrian interlocutor had been forced to flee to a country that the United States had torn asunder because officials in Washington believed that US power could be harnessed to remake a society into a democracy and thus ensure America's security. Of course, it did not turn out as hoped. Saddam Hussein's Iraq was murderous and tyrannical, but liberated Iraq was violent and chaotic.

The Syrians at Bardarash had sought safety in Iraq because of Turkish airstrikes, but that was only part of Syria's problems. That country had become one of the world's worst humanitarian disasters. It became that way over the previous decade because Syria's leader, Bashar al-Assad, responded to a peaceful uprising against his rule by pulverizing cities and towns in an escalating spiral of blood. As he did, Assad justified his indiscriminate violence as a war against terrorists in a cynical and deliberate link to America's Global War on Terror and its "either with us or against us" ethos.

Despite the death and destruction that Assad visited on his fellow Syrians, the United States did not act. To officials in the Obama administration, there were no discernible American interests that could be served by an intervention in the Syrian uprising, though others outside of government argued otherwise.[1]

President Obama's aversion to military action was directly related to Washington's searing failures in Iraq. No matter how different the circumstances and no matter how many deaths could have been prevented or how the Middle East and Europe could have been spared instability, it became paramount in Washington to avoid "another Iraq." The question of intervention in Syria was an issue that few in Washington had even bothered to consider, anyway. In the early days of the uprising, American officials believed that Assad would fall quickly, as authoritarian leaders had in Tunisia and Egypt. And once the Syrian dictator was gone, Americans could roll up their sleeves and help make the country democratic.

As I encountered one tragedy after another while crisscrossing Iraq in late 2019, it became clearer to me that many of the ideas and assumptions that functioned as pillars of US–Middle East policy over the preceding three decades were little more than ambition-fueled delusions. It was disconcerting. It was also a puzzle: how was it that American foreign policy had arrived at the intersection of fantasy and failure in the Middle East, especially after previous years of success in the region? And now, in the wake of the stark reality of those failed efforts—not just in Iraq—how should the United States approach the Middle East? There was a strong pull within the American foreign-policy community for some form of withdrawal, which was understandable after so little return on America's investment in the Middle East, but what did that mean for America's interests in the region?

These questions frame the central concerns of this book, which advances three basic arguments. First, the United States successfully secured its interests in the Middle East throughout the Cold War. Those interests were preventing the disruption of oil exports from the region, helping to forestall threats to Israeli security, and, during the Cold War, containing the Soviet Union. To some analysts and observers, this distillation may read as exceedingly narrow. It is, but it is not arbitrarily so. By tracing the arc of America's encounters with the Middle East in the second half of the twentieth century, it is clear that US presidents, members of Congress, and mainstream analysts made these goals America's primary concerns in the region. That US policy succeeded is not a subjective judgment, but rather a conclusion based on a comparison of what policymakers sought to do in the Middle East and what they achieved. American diplomatic, economic, and military power prevented disruption to the flow of oil, helped Israel stave off threats to its security, and, for as long as it existed, prevented the Soviet Union from trying to dominate the region. There were setbacks and significant—mostly moral—costs, but from the perspective of America's elected leaders, officials, foreign-policy analysts, and other elites, the price was worth paying.

Second, beginning with the Clinton administration, American officials and the foreign-policy community sought to transform politics and society in the Middle East, which led to policy failures. The primary insight to be gleaned from these two track records is that when the United States sought to prevent "bad things" from happening to its interests, it succeeded. However, when Washington sought to leverage its power to make "good things" happen in the service of its interests, it often failed.[2]

Finally, although America's transformative agenda for the Middle East failed, withdrawal or retrenchment from the region is too radical a solution for the dilemmas Washington confronts in the Middle East. Indeed, to pivot away from the region would be self-defeating for the United States. That is because the Middle East remains important to the United States. This was a view that was decidedly out of step with the prevailing Washington zeitgeist of the late 2010s and early 2020s. Yet rather than "de-emphasize" the region, as US Secretary of State Antony Blinken once promised, the challenge for policymakers is to develop a set of achievable goals in a part of the world that will remain critical in global politics and thus to the United States. Beyond the primary issues around which US policy has long revolved, the region is—at the risk of cliché—at a crossroads. From an American gaze, the Middle East is truly the middle, connecting as it does core US global interests in the stability of Europe, the extraction and transport of energy resources (for now), with opportunities in Asia. It is also a region comprising countries that are most vulnerable to the climate crisis, where extremism persists, and the danger of nuclear proliferation remains.

The Middle East will also likely play a role in the development of a new global order precisely because the great powers continue to be interested in the region. This may sound exploitative, but it is important to recognize that actors in the region have agency, too. For all of the region's myriad challenges, governments in the Middle East are determined to shape their own neighborhood rather than watch the Americans, Russians, Europeans, and Chinese do it for them. Washington must partner with countries that—for better or worse—will play critical roles in international security, the global economy, and world culture. Few within the foreign-policy community seem to realize it, but countries in the region—Saudi Arabia and Iran, to name two notable examples—have the ability to affect US interests. Consequently, it behooves Americans to jettison both the transformative policies of the recent past as well as the desire, in response to the failures of the recent past, to withdraw from the Middle East. It is time not for retrenchment, which analysts often use synonymously with withdrawal, but rather a renewal of America's purpose in the Middle East. The United States must have a vision for its role in the Middle East that dispenses with idealist romance about remaking the world in favor of a strategy based on prudence, discretion, and a balance of resources.

The Way the World Is

This book approaches the Middle East and the American encounter with it from the realist-tinged perspective that the United States has a better chance of foreign-policy success when policymakers view "world politics as they *really* are, rather than describe how they *ought to be* [italics in original]."[3] It is not intended to be an exposition on realism, which is a school of thought that explains international politics in terms of state power, the quest for security, and the inescapable competition among states in an "anarchic" international system, however.[4] Instead this study borrows and benefits from insights that realism provides, with the explicit understanding that it is not a theory of foreign policy and as a result cannot accommodate the complex interplay between geopolitics, competing ideological worldviews, domestic politics, and economic concerns that are factors in the development of America's approach to the world. Still, viewing the world as it is provides analytic traction for understanding the successes and failures of US–Middle East policy past and present as well as the lessons they provide for the future.

This realist outlook stands as a dispassionate—and even dark—alternative to the ideas that animate much of Washington about good versus evil in foreign policy, the universality of liberal values, and the responsibility of the United States not only to protect its own democracy, but also to spread democratic ideals around the world. In the Middle East, however, when policymakers understood the limits of what the United States could achieve despite its great power and used that power in the service of limited goals, they succeeded. No doubt there is something tragic about this approach to the world. It means conceding that Washington can do little to compel its often-problematic partners to improve their human right records, pursue political reform, and embark on more-inclusive economic policies.

Not the Way It Ought to Be

The idealist impulse to do good in the world is laudable, of course, but America was both ill-equipped and misguided in its transformational project for the Middle East. Not only did Washington have few, if any, policy tools to realize its vision for the region, but also US officials confronted an entirely predictable conflict between US interests and American values, which always favored the former at the expense of the latter. Although affirmations of values are a regular feature of the rhetoric of American foreign policy, fidelity to them was always difficult. Consider briefly President Joe Biden's approach to Saudi Arabia. Much to his credit, he sought to maintain consistency between American values and his foreign policy, but he abandoned his principled position on Riyadh's human rights record and sought help from the Saudis when oil supplies grew tight—and gasoline prices spiked—in response to the twin shocks of America's post-COVID-19 travel frenzy and Russia's invasion of Ukraine.

Another set of problems that undermined Washington's transformational vision for the Middle East were the political and sociocultural conditions of the region. This is not to suggest that Arabs, in particular, were "not ready" for democracy, as Middle Eastern elites often argue, but rather that the kings, presidents, crown princes, and generals of the region were hardly willing to reform themselves out of power through the changes that Washington was advocating. At the same time, there were talented and courageous activists throughout the region who sought democratic change, but they had few resources and relatively modest followings. Leaders in the area did much to undermine American efforts to boost the effectiveness of pro-democracy groups. As the story of the 2011–2012 uprisings across the Middle East indicates, even when mass protests could topple several Arab leaders, democracy advocates were no match for the defenders of Middle Eastern regimes who had resources to beat back political change.[5] And in response to US efforts, regional leaders and political entrepreneurs alike played easily on cultural norms and historical precedent to portray America's ambitions for the Middle East as yet another in a line of colonial efforts to reshape their societies. In making the charge of "neocolonialism," Islamists, nationalists of all stripes, secularists, and even liberals were not entirely wrong.

Underlying America's transformative vision for the Middle East was a set of faulty assumptions that few bothered to question. These included the notions that democracy could flourish without democrats; that culture and identity do not matter; that all people everywhere want the same things; that peace would produce democracy and its obverse, that reform will produce peace; and, importantly, that the United States had the power and its officials possessed the insight and wisdom to overcome the inevitable obstacles to regional transformation. These assumptions were appealing to American officials and analysts, but they obscured the hard realities of the Middle East that contributed to the failure of Washington's effort to redeem the region.

It has become conventional wisdom that America's sins in the Middle East began in the post-9/11 era, but that is not accurate. Bill Clinton entered the White House on the optimistic notes of Fleetwood Mac's "Don't Stop Thinking about Tomorrow," the American economy hummed, and the United States straddled the globe with no peer competitor. Russia was weak as it struggled with political and economic crises of the immediate post-Soviet era, and China had barely begun its meteoric rise. It was at that moment, when Washington had a surfeit of power, that the seeds of American ambition in the Middle East were sown. The region that seemed most in need of American help was the Middle East because it seemed to defy global trends toward more just, open, and prosperous societies. The view among American officials at the time was that resolving the conflict between Israelis and Palestinians would catalyze political and economic reform in the Middle East.[6]

Everyone knew—or supposedly they did—what peace would look like, but getting there was the challenge. Americans were there to bridge that gap. It meant finding ways to divide land that each side claimed as its own and, in the process, disentangle knotty and poorly understood concepts such as nationalism, historical memory, identity, and dignity in a way that set aside a century of mutual recrimination, mistrust, and at times great violence. In addition, US officials had to accomplish this all within the context of the complex interplay among American, Israeli, and Palestinian politics. Against all odds, policymakers believed they could make peace and, with conflict between Israelis and Palestinians finally resolved, democratic political change would blow through the entire Middle East because the national-security states of the region would have no reason to exist. This sequencing was elegant and made a certain amount of sense given how Arab leaders framed these issues. Yet the approach misapprehended the nature of politics in the region and the roles Israel and Palestine played in the authoritarian systems of the Middle East. Whether the conflict between Israelis and Palestinians was resolved or not, it was likely to have little bearing on the authoritarian politics that was the norm among countries in the region. Of course, it did not matter in the end. For all the effort put into forging peace between Israelis and Palestinians, it came to naught with the eruption of an uprising—the second intifada—in late 2000 that engulfed the West Bank, Gaza Strip, and Israel in violence.

Then, in the aftermath of the 9/11 attacks, which seemed to demand a whole new approach to the Middle East, the United States embarked on another ambitious effort to transform the region. The goal was to promote democratic change directly in the Middle East, which, it was believed, would mitigate terrorism and bring reconciliation to a part of the globe that had experienced too much conflict. The American endorsement of a Palestinian state and the invasion of Iraq—especially after US forces discovered that Saddam Hussein did not possess weapons of mass destruction—were central to this endeavor, yet democratic change never happened in the Middle East as a result. And the one place where it did emerge, Tunisia, subsequently slid back into authoritarianism.

By the mid-2000s, as Iraq burned and regime change became discredited, American foreign-policy thinkers and officials began debating the idea of "engaging" Iran, which had extended and reinforced its already considerable influence in the region after the United States toppled Saddam. Supporters reasoned that the United States and Iran were such critical actors in the Middle East that hostility was no longer tenable. The ample anecdotes from journalists and occasional visitors to Tehran that large segments of Iran's population were eager for better relations with the West, especially the United States, heightened the expectations for engagement. Yet Iran's nuclear-development program, which posed a threat to Israel and other American partners in the region, remained an obstacle to improved ties. The answer was a 2015 agreement that included Russia, China, France, the United Kingdom, Germany, the United States, and Iran called the Joint Comprehensive Plan of Action (JCPOA), which sought to arrest Iran's nuclear activities for about a decade. Implicit in the agreement was President Barack Obama's belief—or perhaps more accurately, his hope—that when the clauses restricting Tehran's program expired a decade later, Iran's leaders would determine that the gains of engagement outweighed those of resuming their nuclear program.[7] This, then, would fundamentally transform regional dynamics, paving the way for a period of Iran's economic, diplomatic, and security cooperation with its neighbors. Yet the Iranians did not see things quite the same way. After Iran's foreign minister signed the agreement, Tehran continued its destabilizing activity around the region. And two years later, President Donald Trump walked away from the JCPOA. He did so primarily for domestic political reasons, but his administration cited Iran's provocations and accused Tehran of hiding ongoing nuclear research—including weapons development—from international inspectors. It was hard to know whom to believe: the people who had a vested interest in preserving the agreement or those motivated to undermine it. Regardless, the transformational ambitions of the United States were thwarted both because of an American overestimation of Washington's power to make it happen and because the JCPOA was too great a load for America's polarized politics to bear.

When President Trump left office, the number of problems roiling the Middle East was unprecedented. Iraq lurched from crisis to crisis. The much-ballyhooed Freedom Agenda of 2003 and the effort to support demands for democratic change that emerged from the 2011 Arab uprisings came to naught, as state failure and resurgent authoritarianism became the dominant features of the region's politics. Palestinian statehood remained beyond the Palestinians' grasp, perhaps permanently. Extremism continued to metastasize.

Whatever the intention of Americans, the decades between the end of the Cold War and President Joe Biden's inauguration in 2021 demonstrated simultaneously the awesome nature of American power and its significant limits.[8] Of course, not all of the failures of the Middle East could be attributed to the United States, yet America's record was nevertheless grim. Washington's lack of success from one administration to the next was rooted in the foreign-policy community's overestimation of what the United States could accomplish in the region.

This era of US policy—bookended by the end of the Cold War and arguably the US withdrawal from Afghanistan (a non–Middle Eastern country)—marked by costly and unrealistic efforts to harness American power to transform the Middle East, stands in stark contrast to the one that preceded it. Until the mid-1990s, American officials sought to prevent challenges to those objectives that were deemed in the national interest—the free flow of oil from the region, helping to ensure Israel's survival, and during the Cold War, challenges to regional stability from the Soviet Union. An argument can be made that this was an ambition in and of itself, but the difference is that, unlike the transformative approach to the region that began with Iraq's defeat in 1991 and the Soviet collapse ten months later, the preventive policies of the past were achievable given the capabilities of Washington and of its adversaries, along with the politics of US–Middle East policy at the time.

What Follows

Answering questions about where the Middle East is headed and what the United States should do in the region is more difficult than it might seem. It is not for lack of trying. The failures that have piled up in the Middle East over the course of thirty years forced a certain amount of soul-searching among many within the American foreign-policy community. Analysts and officials, some of whom had been enthusiastic about the use of American power to change the world, now thought better of it. Journal articles, opinion pieces, editorials, blog posts, and podcasts began exploring ideas like retrenchment, reduction, and withdrawal from the Middle East. As terms of art, each of these ideas has a particular meaning, but they all were nevertheless employed in a way to convey the idea that the United States must reduce its military presence and pare back its ambitions in the region. In time, "ending forever wars"—a phrase that presidents Trump and Biden embraced—became the terms of debate about US policy in the Middle East.[9]

Experts were justifiably concerned that America's encounters with the Middle East had drained US resources, eroded its influence, undermined its prestige, and distorted its politics. Yet, taken to their logical conclusions, the various forms of withdrawal that analysts and policymakers proposed were both flawed and unlikely to resolve America's predicament in the Middle East. Some of this work started backward from the unhappy place Washington found itself in the region after years of failing to achieve its transformative goals there. Implicit in the idea of withdrawal was the view that the United States was the problem in the Middle East. Of course, Washington had done its fair share of damage in the Middle East, but America's failures had come mostly after the end of the Cold War when the foreign-policy community advocated for and implemented an effort to remake the Middle East. As a result, commentators lost sight of America's record of achievement in the region and the lessons it provides.

The six chapters that follow explore the arguments and themes outlined above. They begin with a pair of chapters that examine the origins of America's core national interests in the free flow of oil, Israel's security, and ensuring that no other power or group of powers could do harm to either goal. The underlying rationale for chapters 2 and 3 is straightforward: in addition to advancing and supporting the claim that Washington was effective in ensuring its regional interests when it pursued policies that placed a premium on prevention, it is important for readers to understand how these objectives came to be national interests in the first place.

Of course, America's accomplishments did not come without costs. Accordingly, both chapters discuss the price the United States has paid for its willingness to invest in energy security from the Persian Gulf and Israel's well-being. These chapters are overviews aimed at providing readers with historical context for the arguments made throughout this book. They are not intended to be comprehensive histories of the region or of America's role in the Middle East. Many works of history already address these issues in fine detail.[10] It is important to note that I made the editorial decision not to include a chapter specifically on the Cold War in the Middle East for several reasons. The major events and stories of that era are told in the chapters on oil and Israel. And, beyond my concern about being repetitive, it struck me that retelling, even in a succinct way, the complex story of how the global competition between the United States and Soviet Union played out in the Middle East would overwhelm the overall analysis presented here and thus detract from it.

The fourth chapter explicates how the combination of America's successes in the Middle East and the collapse of the Soviet Union in 1991 drove Washington's subsequent failures in the region. Forging a Palestinian state, remaking Iraqi society, and promoting democracy in the Arab world were the results of a toxic brew of America's unbounded power and faulty assumptions about the Middle East that produced an ambitious effort to transform the region. These stories are well known but are often viewed individually or through a partisan lens. The chapter makes it clear that each of these efforts was part of a broader pattern of both Democratic and Republican administrations that led to a series of failures. The fifth chapter highlights the unsuccessful efforts on the part of presidents Barack Obama and Donald Trump to rectify this unfortunate situation. In their desire to retrench, one president sought to refashion the region's politics and geopolitical dynamics through an arms control agreement with Iran; the other lacked a coherent strategy to undertake the withdrawal he had promised.

The sixth chapter evaluates the ideas for future US–Middle East policy that analysts, policymakers, and commentators have proposed while explaining how America's partners have responded to debates about retrenchment and withdrawal from the region. The final chapter provides a reckoning or accounting of the two eras of American foreign policy explained in the preceding chapters, highlighting the successes of an approach steeped in an understanding of the Middle East as it actually exists, the limits of US power, and the disastrous consequences of Washington's attempt to transform the region for its people and Americans as well as the power and prestige of the United States. The chapter also outlines how a policy based on preventing "bad things" from happening to US interests can be constructive for the Middle East, rebuild and refashion Washington's relationships in the region for a new era of global politics, and free up American resources for new challenges in other parts of the globe.

There is an opportunity for Washington to shift away from the transformative and destructive policies of the past in favor of a more modest, pragmatic approach that will render the United States successful in the region once again. No doubt, US policy will often lack elegance and there will be setbacks provoking fierce criticism among Americans and Middle Easterners alike, but the costs of policies based on the world as it exists are likely to be far less than the bill for Washington's past ambitious effort to transform the region.

I often think of my afternoon at the Bardarash refugee camp in 2019. It is uncomfortable but serves as a reminder that, as awesome as US power is and as high-minded as America's ideals may be, the combination of the two can wreak havoc on the world. This book is a response to that reality. My purpose—my hope—is that the ideas, proposals, and prescriptions I set out will help Americans think more cogently about the Middle East and the stakes for the United States in that region. The collective desire to de-emphasize the Middle East is understandable, but like retrenchment, this idea has become shorthand for withdrawal. The goal should not be to de-emphasize the Middle East in US foreign policy, but rather to approach the region with both a clearer understanding of what matters to the United States and how best to achieve those goals. Of course, Americans should want to avoid the calamities of the post–Cold War era that came together for me in a cold rain among people with no place to go, but there is a better way forward than leaving. It is hard to imagine, given the frustrations, lives lost, and those lives forever changed, but Americans can be constructive in the Middle East if they can avoid the temptation to want to make the world as they believe it ought to be.

2

Prime Directive

On a seasonably chilly and cloudy Sunday in late January 1991, seventy-five thousand people traveled to Washington, DC, to bring their concerns about American foreign policy to President George H. W. Bush's doorstep. As they marched past the north lawn of the White House, they held placards and banners aloft that declared, "Minnesota for People Not War," "Vermont Says No to War," and "Stop War . . . Bring Our Troops Home Now." Some demonstrators also chanted "No blood for oil!"[1]

Similar scenes played out in cities around the country. The United States had been engaged in military operations to push Iraq's army out of Kuwait for ten days.

A little more than a decade later, far larger crowds descended on the nation's capital and some six hundred other cities around the world to denounce what would become Operation Iraqi Freedom. The day featured addresses from the likes of singer, actor, and racial-justice advocate Harry Belafonte, the renowned actor and antiwar activist Susan Sarandon, the director and champion of liberal causes Rob Reiner, the singer Jackson Browne, the famed British playwright Harold Pinter, three members of the German government, and global voices of conscience such as South African Bishop and Nobel Peace Prize winner Desmond Tutu.[2] In New York City, organizers claimed 375,000 protesters took to the streets.[3]

There were many themes that pervaded the antiwar demonstrations in 1991 and 2003, but the idea that the United States was undertaking military operations in the Middle East for the sake of oil was visceral for protesters. While both Bush administrations denied the claim, and indeed, oil may not have been top of mind for each president, the charge was not baseless either. After all, the effort to exploit and maintain access to oil reserves around the globe had been a goal of both American private enterprise and the US government for the better part of the preceding century.

Because the United States has sustained a significant military presence in the Middle East for decades, Americans could be forgiven for believing that this had always been the case. Rather, America's entanglement in the region developed over eight decades, and Washington only took on the role of primary guarantor of the region's energy resources in the 1970s. This chapter tells that story, underlining both how successful the United States was at preventing disruptions to the flow of energy resources from the Middle East and the costs associated with pursuing this core national interest.

Origin Stories

American dependence on oil dates back to the mid-1850s, when a New York lawyer named George Bissell intuited that "rock oil" could be processed into kerosene and used as an illuminant.[4] The widespread adoption of kerosene in ensuing years led to an expansion of the American economy and innovations in the exploration and exploitation of oil. Yet it was not until the years leading to World War I that oil became a strategic commodity. That is because the Great War was a hinge conflict. When it started, it was closer to the warfare of the previous century, dependent on cavalry and open fields of battle. By the time the guns fell silent in November 1918, the mechanized, combined-arms militaries of the twentieth century had come into view.

During the war, the British military began converting its naval fuel from coal to petroleum. The United States followed soon thereafter, leading to an ever-increasing demand for the black, viscous goo.[5] Other changes also increased demand. At the start of World War I, airplanes were used primarily for reconnaissance purposes, but as the conflict progressed, both Allied and Axis powers engaged in air-to-air combat, close-ground support, and strategic bombing. Meanwhile, in September 1916, the British deployed the first tank at the Battle of the Somme. Though the tank was an underwhelming early performer, given its modest speed and propensity for breakdowns, its effectiveness improved rapidly throughout the rest of the war. German submarines—the infamous *Unterseeboot*, or U-boat—hunted merchant ships supplying the Entente powers and sought to break a British blockade that prevented war materiel, including fuel, from reaching the Axis countries. And when the opportunity presented itself in August 1916, Germany attacked Romania and seized the country's oil fields, the largest producers of the increasingly important commodity in Europe. The lesson was clear: World War I portended a future in which the world's oil reserves would receive the sustained attention of global powers.

During the conflict, the United States satisfied 80 percent of the Allies' petroleum needs. Yet, despite the bountiful supply of America's oil fields and the reserves that US companies controlled elsewhere in the Western Hemisphere, officials in Washington fretted—not for the last time—that the country would soon run out of petroleum.[6] As a result, both policymakers and oil executives began the search for new reserves around the world, especially in the Middle East.[7]

Redrawing the Map

Jockeying for the world's oil resources began immediately after World War I. Discussions among the victorious powers in San Remo in 1920 addressed, among other things, how to dispose of the territories and other assets of the losing side, including their oil fields. The British and French signed an agreement that granted themselves preferential access to major fields in former Ottoman territories in the Middle East.[8] This led American oil executives and diplomats alike to worry that the Anglo-French deal would be just the first by European countries to freeze the United States out of the effort to secure stable and consistent supplies of petroleum. In response, the US Congress passed the Mineral Leasing Act of 1920, which denied drilling rights domestically on public lands to any foreign government that denied such access to Americans. It was mostly a symbolic gesture since neither the British nor French sought to prospect for oil in the United States.

As important as oil was to their respective economic and strategic futures, Britain, France, and the United States did not wish to threaten their relationships over the issue. Under President Calvin Coolidge, Washington struck a deal with London and Paris to ensure access to the Middle East for a group of American companies through what is called the Red Line Agreement (1928).[9] This accord gave a consortium of major oil companies the right to operate anywhere in the region between the Suez Canal and Iran (not including Kuwait) under the banner of the Iraq Petroleum Corporation. There was an important proviso, however: all participating companies had to agree before any single firm or group of member firms could develop oil fields within the territory covered in the agreement.[10] This was clearly meant to prevent any company or country from gaining an advantage in the exploitation of the Middle East's oil fields. Yet negotiators failed to include a mechanism to keep nonmember companies out of the area.

That flaw in the Red Line Agreement allowed the Standard Oil Company of California to secure an oil concession in the Persian Gulf emirate Bahrain in 1930. And in 1933 the same company obtained prospecting rights in the eastern reaches of the newly established Kingdom of Saudi Arabia under a subsidiary called California Arabian Standard Oil Company.[11] It was the concession in Saudi territory, more than any other commercial agreement in the region, that would have the most far-reaching effects for the United States in the Middle East. Within five years, and with a second global conflagration on the horizon, a well in Saudi Arabia called "Dammam-7" began to gush oil, confirming the viability of Saudi reserves.

Even as World War II was being waged, the belligerents knew it would re-shape the world for generations. That was no less true in oil than for global politics. American oil companies, producing both domestically and from US-controlled oil fields in Latin America, supplied the bulk of the fuel that defeated Nazi Germany and imperial Japan, but both sides in World War II understood the long-term strategic importance of Middle Eastern oil. Reflecting on the issue in his memoirs, Cordell Hull, who served as Franklin D. Roosevelt's secretary of state from 1933 to 1944, proclaimed "the Near East, in which our government has evinced only a slight interest for a century and a half, became through demand of WWII[,] a vital area in the conduct of our foreign relations."[12] He went on to say that countries of the Middle East had become "cogs in the machine of war," principally because of the vast amount of oil that was soon to come online from the region.[13]

Hot War, Cold Peace

One of the most important cogs was Saudi Arabia. In 1945, not long after President Roosevelt met King Abdulaziz bin Abdulrahman Al Saud (aka Ibn Saud) aboard an American naval vessel in the Suez Canal during which they discussed the Palestine problem, the United States began constructing an airbase on Saudi Arabia's eastern coast in what was then a frontier town called Dhahran. The State Department justified the project, which began too late to be useful during World War II, as a means to protect Saudi Arabia, its oil fields, and the interests of American companies prospecting there.[14] This would prove to be prescient.

Just three years after the Dhahran airfield project got underway, the Arabian American Oil Company (Aramco), the successor of California

Arabian Standard Oil Company, struck oil at Ghawar, which turned out to be the world's largest oil field. The effects of this discovery were profound: in the second half of the 1940s, Saudi Arabia's gross output of oil increased from 21,000 to 548,000 barrels per day.[15] Although only a small percentage of US petroleum imports came from Saudi reserves, the United States was nonetheless a major beneficiary of the region's oil boom. By 1960, five of the seven top oil companies in the Gulf were American.

Unlike the United States, Western Europe relied almost exclusively on Middle Eastern oil. Much of the petroleum imported to Europe for the Marshall Plan came from the region.[16] Indeed, Europe's postwar economic development and expansion depended almost entirely on access to inexpensive oil from the Persian Gulf. Making sure oil flowed to allies in Europe and Asia, therefore, was a major preoccupation of American policymakers as the confrontation with the Soviet Union deepened. If the oil was diverted and capitalism failed, Europe would become even more vulnerable to the appeal of communism.

At the time, the American strategy did not include a large military presence in and around the Middle East because the British remained the primary external power in the region. Still, the United States sought to collect allies that policymakers in Washington hoped would become regional bulwarks against the Soviets. These included Egypt, Saudi Arabia, and one of the Persian Gulf's other preeminent oil producers, Iran.

Like many of America's relationships in the Middle East, its ties with Iran were a legacy of the British presence in the region. When oil was discovered just outside an Iranian town called Masjed Soleyman in 1909, a British company partnered with the Iranian government to create the Anglo-Persian Oil Company. Later renamed the Anglo-Iranian Oil Company (AIOC), the firm began production in 1913 under inequitable royalty terms. Iranians garnered only 16 percent of the net profit from the sale of their oil, a grossly lopsided arrangement that generated political discontent among Iranians and mistrust between British leaders and Iran's ruler, Reza Shah Pahlavi. Oil was not the only sticking point in the relationship, however. Britain also suspected that Iran's leader harbored Nazi sympathies. As a result, in 1941, as the Germans made advances in the Middle East, the Russians and British forced the Iranian leader from power in favor of his son Mohamed Reza Pahlavi.[17] Decision makers in London and Moscow hoped that Iran's new head of state would be friendlier to the Allied powers than was his father.[18]

The royalty agreement reared its head again in the early 1950s with far greater consequences for the United States, Iran, and the American role in the Middle East.[19] In April 1951, the Iranian parliament elected a European-trained academic and lawyer named Mohammed Mossadegh to be prime minister. Within a month of taking office, Mossadegh announced the nationalization of the AIOC and the withdrawal of all of its British employees.

The standard history of the subsequent events contends that the CIA feared a leftward drift in a country of vast oil reserves and growing strategic importance to the West. So, along with Britain's foreign intelligence service, MI6, it engineered a coup d'état that toppled Mossadegh and brought the young shah back to the country after a brief period of self-exile. There is much truth to this narrative: officials in Washington and London were concerned about Moscow's influence in the country. Iran's nationalization of the AIOC, which precipitated a significant disruption of Iran's oil exports and took a toll on the Iranian economy, helped to sow these perceptions.[20] It is also true that American and British intelligence agencies were involved in the coup. But Mossadegh's overthrow was more complicated than most journalists, academics, and Iranians have long suggested. The CIA and MI6 did not so much manufacture opposition to Mossadegh as they did leverage existing hostility toward him from important sectors of Iranian society, including the military, the clerical establishment, parliamentarians, and the prime minister's fellow elites.[21] Mossadegh's ouster would not have been possible had the Iranian political environment not been conducive to it.

Still smarting from the decades-long controversy concerning AIOC's royalty agreement, however, Iran did not welcome the British back to Iran even after Mossadegh was toppled. As a result, Washington stepped in as the West's primary representative in Tehran. American officials proposed inviting US petroleum companies to Iran to develop the country's oil reserves, which they believed would spur widespread economic development and thus give Iranians a stake in the shah's rule.[22] Yet, for a variety of technical, commercial, and legal reasons, American oil companies were not enthusiastic about this suggestion.[23] Nevertheless, at the behest of the US government, a consortium of the "five majors"—Standard Oil of New Jersey, Mobil, Texaco, Gulf, and Standard Oil of California—entered the Iranian market in the 1950s, helping bring Iranian oil back online. Those companies and smaller independent firms would in time become fixtures of Iran's petroleum industry.

Throughout the 1950s and 1960s, the United States relied primarily on commercial and diplomatic tools to ensure the free flow of oil from the region. Although geopolitical competition with the Soviet Union was a major concern, the American military commitment to the Persian Gulf remained modest. From the late 1940s until the 1970s, the US presence in the Gulf amounted to a three-ship flotilla showing the flag from what was a rented corner of a British naval port in Bahrain.[24]

Turning Points

In January 1968, British prime minister Harold Wilson announced that the United Kingdom would begin withdrawing all its military forces from the Persian Gulf. Exhausted and financially strapped, the British could no longer afford to protect the remnants of their once mighty, globe-spanning empire. Wilson's decision caused consternation in Washington. The United States had long supported Great Britain's forward position east of the Suez Canal diplomatically, politically, and materially. American officials relied on the British to guarantee the free flow of oil and prevent Moscow from expanding its influence in the region. Given the long-standing Soviet interest in establishing warm-water ports, Washington feared a British withdrawal might invite Soviet military activity in the area, giving Moscow the capacity to threaten the security of the sea lanes. This would jeopardize both the safe export of the oil that fueled capitalist economies and American commercial interests in countries like Saudi Arabia and Iran. Washington was so alarmed by the British intent to withdraw that just before Wilson made his government's decision public, Secretary of State Dean Rusk, Ambassador-at-Large Averell Harriman, and President Lyndon Johnson himself all sought to talk the British leader out of it.[25] They failed.

American policymakers were afraid that a fundamental geopolitical shift was underway. Britain's military withdrawal came on the heels of the 1967 establishment of the Soviet-influenced Democratic Republic of Yemen, close to the Mandeb Strait at the southern stretch of the Red Sea and the gateway to the Suez Canal. American anxiety intensified when, not long after Wilson's announcement, a small Soviet naval force entered the Indian Ocean. Without the British standing watch, Moscow would be well positioned to establish its own presence on the Arabian Peninsula and in the Persian Gulf, threatening what had been a long period of Western domination of the region.[26]

By the time British military forces completed their withdrawal in 1971, the Pentagon was able to place an aircraft carrier task force on rotation in the

Indian Ocean to augment the "presence operations" that the United States had long maintained in the Gulf with three aging naval vessels. Beyond that, the US military maintained "limited-access agreements" that permitted the use of port facilities in Bahrain and both ports and airstrips in Saudi Arabia. There had been some discussion within President Richard Nixon's administration about deploying a larger naval force to the Arabian Sea, but it proved to be impractical. Not only were there no countries willing to commit publicly to providing the United States with homeport facilities, but there was likely to be American domestic opposition to a new foreign-military commitment as the United States remained bogged down in Vietnam. The idea also violated Nixon's preferred approach to foreign policy.

The Nixon Doctrine

At a press conference in Guam in 1969, Nixon laid out the terms of what was later dubbed the "Nixon Doctrine." Facing stiff and rising domestic opposition to the Vietnam War, the president announced that, while the United States would continue to abide by its treaties, provide a nuclear umbrella for its allies, and offer economic and military support to friendly countries around the world where required, Washington would expect other countries to be the primary guarantors of their own defense. In the Middle East, the Nixon Doctrine was manifested most importantly in what came to be known as the "Twin Pillar" strategy that poured economic and military aid into Saudi Arabia and Iran.[27] Neither country was democratic, nor did its leaders share American values, but that was not as important to US policymakers as was their apparent strategic value in helping the United States prevent disruption of the free flow of oil from the Gulf.

It is important to note that the word *twin* suggests an equivalent value ascribed to the two countries that was not actually the case. Washington privileged Iran, which became America's policeman in the Gulf. With the Nixon administration's blessing, Mohamed Reza Pahlavi dramatically augmented his armed forces. As he was building what was intended to be the region's most powerful military, the shah deployed naval and ground forces along the shores of the Gulf to ensure it remained open to shipping. In 1973, he sent Iranian soldiers across the Strait of Hormuz to help Oman's sultan quell what became known as the Dhofar Rebellion, which was receiving support from both the Soviet Union and the People's Republic of China. This raised the specter of a radical regime aligned with the two major communist powers at the place where the Arabian Sea meets the Strait of Hormuz, which could jeopardize the free flow of oil from the region.

The United States was less generous with Saudi Arabia, its other pillar. Washington's goals in Riyadh were more limited, focused on the preservation of a Saudi regime that had been instrumental in facilitating Western (and especially American) access to its oil fields. Beginning in 1973, Washington helped the Saudis reorganize the Saudi Arabian National Guard (SANG)—a praetorian force dedicated to preserving the House of Saud. A well-equipped and well-trained SANG would reduce the likelihood of a coup d'état or other challenges to the ruling family. Indeed, the overall security relationship at the time was geared toward internal security. From the American perspective, regime survival was paramount lest Saudi Arabia's vast oil reserves fall into the hands of radical elements aligned with the Soviet bloc.

The Oil Weapon

Despite the American effort in support of Saudi security, a series of geopolitical and domestic shocks in the 1970s severely tested the US-Saudi bilateral relationship. First, on the morning of October 6, 1973, Egyptian troops swept across the Suez Canal and Syrian armored units poured over the Golan Heights, initially overwhelming the Israeli Defense Forces. It was an extraordinary moment. If the United States intervened to help Israel, it risked provoking the hostility of oil-producing governments across the region. If it stayed neutral, it risked the destruction of Israel. America's core interests in the Middle East had collided in a way that put policymakers in the unenviable position of having to choose one at the potential expense of the other. Watching the war unfold, Secretary of Defense James Schlesinger wrote to Secretary of State/National Security Advisor Henry Kissinger expressing concern over a nightmare scenario in which Washington resolved this dilemma by force. "The fundamentals are," he said, "that we may be faced with the choice that lies cruelly between support of Israel [and] loss of Saudi Arabia and if [our] interests in the Middle East are at risk, the choice between occupation or watching them go down the drain."[28]

The Nixon administration did not take the drastic step of seizing Saudi oil fields—the "occupation" to which Schlesinger was referring. Instead, it picked sides, choosing to support Israel during the war. In the initial phase of the October War (also known as the Yom Kippur War and Ramadan War), Israel's vaunted armed forces were caught by surprise and badly beaten, prompting Israeli officials to appeal to the United States for material assistance. President Nixon responded by making $2.2 billion of emergency assistance available to Israel and establishing an "air bridge" to resupply Israeli forces.[29] This prompted the Saudis—along with Arab members of the Organization of Petroleum Exporting Countries (OPEC)—to impose an oil embargo on the United States, which brought a halt to American imports from participating countries. Arab oil producers also slashed production, compounding the effects of the embargo.

Anyone who was alive and old enough at the time of the 1973 war remembers the long lines for gasoline at American service stations as the iron laws of economics were laid bare. The precipitous cut in Middle Eastern petroleum supplies quadrupled the world price of a barrel of oil—from $2.90 in mid-1973 to $11.65 by January 1974, the equivalent of a jump from $18.45 to $70.29 in 2022 dollars. This was, in turn, reflected in sharp price increases at the gas pump. In the nine months prior to the conflict, Americans were filling their tanks up for, on average, twenty-six cents a gallon (equivalent to $1.45 in 2022). At the peak of the five-month-long embargo it cost them just shy of forty cents per gallon—a 54 percent increase—which was equal to $2.35 in 2022.[30] Even after the embargo was formally lifted, prices continued to rise through the summer before pulling back to about forty cents a gallon a year after the October War ended.

The 1973 oil embargo is often referred to as a "shock," a term of art that economists use to convey a sudden, dramatic, and adverse development, but it was also a shock to Americans in the more conventional sense of the word. In the roughly three decades between the end of World War II and the outbreak of hostilities in the Middle East in October 1973, Americans registered seventy-five million cars. There was also a surge in the number of trucks on American roads as the US government built the federal highway system, helping to fuel America's postwar economic expansion.[31] At the same time, the automobile became not just a means of transportation but also a cultural icon.[32] The auto industry created a narrative that rendered the car a symbol of freedom, individualism, and adventure limited only by the distance between gas stations.[33] This story worked well in the 1950s and 1960s because the fuel to power all the new Ford Thunderbirds, Cadillac Coupe DeVilles, Chevrolet Corvettes, and Buick Rivieras was plentiful and cheap.

In the early 1970s, however, a combination of aging oil fields and the sheer volume of vehicles on American roads meant that even as US producers pumped more oil, their spare production capacity was falling. So, when the Saudis and their partners imposed an embargo over the Nixon administration's support for Israel, American oil producers were unable to make up the difference. The result was not just long lines at gas stations and the realization of just how dependent Americans had become on foreign oil suppliers in unstable parts of the world, but also a deep and painful recession, which took a toll on Americans.[34]

The embargo itself turned out to be unsustainable, however. King Faisal bin Adbulaziz Al Saud had put himself in the awkward position of harming the one country that could guarantee Saudi security. Officials in Riyadh grew concerned that a prolonged rift between the United States and Saudi Arabia would invite Soviet adventurism in the region.[35] As a result, even during the embargo, the king quietly permitted the export of oil for the use of the US military. And although not all its OPEC allies agreed, in March 1974, the Saudis brought the embargo to an end.

This return to the status quo gave American policymakers an opportunity to move forward with Middle Eastern oil producers even if a return to business-as-usual defied public opinion. In a January 1974 poll, 22 percent of Americans believed that Arab governments deserved "major blame" and 45 percent assigned them "some blame" for fuel shortages.[36] A year later, 63 percent of respondents said that Arab countries were "very much" to blame for the recession that resulted from the energy shock.[37] In the same survey, when asked whether the United States should supply military aid to Arab countries, 77 percent said "no."[38] In mid-1975, 64 percent of Americans said Arab countries were the "major cause" of inflation.[39] Despite public resentment, US policymakers recognized the world as it was: the Persian Gulf's plentiful oil was simply too important to the United States, and other available policy options—like energy conservation and innovation—were too difficult to forsake relations with the Saudis and others.

Seven Weeks to Change the World

Less than a decade later, an extraordinary series of events would drive home again for the United States the critical importance of Middle Eastern oil, the countries that produce it, and the need to prevent disruption to the commodity's production and export. First, in January 1979, the shah was forced to flee Iran, toppling one of the United States' twin pillars and scrambling its security arrangements in the Middle East. The shah's flight was the culmination of a thirteen-month-long revolution, led by a fractious coalition of nationalists, intellectuals, and clerics that ultimately ushered in the Islamic Republic of Iran under the leadership of Ayatollah Ruhollah Khomeini. The leaders of the new regime in Tehran harbored a long list of grievances against the United States, including the overthrow of Mossadegh, Washington's patronage of the shah, and America's support for Israel. The Islamist faction of the revolution, which soon became preeminent, also sought to export its revolutionary fervor throughout the Middle East. These developments were deeply disquieting to American officials. Not only had the United States lost a partner in Tehran, but it also faced the possible spread of a destabilizing revolutionary ardor.

The sense of threat only intensified with three developments at the end of that same year. On November 4, Iranian revolutionaries stormed the American embassy in Tehran and took fifty American diplomats and their Marine guard hostage. They remained in captivity for 444 days. The hostage crisis seemed to overwhelm President Jimmy Carter and irretrievably painted his administration as impotent in the face of Iran's provocations. The loss of one of Washington's twin pillars also rendered the remaining one—Saudi Arabia—more important.

Yet Saudi Arabia was not immune to crises of its own. On November 20, just two weeks after the hostages were taken in Tehran, a group of Islamist extremists seized the Grand Mosque in Mecca. This is the holiest site in Islam, which houses the Kaaba, the focal point toward which Muslims the world over pray. The group, led by a former low-ranking member of the Saudi Arabian National Guard, sought to overthrow the House of Saud, impose a strict interpretation of sharia, and enact radical changes in the country's foreign policy, which included severing diplomatic relations with the West. These terms were, obviously, nonstarters for the Saudis. As the "custodian of the two holy mosques"—the Grand Mosque and the Prophet's Mosque in Medina—the Saudi monarch ordered the liberation of the building by force. On the morning of December 3, security forces stormed the Grand Mosque. They eventually prevailed over the attackers after fierce fighting, but the siege raised questions among American officials about the country's stability.

Then, on Christmas Eve, the Kremlin ordered 280 transport aircraft carrying three divisions (approximately twenty-five thousand soldiers) to descend on the Afghan capital, Kabul. Within a matter of days, the Soviets had installed a puppet government in Afghanistan. From their new position in Kabul, the Soviet military was within striking distance of the Strait of Hormuz and the Gulf of Oman. This potential threat had major implications for Western economies. Americans were already struggling—as they had been in 1973—with long lines and higher prices at the gas pump because the instability associated with the Iranian Revolution had taken 7 percent of global production off the market at a moment when demand for oil around the globe was surging. If Soviet military forces chose to menace oil producers and the waterways through which their product flowed, Western economies would suffer significant dislocations.

President Carter addressed these mounting crises in his 1980 State of the Union address when he proclaimed:

> The region which is now threatened by Soviet troops in Afghanistan is of great strategic importance: It contains more than two-thirds of the world's exportable oil. The Soviet effort to dominate Afghanistan has brought Soviet military forces to within three hundred miles of the Indian Ocean and close to the Straits [sic] of Hormuz, a waterway through which most of the world's oil must flow. The Soviet Union is now attempting to consolidate a strategic position, therefore, that poses a grave threat to the free movement of Middle East oil. . . .
>
> Let our position be absolutely clear: An attempt by any outside force to gain control of the Persian Gulf region will be regarded as an assault on the vital interests of the United States of America, and such an assault will be repelled by any means necessary, including military force.[40]

This new policy had been the subject of a bruising battle within the administration over the previous six months, and questions remained even after President Carter's speech.[41] Some analysts wondered whether the United States had the military wherewithal to carry out this new mission, and other observers questioned whether it amounted to an oversimplification and over-investment in the region. Yet the "Carter Doctrine" became the unquestioned guiding principle of American foreign policy in the Middle East over the following four decades.[42]

Carry a Big Stick

If the 1950s and 1960s were characterized by the United States' expanding commercial involvement in the Middle East, the 1970s saw the beginning of American military engagement in the region. In the decades that followed, that commitment would deepen. Throughout the 1980s, US forces undertook a number of operations in the Persian Gulf to guard against threats coming from within the region. Although never articulated formally like the Carter Doctrine, collectively these operations are sometimes referred to as the "Reagan Corollary," which added a new dimension to American policy in the Middle East: Washington would defend the oil fields of the region not only from external threats but also from malevolent regional actors.[43]

The decade began tumultuously, with Iraq's September 1980 invasion of neighboring Iran. Iraqi president Saddam Hussein hoped to weaken Iran's new revolutionary government and to replace Tehran as the region's dominant power. As the war ground into an eight-year stalemate, President Ronald Reagan began to provide support to Baghdad to reduce the likelihood of an Iranian victory. He also pursued a wider policy of intervention to deter Iran's attacks on Gulf shipping, which had become part of Tehran's war strategy. In 1984, for example, an American warship fired on an Iranian plane patrolling the skies above the Persian Gulf; that same year, American air controllers helped Saudi F-15 pilots destroy two Iranian warplanes. Though each individual action was relatively minor in the grand scheme of war, they nonetheless enmeshed the United States ever more deeply into direct military protection of the Gulf's shipping routes.

Despite American intervention, Iranian attacks on oil tankers continued. By early December 1986, infuriated by sustained Iranian attacks on its ships and those sailing to its ports, the Kuwaiti government, which played a significant role in financing the Iraqi war effort, had had enough. Kuwait's leaders reached out to the United States, the United Kingdom, France, the Soviet Union, and China, seeking their protection. When, in early March 1987, officials in the Reagan administration heard of a possible deal in which the Soviet Union would.ensure the security of Kuwait's tankers, the administration's decision-making processes caught up with the urgency of the situation. The Kuwaiti request, which had been languishing at US Coast Guard headquarters for several months, leaped to the attention of the White House. Just before the Kuwaitis were to finalize the deal with the Soviets, American secretary of defense Caspar Weinberger informed Kuwait's emir that the United States would both allow Kuwaiti tankers to fly under the US flag and provide a naval escort for them. Had the Kuwaitis and Soviets moved forward with their agreement, it would have dramatically expanded the Soviet Union's presence in the Gulf, posing a possible threat to the energy supplies vital to Western economies.[44]

The naval escort, code-named Earnest Will, would grow to become the largest operation of its kind since World War II. It lasted for thirteen months and involved an aircraft carrier, three frigates, four destroyers, and a guided-missile cruiser, in addition to aviation units and special-forces operators. In parallel with Earnest Will, the United States undertook three additional military actions during that period, of which Operation Prime Chance was the most consequential. In an effort to destroy Iran's ability to threaten shipping, Navy SEALs destroyed platforms in the waters of the Gulf from which Iranian forces fired anti-ship missiles and hunted down vessels that laid mines in the path of the Kuwaiti—now American—tankers and their US Navy escorts. By September 1988, American forces had so battered the Iranians in Gulf waters that Iran's Supreme Leader, Ayatollah Khomeini, sued for a ceasefire, effectively ending the Iran-Iraq War.

When Saddam Hussein invaded Kuwait in August 1990, important elements of America's contemporary presence in the Middle East were already in place. The Carter Doctrine and the Reagan Corollary legitimized the use of force to protect the oil fields of the region. Toward that end, Central Command (CENTCOM)—a combatant command within the US military responsible for the Middle East—was established in 1983.[45] Still, the US military lacked permanent basing in the region. Instead of the shores of the Persian Gulf, CENTCOM was based on the shores of the Gulf of Mexico in Tampa, Florida. That is where it remains forty years later, though Operation Desert Storm/Desert Shield, which spanned from August 1990 until February 1991, broke down opposition among Gulf leaders to hosting American forces, which expanded their presence in the region after the war.

After Iraq invaded Kuwait, President George H. W. Bush stood publicly on principle to justify the deployment of more than half a million American troops to Saudi Arabia. If the Iraqis were permitted to swallow up their smaller and weaker neighbor, it would create a dangerous precedent in global affairs. In a joint statement with Soviet president Mikhail Gorbachev in early September 1990, the two leaders announced: "We are united in the belief that Iraq's aggression must not be tolerated. No peaceful international order is possible if larger states can devour their smaller neighbors."[46]

That was certainly true. But oil was an additional critical, though unstated, factor in the American decision to go to war.[47] Had the United States not liberated Kuwait, Iraq would have been in the position to menace and intimidate the Saudis from its newly declared "nineteenth province."[48] This raised the possibility that Saddam Hussein could gain effective control over two of the world's largest oil-producing states in addition to Iraq's own vast petroleum reserves, putting him in a position to manipulate global energy supplies. Washington could abide neither Iraq's violation of the international order nor its power over such a significant amount of oil. So, on the night of January 17, 1991, President Bush ordered American forces into battle. After forty-six days of being hammered from the air and a hundred hours of pummeling by American ground forces, Iraq's military made a headlong retreat out of Kuwait.

Dual Containment

The American-led effort to push Saddam Hussein from Kuwait was the apotheosis of the explicit American commitment to ensure a steady and stable supply of Middle Eastern oil over the previous dozen years. Saddam's invasion reinforced to American policymakers just how quickly the region's stability could be broken. And the war's quick end, with relatively few coalition casualties, suggested that the Persian Gulf could be protected by US troops at a bearable cost. The conflict was also a reflection of profound changes to regional and global politics. Up until then, US priorities had often been preventive: avoiding interruptions to oil transit, for example, or ensuring that other countries could not exercise predominant political influence in oil-producing capitals. With the Cold War coming to an end, Washington could, in principle, have pulled back from the region, supporting partner governments but not taking an active role in their affairs. Instead, the United States took the opposite approach. Its attention began to shift from what it hoped to avoid to what it aimed to achieve. Washington's diplomatic and military commitments in the region deepened as it embarked on a new and ambitious effort to remake the politics of the Middle East.

Not long after President Bill Clinton took the oath of office, his senior director for Near Eastern and South Asian Affairs at the National Security Council, Martin Indyk, addressed the Washington Institute for Near East Policy's annual Soref Symposium. It was a homecoming for Indyk, who had helped found the organization and served as its executive director until Clinton appointed him to be his principal advisor on Middle East policy. In his speech laying out the new administration's goals to the region, Indyk noted the Clinton team's intention to pursue America's long-standing interest "in the free-flow of Middle Eastern oil at reasonable prices," but also asserted that "in the wake of the demise of the Soviet Union and the Gulf War, the United States stands as the dominant power in the region, uniquely capable of influencing the course of events."[49] Indyk offered a three-pronged strategy that included " 'dual containment' of Iraq and Iran in the east; promotion of Arab-Israeli peace in the west; backed by energetic efforts to stem the spread of weapons of mass destruction and promote a vision of a more democratic and prosperous region for all the peoples of the Middle East."[50]

Of the three prongs, dual containment was consistent with past policies aimed at preventing the disruption of oil flows from the region, but its details reveal a significant policy departure. In previous decades, Washington sought a balance of power between Iran and Iraq. When Iraq was deemed a threat to Gulf stability in the 1970s, Iran was a US partner that would check Baghdad's regional ambitions. When the shah fell, making way for the Islamic Republic, American policymakers provided intelligence and non-US military equipment to Baghdad during the Iran-Iraq War. The new president's advisors determined that not only had the policy contributed to instability, but also that the United States was now confronted with two "rogue states." Moreover, even if US officials had wanted to continue a balance-of-power approach, they would not have partners in either Tehran or Baghdad with whom to work. The White House thus concluded that the best way to ensure the flow of energy resources from the Persian Gulf was to deter and contain both Iran and Iraq simultaneously. Both countries would be placed under sanctions and the US military would keep a watchful eye on both, so that neither could threaten the stability of the Gulf.

Dual containment benefited from the fact that in the aftermath of Operation Desert Shield/Desert Storm, Arab leaders dropped their prior reluctance to hosting American forces in the region. The Iraq crisis taught them that the public reservations they had previously held about America's commitment to regional security were no longer valid. As a result, they swung the doors open to American forces. Within two decades of the British departure from the Persian Gulf, the United States had taken up a roughly similar position east of Suez. Although CENTCOM's headquarters remained in Florida, the command also maintained a massive forward-operating base in Saudi Arabia before relocating to Qatar. The US military also operated out of facilities or had access to bases in the United Arab Emirates, Oman, Kuwait, and Bahrain—a far cry from the three-ship flotilla that plied the Gulf before 1971.

By the 2010s, America's seemingly permanent presence with tens of thousands of service personnel in the Persian Gulf alone represented a marked evolution of US involvement in the region, from its initial commercial interests in Middle Eastern oil to establishing itself as the sole guarantor of the region's security and stability. Throughout America's encounter with the Middle East since World War II, but beginning in earnest in the 1970s, American officials may have called their policies by different names—Nixon's Twin Pillars, the Carter Doctrine, the Reagan Corollary, Dual Containment—but they were all designed to achieve a basic core objective: preventing disruptions to the flow of oil from the Middle East to the West.

Investment, Sacrifice, Defense

Was the United States successful preventing any effort to undermine Middle Eastern energy security? Measured against what American policymakers sought to achieve, the answer is yes. They consistently chose to prioritize energy security, and throughout the post–World War II period interruptions in the supply of oil were rare and temporary. Price increases were more common, but more often the result of the emotion of market players than of real-world circumstances in the energy-producing regions of the Middle East.[51]

It is possible to draw one of two conclusions from the fact that, for most of the time since the first Saudi oil shipment left the terminal at Ras Tanura in 1939, oil has flowed unimpeded from the Middle East. The first possibility is that American activities in pursuit of this goal, especially beginning in the 1970s, were mostly unnecessary and wasteful. After all, oil was employed as a weapon only once—in 1973. And the logic of market forces suggests that oil-producing states will sell their product and oil consumers will buy it regardless of the domestic politics of sellers or their foreign policies. This was the argument that some opponents to military action advanced in the runup to Operation Desert Storm in 1991. Iraq would want and need to sell oil; therefore, it did not matter whether Kuwait was Kuwait the nation-state or a province of Iraq. Supply would meet demand, no matter who was pumping the oil.[52] There is a certain appeal to this line of reasoning: By stripping out the geopolitics, it suggests that the United States and its allies can continue to reap economic benefits from Middle Eastern oil without having to sacrifice any more than the price of a barrel of oil.

The second possible conclusion one could draw from the history of the region is as follows: without the order provided by a predominant, external, military power committed to open markets, the region would be vulnerable to forces—both internal and external—that could disrupt the oil supply, with all the attendant economic consequences that would follow. It is hard to imagine how, had the United States not intervened in the region, its interest in energy security would have been achieved. Had the United States not kept the Soviets out of the Gulf, preventing Moscow from interfering with the Western capitalist economic order; had American officials not twisted the arms of oil executives to enter Iran in the 1950s; had the United States not been a guarantor of Saudi security; had the US Navy not escorted Kuwaiti tankers and taken military action that helped bring an end to the Iran-Iraq War; and had Washington not led a global coalition to push Iraq from Kuwait, the world would likely look different from the way it did throughout the triumphant 1990s. Indeed, the United States would likely be less prosperous and thus less powerful.

There were other choices available to American policymakers, of course. They could have, for instance, pursued domestic-energy policies that favored energy efficiency, expanded renewable and nuclear energy, and/or increased domestic oil and gas production to limit US dependence on international energy sources. Washington also could have chosen to put in place multilateral security arrangements in the Middle East rather than relying on its own military power. But, at each turning point—Britain's departure from the region, the Iranian Revolution, instability threatening Saudi Arabia, and the Iran-Iraq War, among others—the United States consistently opted to use its own military power. It received help from partners and clients throughout the region, which rendered the pursuit of American interests relatively easier and less expensive than it might have been otherwise, but the United States always maintained the capacity to defend oil exports on its own.

For decades this policy remained mostly uncontroversial, garnering the support of majorities in both houses of Congress. That is because the United States benefited politically and economically from the implicit bargain at the heart of American regional dominance: the stable supply of oil at relatively inexpensive prices that fueled American cars and trucks as well as the global capitalist system.

For all of its success preventing the disruption of the flow of oil from the Middle East, it would be remiss not to account for the negative impact of America pursuit of this interest. Indeed, the United States has hardly been enlightened in the Middle East, sowing great damage in the process of securing sea lanes and oil fields. From administration to administration—regardless of party—the United States has supported authoritarian leaders whose commitment to tolerance; the rule of law; and freedoms of the press, of association, and assembly, among others, was nil. Iran's shah held himself up as a great reformer and modernizer, but he also applied force and coercion to ensure political control in a way that ultimately contributed to his undoing. The brutality of his security services was well known to American officials.

America's indifference to human rights and democracy in the region was consistent during the post–World War II period. At around the same time the United States helped enable the overthrow of Mohamed Mossadegh and facilitated the return of the shah, officials in the Eisenhower administration courted Egypt's ruling junta—the Free Officers—because Washington believed that Egypt could be important to an emerging Western security system during the early Cold War. President John F. Kennedy, often romanticized in American culture as having embodied American ideals, also sought good ties with the Egyptian government even though its leader, Gamal Abdel Nasser, built the archetypal Middle Eastern national security state. The strategic relationship did not materialize during the early Cold War. But it did in the mid-1970s and, since that time, the United States has supplied tens of billions of dollars in economic and military assistance to Nasser's successors. Throughout this time, Egypt's human rights record has been consistently deplorable.[53]

To varying degrees of severity, America's strategic partners in the region—including Iran under the shah, Saudi Arabia, the small Gulf states, Jordan, Morocco, and Israel—all have problematic human rights records. The State Department's 2020 *Country Reports on Human Rights Practices* documents unlawful and arbitrary killings (Egypt, Saudi Arabia, Israel), torture (Egypt, Saudi Arabia, Bahrain, UAE), accusations of torture (Morocco and Kuwait), degrading treatment and/or harsh prison conditions (Egypt, Saudi Arabia, Jordan, Bahrain), arbitrary detention (Egypt, Saudi Arabia, Israel, UAE, Jordan, Bahrain), and restrictions on freedom of the press, expression, movement, and/or assembly (Egypt, Saudi Arabia, Kuwait, Israel, Qatar,

Jordan, Oman, Morocco).[54] Previous and subsequent iterations of the State Department's report outline many of the same problems.

The underlying rationale for supporting perennial abusers of the values that Americans ostensibly hold dear is national interest. It is a double standard that has long been a dilemma for policymakers, more often than not being resolved at the expense of principle in favor of cold calculation about how best to advance US goals.[55] If regional actors are authoritarian, but friendly to the exercise of American power, Washington does not have to spend as much, in terms of both money and effort, as might otherwise be required to achieve its interests. Indeed, friendly authoritarians have often proven helpful to the United States, where more democratic countries may not have been given the greater relative importance of public sentiment in democracies. The paradigmatic example of this is Egypt after it became an American client in the early 1970s. Presidents Anwar el-Sadat and Hosni Mubarak became linchpins of a regional order—including Jordan, Saudi Arabia, Bahrain, the United Arab Emirates, Qatar, and others—that made it easier for the United States to exercise its power in the region. A more democratic Egypt would not likely have signed a peace treaty with Israel or deployed thirty-five thousand soldiers to Saudi Arabia in 1990 to take part in Operation Desert Shield/Desert Storm.[56] Both Egypt-Israel peace and Egyptian participation in the effort to push Iraq from Kuwait were critical to Washington's core interests in the region. Both events reinforced the importance of friendly authoritarians in American foreign policy, leaving the United States in a strategically tenable, but morally questionable, position.

The effects of US support for authoritarians have not been limited to moral injury. Blood has also been shed. The pursuit of Washington's core interests in the region has led to the death of innocents, both indirectly and directly. In recent years, sophisticated surveillance technologies have targeted peaceful opponents of regimes, and ostensibly defensive American weaponry has been unleashed on civilians. Among the iconic photos of Egypt's tumultuous eighteen-month-long uprisings, street protests, and coups d'état between 2011 and 2013 were images of spent tear gas canisters that security forces rained down on pro-democracy protesters. Almost always these munitions were stamped "Made in the USA."

Saudi Arabia's 2015 intervention in Yemen exacerbated a humanitarian disaster in the region's poorest country and was undertaken exclusively with American-supplied weaponry. American officials will regretfully dismiss the loss of life and injuries as "collateral damage" or underscore the "nonlethal nature" of American-supplied equipment. This is mostly sophistry. Policymakers know exactly how the materiel they sell will be used. The Saudis, after all, sought to pound their Yemeni adversaries into submission to prevent Iran from gaining a foothold in the Arabian Peninsula—a goal that Washington shares.

Yet, the United States' responsibility for death and destruction in the Middle East is not limited to activity through its regional clients. In 1988, an American warship fired two antiaircraft missiles at Iran Air Flight 655, a civilian airliner carrying 290 passengers and crew from the Iranian city of Bandar Abbas to Dubai. Everyone on board perished. The Pentagon called the attack a "tragic and regrettable error," resulting from the heat of battle and Iran's own recklessness. According to this version of events, the USS *Vincennes*—the ship that fired the missiles—was engaged in combat against Iranian gunboats at the same time its sailors misidentified an ascending civilian airliner in a commercial air corridor for a descending Iranian fighter plane in attack mode.[57] The American commander concluded that his ship was at risk and ordered the plane to be shot down. Investigative journalists and the testimony of other American naval officers subsequently cast doubt on this story, laying blame on the combination of an overly aggressive commander and crew in pursuit of retreating Iranian gunboats—in Iran's territorial waters—with hubris-inspired incompetence.[58]

Regardless of which account reflects reality, the result was the same. The American pursuit of energy security in the Middle East came at the cost of innocent lives. The *Vincennes* was in the Persian Gulf because oil from the region was critical to Western economies. Although the 290 people killed is a fraction of the lives lost as a result of US policy in the region, the event was among the most horrific, given the banality of being a passenger aboard a commercial airline flight. Those killed aboard Flight 655 were never much of a concern to Americans. The Gulf is seven thousand miles from the East Coast of the United States, and as long as Americans have access to inexpensive gasoline, they evince no real interest in how it is obtained. There was saturated media coverage of the Iran Air tragedy, but it reflected the official views of the Department of Defense and faded as the news cycle changed. More broadly, armed as the United States is with unrivaled diplomatic, economic, and military power, Americans almost never have to grapple with the consequences of their country's actions. After the *Vincennes* incident, the Iranians gave up their tanker war and accepted a UN-sponsored cessation of hostilities that brought the Iran-Iraq War to an end, tantamount to yet another success in the American effort to ensure that oil flowed from, through, and out of the Persian Gulf.

3

Unbreakable Bonds

On April 25, 2023, Israelis marked the seventy-fifth anniversary of the founding of their country. Even in the political turbulence of the moment, stemming from Prime Minister Netanyahu's effort to weaken judicial oversight and thus alter the balance of power between the branches of government, Israelis (and many Jews around the world) could step back and marvel at Israel's achievements. The country was hot, and not just because of its Mediterranean weather or its politics. In the early 2020s, investors poured billions into Israel; four Arab countries normalized ties with Jerusalem and several more, including Saudi Arabia, moved in that direction. Quirky, boxy, blocky, Bauhausian Tel Aviv had become a gleaming city of glass towers. Israel was not only the "land of milk and honey" as Exodus declared, but also of start-ups, venture capital, and initial public offerings. Israeli television programs like *Fauda*, *Tehran*, and *Shtisel* were international hits. Israel still had many opponents around the world, but it was also integrated in the global community like never before.

It is hard to grasp how vulnerable the country was at the time of its independence given the wealth and power that contemporary Israel enjoys. The country was poor in natural resources and human capital, having meager financial resources.[1] The hostility of its neighbors added to the nascent state's challenges. When the Jewish community in Palestine proclaimed the establishment of the State of Israel on May 14, 1948, the combined forces of Egypt, Transjordan, Syria, Lebanon, and Iraq—with detachments from Saudi Arabia and Yemen—attacked. These were hardly mighty armies, though the British-trained and -equipped Transjordanian Arab Legion was a proficient military. Even so, Israel did not initially fare well on the battlefield. In time, however, the Israelis were able to equip and organize themselves into a formidable force and, in March 1949, Israel's soldiers raised the flag of their new state in Eilat—a town at the southern tip of the country—sealing the country's independence. After the conflict ended, Israel was significantly larger and more contiguous than the country that was envisioned in UN Resolution 181 of 1947, which partitioned Palestine into Jewish and Arab states.[2] The area of

Galilee, from Nazareth to the Lebanese border that had been intended for the Arab state, was now in Israeli hands. In the south, Israel's defenders pushed the Egyptians out of the Negev region, leaving Egypt in control only of the Gaza Strip. To the south and west, the Israelis widened a corridor between the Mediterranean Coast and the Judean Hills. Jerusalem, however, was divided in two, with the Jordanians administering the eastern part of the city, including the holy sites, and the Israelis in possession of the western sector.

Despite this expansion, Israel remained exposed in a variety of ways. The Syrian army enjoyed commanding views of the Galilee region from the Golan Heights, and north of Tel Aviv, Israel's width left a slim eight miles between it and the Jordanian-controlled West Bank and the coastal town of Netanya. Demographically, the influx of Jewish refugees from Europe and the Middle East posed unique challenges of absorption. Not only did they hail from a huge variety of linguistic, national, and cultural traditions, but many of them were also too old, too sick, too young, or otherwise unable to contribute to building a new society and thus likely to become a drain on scarce resources. Then there were the approximately 150,000 Palestinians (19% of the country's 805,000 inhabitants) who were now Israeli citizens and who did not share the belief that Jews had a "natural and historic right" to establish a state in Palestine.[3] They were the remnants of a larger Arab population that, depending on whose narrative one believes, either fled the 1948 war or were forced from their homes in a determined effort to cleanse Palestine of its Arab population.[4] Despite a commitment to equal political and social rights in Israel's founding texts, Israeli authorities regarded their Arab citizens with great suspicion—so much so that during the first eighteen years of Israel's existence, its Arab inhabitants lived under military rule.[5]

Meanwhile, Israel remained in a state of war with its immediate neighbors, while the countries of North Africa and the Persian Gulf refused to recognize its existence. In 1948, just twelve countries around the world extended recognition to Israel's provisional government, and three—Costa Rica, Czechoslovakia, and Uruguay—established diplomatic relations. After Israel's war of independence ended the following year, those numbers increased to twenty-nine and six, respectively. Among them were the major powers of the day, including the Soviet Union, Great Britain, France, and the United States—but relations with these countries were often fraught. When it came to the kind of support Israelis needed to ensure their survival, it was not the United States, but rather France, that provided the bulk of security assistance in Israel's first decade and a half of existence.

What follows sketches Israel's development and the parallel role that the United States played in helping to prevent challenges to the Jewish state's security and integrity. The story emphasizes the evolution of the relationship. It traces an arc from the years immediately after the country's founding, during which American policymakers regarded Israel's greatest challenges to be economic, through the years leading up to the June 1967 War, when a gradual shift took place producing enhanced military ties. In the years following that six-day conflict, American policymakers prioritized Israel's security with not just copious amounts of military aid but also critical assistance to the Israeli economy and tech sector. Over time, the American effort to help guarantee Israel's survival became institutionalized. Each of these phases in the relationship reflected the way American leaders recognized the world at that moment, including the political and strategic realities of the Middle East as well as their own politics. The chapter culminates in an exposition of how America's success bolstering Israel's security came with moral costs.

The Early Years

President Harry S. Truman's 1948 decision to recognize Israel was not uncontroversial. He did so over the objections of some of his most senior advisors, who worried about the effect on America's relations with Arab countries at a pivotal moment. World War II had only just ended, and the United States and the Soviet Union were in the earliest days of the Cold War, competing for influence all over the globe and especially in the Middle East, where energy resources were of great and growing strategic importance. Truman weighed a combination of moral, historical, religious, and political factors, as well as the new geostrategic context, as he wrestled with whether to support the creation of Israel. In the end, however, while Truman understood the strategic importance of the Arab world, he also believed that formal recognition of Israel was required as a matter of justice.[6] Of course, absent from the president's calculation was the concomitant injustice that would result from Israel's creation inflicted upon the Arab population of Palestine.

This blind spot likely stemmed from the fact that Truman was deeply moved by the plight of Holocaust survivors and refugees in Europe. As a senator, he had advocated for efforts to save Europe's Jewish community during the war, and for the fulfillment of Britain's 1917 Balfour Declaration, which had promised a Jewish state in Palestine. At a personal level, the president—like many Americans—interpreted the Bible in a way that lent support to Zionist goals.[7] At the same time, the agonies of Jewish refugees and Truman's world-view intersected with geopolitical calculation and domestic politics. When he recognized Israel's provisional government, Truman was six months away from the 1948 presidential election year. The American Jewish community—which, much to the president's ire, had applied tremendous political pressure on him regarding the Palestine issue—was growing in number, becoming prosperous, and located in states rich with Electoral College votes. In the biggest prize of all, New York, with its forty-seven Electoral College votes, had more than two million Jewish voters.[8] The president also wanted to beat the Soviet Union to the punch.[9]

Truman remains a giant among many Jews around the world for his rec-ognition of Israel, but after lending the imprimatur of the United States to the new state, his administration was cautious about the type of support it was willing to offer. He did authorize badly needed economic assistance in the form of loans intended to help Israel resettle refugees from Europe and the Arab world.[10] When it came to security guarantees, however, Truman rebuffed the Israelis. The White House calculated that, given the hostility of Arab countries toward the Jewish state, closer ties with Israel would provide the Soviet Union with a political advantage in the region.

After Dwight D. Eisenhower succeeded Truman as president in January 1953, he sought to upgrade ties with Arab countries generally, and Egypt in particular, in an effort to construct a regional security order that would keep the Soviet Union out of the region. The new administration also sought to maintain ties with Libya and Saudi Arabia, two major oil producers. Eisenhower, the supreme Allied commander in the European theater during World War II and hero of D-day, was notably cool to Israeli concerns and requests for security assistance. Even after Egypt dramatically increased its military capabilities with the purchase of 200 tanks, 150 artillery pieces, 120 fighter jets, 50 bombers, 2 destroyers, 2 submarines, and thousands of small arms and munitions from Czechoslovakia in 1955, Eisenhower stood firm. He believed that the 1950 "Tripartite Agreement" among the United States, France, and the United Kingdom aimed at keeping weapons out of the region was the best way to prevent war and calculated that the Israelis possessed suf-ficient capability to defend themselves adequately.[11] Moreover, the American president believed that Arab leaders would have greeted arm sales to Israel with hostility, complicating Washington's efforts to counter the Soviet Union in the Middle East.

The American unwillingness to provide weapons to Israel added tension to the bilateral relationship, which became a crisis in 1956. In late October and early November of that year, Israel, Britain, and France conspired to precipitate an armed conflict with Egypt that would, they hoped, reap strategic benefits. Britain aimed to regain control of the Suez Canal, which Egyptian leader Gamal Abdel Nasser had nationalized earlier that year. The Israelis hoped to open the Strait of Tiran—a gateway to the Israeli port of Eilat—which the Egyptians had closed to Israeli shipping in 1950.[12] And the French wanted to deal a blow to an important supporter of the Algerian revolution.

The Israeli-British-French action infuriated President Eisenhower. Just the day before British and French paratroopers landed in the Canal Zone, Soviet forces entered the Hungarian capital, Budapest, to put down an uprising against the communist government there. The invasion of Egypt by two colonial powers—and NATO allies—undercut American opposition to Moscow's aggression in Hungary. The president moved swiftly to force the three aggressors from Egypt, though the Israelis did not fully withdraw until March 1957, prompting Eisenhower to propose, but never submit, a UN resolution punishing Israel for dragging its feet. The relationship only improved slightly after the Suez episode. In 1958, the Israelis convinced the administration to sell them anti-tank rifles, though Secretary of State John Foster Dulles made clear that it was a one-time agreement.[13] Indeed the long-sought security relationship with the United States never materialized and during the early years of Israel's existence, presidents Truman and Eisenhower prioritized Washington's relationships with oil producers and containing the Soviet Union. Instead of American arms, the Jewish state sourced its weaponry from France, Great Britain, and other countries in Europe. Washington's approach to the region at the time reflected the world as it was. The primary concerns of policymakers were ensuring access to the Middle Eastern oil necessary to fuel Europe's reconstruction and containing Soviet influence. Israel was now part of that world, but to the Truman and Eisenhower administrations, the Jewish state's economic well-being was most important for its survival. That view would slowly begin to change in the 1960s.

Special Relationship

However difficult Israel might have found the Eisenhower White House, it did have friends in the halls of Congress. Among those in the late 1950s and early 1960s was the junior senator from Massachusetts, John F. Kennedy, who understood the growing political importance of Israel's American constituency.[14] Throughout his fourteen years in the House and Senate, Kennedy perfected a studied balance between Israel-friendly positions and the desire to develop and preserve America's relations with the Arab world. In 1951, for example, he expressed regret that relations between important countries in the region, such as Egypt, and the United States had soured. Kennedy was also a consistent supporter of economic-assistance packages to Israel.

In time, however, the senator advocated for security assistance to Israel as well. In 1956, Kennedy wrote a letter to Secretary of State Dulles arguing that the Tripartite Agreement's embargo on arms sales to Israel should be lifted.[15] In April of the same year, he traveled to the Bronx and its secular temple of the American pastime, Yankee Stadium, to speak at a rally marking eight years since Israel's establishment. There, Kennedy gave a rousing speech to forty thousand supporters of the Jewish state, extolling the redemption of Zion while reciting, chapter and verse, the mythology that surrounded the "ingathering of exiles" in "a land without a people . . . for a people without a land." A little more than four years ahead of the 1960 presidential election, Kennedy drew a sharp contrast between his views and those of President Eisenhower, culminating in a vow to ensure Israel's security: "It is time that all the nations of the world, in the Middle East and elsewhere, realized that Israel is here to stay. She will not surrender—she will not retreat—and we will not let her fall."[16] This was the first time an American politician publicly uttered a commitment that would, over ensuing decades, become a core interest of the United States in the Middle East.

It was a theme to which Kennedy would return as he made his run for the presidency. On August 26, 1960, Kennedy appeared at the Statler Hilton Hotel in midtown Manhattan to give an address at the annual convention of the Zionist Organization of America (ZOA), an umbrella for several related pro-Israel groups whose leadership boasted a roster of American-Jewish eminences. In his speech, he stressed that Israel was a cause that transcended ethnicity, religion, and political affiliation and in the process laid the foundation for an enduring narrative that has made the bilateral relationship worthy of significant American investment:

> It is worth remembering, too, that Israel is a cause that stands beyond the ordinary changes and chances of American public life. In our pluralistic society, it has not been a Jewish cause—any more than Irish independence

was solely the concern of Americans of Irish descent. The ideals of Zionism have, in the last half century, been repeatedly endorsed by presidents and members of Congress from both parties. Friendship for Israel is not a partisan matter. It is a national commitment.[17]

The Republican nominee, Vice President Richard M. Nixon, opted not to appear at the Statler and instead sent a message to the ZOA delegates the day after Kennedy met them. Nixon's missive was decidedly less rapturous in tone than Kennedy's speech, offering a business-like recitation of the Eisenhower administration's Middle East policies. The vice president ended with an assurance that a goal of his administration would be the "preservation of the State of Israel."[18] By today's standards, this seems like unremarkable fare for politicians meeting or communicating with pro-Israel groups, but the commitments to Israel's security that both Kennedy and Nixon made during the 1960 presidential campaign were new.

A little more than two months later, Kennedy beat Nixon by a narrow 0.17 percentage point of the popular vote. The pro-Israel positions he had staked out on the campaign trail accurately foreshadowed the way his administration would alter the course of US–Middle East policy. Kennedy blocked pro-Palestine efforts at the UN, designated Fatah—the main faction of the Palestine Liberation Organization (PLO)—as a terrorist group, and sold Israel the Hawk air-defense system that its leaders had coveted throughout the Eisenhower period. Kennedy's embrace of Israel was the result not just of political calculation, but also of statecraft.[19] The new American president was concerned that without the reassurance of the United States, the Israelis would develop nuclear weapons, setting off a destabilizing cascade of regional proliferation.[20]

In line with both his politics and strategic concerns, Kennedy became the first president to describe the US-Israel relationship as "special" in a conversation with Israeli foreign minister Golda Meir in 1962. This effectively placed bilateral ties on par with those the United States enjoyed with the United Kingdom.[21] These changes were not just a departure from his predecessor, but also set out the contours and trajectory of the relationship for the ensuing sixty years.[22] When subsequent presidents reaffirmed the "unbreakable bond" between the United States and Israel, shielded the Israeli government from international censure, and sent abundant amounts of military assistance to Jerusalem, they were following the precedent that Kennedy established during his 1,036 days in office.

President Lyndon B. Johnson picked up where Kennedy left off. As both minority and majority leader in the Senate from 1953 to 1961, he had been a supporter of Israel, having advocated—like his Senate colleague Kennedy—that the Eisenhower administration drop its opposition to arms sales to the Jewish state. When Johnson became president after Kennedy's assassination in November 1963, he made a commitment to the American people that he would carry on the policies of his predecessor. In fact, once he took office, Johnson positioned himself as an even better friend to Israel than Kennedy had been. Upon welcoming Israeli prime minister Levi Eshkol to the White House in 1964, Johnson told him that "the United States is foursquare behind Israel on all matters that affect their vital security interests."[23] This is not to suggest that there were no tensions in the bilateral relationship during the Johnson era; but despite these problems, the president remained positively disposed toward Israel and its survival and helped to expand Western and American arms sales to Israel.

For all of the president's willingness to help ensure Israeli security through the provision of more weaponry, at a moment of crisis, Johnson was unable to provide the kind of support that the Israelis desired.[24] In May 1967, the Egyptian, Syrian, and Jordanian governments undertook a series of provocative moves, including shelling Israeli territory, mobilizing forces, dismissing UN peacekeepers in the Sinai Peninsula, and closing the Strait of Tiran to Israeli shipping. The economic damage from a prolonged closure of the strait would have been untenable for Israel, so Prime Minister Eshkol appealed to Johnson for diplomatic and military assistance to relieve the increasing pressure on his country. Despite his record of support for Israel's national security, the war in Vietnam cast a long shadow on the Johnson White House and the Democrats' losses in the 1966 midterm elections weakened the president politically. Johnson did not want to be drawn into a regional conflict and, as a result, the administration never seriously considered military intervention to force open the strait.

When the crisis came to a head in early June, the White House sought to head off an Israeli preemptive strike with a tortuously worded letter from the president to the Israeli prime minister. To the Israelis, the most important feature of President Johnson's message was its ambiguity. Israel's leaders believed that Johnson was signaling neither a red light nor a green light, but rather a "yellow light."[25] And on the morning of June 5, the Israel Defense Forces (IDF) seized the opportunity.[26] As the early battles in the Sinai Peninsula unfolded and the extent of Israel's successes became apparent, the

United States did little to restrain the IDF.[27] By the time a ceasefire went into effect on June 11, following a Soviet threat to intervene militarily on behalf of its Arab clients, the Israelis controlled the Sinai Peninsula, were within striking distance of Syria's capital, Damascus, and had pushed the Jordanians from the west bank of the Jordan River.

Israel's victory in June 1967 had two significant consequences for US-Israel relations. First, the war gave rise to the idea that Israel could trade territories it conquered in exchange for peace.[28] This notion was codified in UN Security Council Resolution 242 of November 1967 and has served as the basis for American peacemaking in the Middle East. Second, until the June War, America's relations with Israel were intertwined with the moral imperatives of the post-Holocaust world, the centrality of the Jewish return to Zion in Christian theology, and the significance of states with large numbers of Jewish/pro-Israel voters in securing an electoral victory.[29] With the swift defeat of three Arab armies—two of which were Soviet clients— in less than a week's fighting, a new dimension of bilateral ties began to develop: strategic cooperation.

When Nixon became president in January 1969, he inherited a different US-Israel relationship from the one that existed when he left office as vice president eight years earlier. The diplomatic dialogue was considerably warmer, though perhaps not quite as "special" as Kennedy and Johnson suggested to visiting Israeli dignitaries. And though the United States was not meeting every Israeli request for weaponry, military aid was flowing.

Consistent with the concerns of the administration in which he served as vice president, Nixon believed—given the prevailing strategic environment in the region—that the best way to avert war in the Middle East was to ensure that neither side in the conflict could impose its will on the other militarily. This was an era when nuclear strategists dominated the national-security discourse. And while these thinkers were focused on thorny questions about warfighting and peace in a world with nuclear weapons, some of their basic ideas trickled out beyond the realm of superpower competition. Nixon's focus on limiting the transfer of weaponry into the Middle East was, for example, based on the idea of establishing a stable deterrent between Israel and its neighbors. He articulated this point upon welcoming Israeli prime minister Golda Meir to the United States in September 1969: "[This administration] has also urged an agreement to limit the shipment of arms to the Middle East as a step which could help stabilize the situation in the absence of a [peace] settlement. In the meantime, however, I now reaffirm our stated intention to maintain careful watch on the balance of military forces and to provide arms to friendly states as the need arises."[30] Nixon's policy was to calibrate weapons sales to Israel based on Washington's own assessment of Israeli security requirements and what would ensure a rough equilibrium between Israel's military and Arab forces.

American policy would change for good on the morning of October 6, 1973, when Egyptian and Syrian armies attacked Israel across the June 1967 ceasefire lines. Israeli forces were thin that day due to the observance of Yom Kippur—the holiest day on the Jewish calendar—and were quickly overwhelmed on the Golan Heights and across the Bar Lev Line, Israel's massive fortifications along the east bank of the Suez Canal. After a difficult few days for Israel when Syrian forces made significant battlefield gains, the IDF were able to stabilize the battlefield and counterattack on the northern front. Yet even with the significant losses that the Israelis imposed, they were never able to force Syria's military to collapse. In the south, the Israelis mounted a counteroffensive that proved ineffective until October 11, when Egyptian lines began weakening, but even then, the IDF and Israel remained in grave danger.[31]

The Jewish state's defense doctrine had always emphasized taking the fight to the enemy in short, devastating conflicts. Israel's size, available manpower, and economy could not withstand an extended war at full mobilization. Having lost a quarter of its tanks and running low on fuel and ammunition, Prime Minister Meir placed a call directly to President Nixon on October 12 seeking help. Within forty-eight hours of that conversation, the United States began a massive airlift of American military stocks directly to the IDF. Buoyed by American support, the Israelis quickly seized the momentum with their own crossing of the Suez Canal aimed at cutting off Egypt's armies in the Sinai. By October 24, the IDF had surrounded Egypt's Third Army and was tightening its grip on it until the United States prevailed on Israel's government to accept a ceasefire.

The October War produced three significant changes in the US-Israel relationship that underscore how helping to prevent challenges to Israeli security evolved into a core American interest in the Middle East. First, the outbreak of war undermined the idea that if the United States just assured a balance of forces between Israel and its neighbors, it would deter the parties from fighting. Second, this led to an American policy shift, which going forward would ensure that the Israel Defense Forces enjoyed a "qualitative military edge" (QME) over its adversaries.[32] And finally, it underlined the importance of Israeli security to American policymakers. Faced with a choice of providing Israel with the materiel it needed to defend itself or accede to threats from Saudi Arabia and other Arab oil producers (discussed in Chapter 2), Nixon chose to support the Israelis. Recognizing the world the way it was, American policymakers subsequently calculated that a military balance in the Middle East was not the best way to avoid conflict. Instead, forestalling threats to Israeli security and precluding war required a long-term investment in the IDF's military superiority.

Planes, Tanks, and Missile Defense

The most visible sign of the American commitment to Israel's security has been Washington's $107,806,200,000 in total military assistance between 1946 and 2021, dwarfing this type of aid to any other country.[33] The centerpiece of the defense relationship after 1973 was America's commitment to Israel's military superiority of any combination of adversaries. This means providing Israel with access to American technology before others in the region, placing restrictions on weaponry sold to Israeli opponents, and providing Israel with "offsetting" military sales when Washington sold advanced weaponry to other regional powers. These principles were applied consistently from administration to administration for more than forty years—so much so that QME was not actually codified until 2008 with the passage of the Naval Vessels Transfer Act. As the title suggests, the bulk of that legislation set out provisions and requirements for conveying an American warship to another country. Title II—"United States Arms Exports"—addressed a wider set of issues, however. This included a requirement directing the president to undertake an "empirical and qualitative assessment on an ongoing basis of the extent to which Israel possesses a qualitative military edge over military threats to Israel," which legislators defined as:

> The ability to counter and defeat any credible conventional military threat from any individual state or possible coalition of states or from non-state actors, while sustaining minimal damages and casualties, through the use of superior military means, possessed in sufficient quantity, including weapons, command, control, communication, intelligence, surveillance, and reconnaissance capabilities that in their technical characteristics are superior in capability to those of such other individual or possible coalition of states or non-state actors.

This assessment would then be used to review requests for weaponry and defense services under the Arms Export Control Act. Although Republican and Democratic administrations had been faithfully ensuring Israel's military advantage, the sponsors of the Naval Vessels Transfer Act believed that without legislation, there was no way for Congress to compel an administration to uphold Israel's QME if a president chose a different policy. The act, which President George W. Bush signed into law in October 2008, was the way to guarantee that the United States would continue to prevent threats to Israeli security.

The US commitment to forestall threats to Israel's security extends well beyond congressionally mandated executive branch assessments of proposed arms transfers to Middle Eastern countries, however. American assistance has given Israel the ability to acquire and develop (often jointly with the United States) advanced weaponry and defensive systems that more than make up for Israel's disadvantages in manpower. For example, the United States and Israel have worked on the development of a multilayered air-defense system to protect Israelis from missile and rocket attacks. The effort began in 1986 when the United States and Israel signed a secret memorandum of understanding that outlined Israel's participation in the Strategic Defense Initiative (SDI)—known colloquially as "Star Wars"—the Reagan administration's program to build a system that would shoot down intercontinental ballistic missiles. The content of the memo remains classified, but public reporting indicates that funds for SDI were used to help Israel develop what would become the Arrow anti-ballistic missile system. Following the deployment of the first three iterations of the system, in 2021 the United States and Israel announced plans to develop fourth-generation Arrow, which will take advantage of new technologies to provide Israel with even greater protection from missile strikes.

In addition to the Arrow, the United States has contributed to the research, development, and deployment of other systems intended to protect Israeli civilians, infrastructure, and military installations from air attacks. For example, Rafael—an Israeli defense contractor—and its American partner, Raytheon, developed David's Sling with US government financial assistance. It is designed to shoot down planes, drones, cruise missiles, tactical ballistic missiles, and long-range rockets fired from 25 to 190 miles away. It was deployed in 2017.

Perhaps the best-known of Israel's multitiered air-defense systems is the Iron Dome, which, since 2011, the IDF has used to great effect during periodic rounds of warfare against militants in the Gaza Strip. The system is designed to neutralize rockets and artillery at short range. Israel funded the development of the system and the deployment of the first two Iron Dome batteries entirely on its own. But since 2011, the United States has contributed more than $2.6 billion to the production, deployment, and replenishment of the system (after the wars between Hamas and Israel in 2014 and 2021). In exchange for this investment, Israel agreed to share technology and coproduce it with an American defense contractor.

There are many more examples of US military assistance to Israel; the Arrow, David's Sling, and the Iron Dome are just the most prominent examples. This aid is not altruism, of course. A significant portion of the largesse is spent in the United States, through US defense companies. The vast majority of Israel's warplanes, helicopters, command-and-control systems, and aerial refueling aircraft come from the United States. Three of Israel's naval corvettes were built in the United States, and the IDF's ground forces use myriad American weapons and combat engineering equipment. Yet for all the benefit that accrues to the United States from security cooperation with Israel—whether in terms of revenue for American defense contractors, joint technology development, or mutual intelligence sharing—US military assistance to Israel has also been critical in helping to ensure Israeli security.

Innovation Nation (with Help)

In parallel to the evolution of US-Israel defense ties, a critical aspect of the American effort to prevent any country or group of countries from threatening Israel has been Washington's investment in the development of Israel's economy. This dates back to the earliest days of the Jewish state's existence, but in addition to direct budget support (which ended in the 1990s), it included programs to help advance Israel's science and technology sectors. Of course, much of the credit for Israel's modern, thriving, globally competitive, and innovative economy is owed to specific attributes of Israeli society, including its education system, research institutes, and, after 1991 in particular, an inflow of talented immigrants from the former Soviet Union. The country's unique security environment also puts a premium on creativity and innovation.

Yet Israel was not always "Start-Up Nation." As part of an overall effort to help ensure Israel's security, Washington played a role contributing to the country's world-renowned health care, cybersecurity, agricultural, and, importantly, defense technology sectors.[34] For example, in 1972, officials in Washington and Jerusalem oversaw the establishment of the US-Israel Binational Science Foundation (BSF), which has "support[ed] . . . collaborative research across a wide range of scientific disciplines . . . [for] peaceful and non-profit purposes."[35] The organization is independent of both governments, though of the ten-member board of governors (five from each country), half are representatives from various governmental ministries, departments, and agencies, and one is a delegate of the US federally funded National Science Foundation.

By all measures, the BSF has been an extraordinary success. Among the recipients of BSF grants are forty-seven Nobel laureates, seven Turing Award winners, and eight winners of the Fields Medal in mathematical sciences, in addition to a long list of other honorees and awardees. The organization has funded more than five thousand scientific studies with $700 million in grants to American and Israeli scientists, leading to breakthroughs in cell functions, computing and robotics, stem-cell therapies, space exploration, and cancer treatments.[36] Though these grants and discoveries undoubtedly benefited both countries, the relative asymmetry in resource availability between American scientists and researchers and their Israeli counterparts means that BSF funding has been more consequential to Israel's development of scientific talent and infrastructure than it has been for the United States.

The BSF was only the first among several foundations and commissions that the United States and Israel founded in pursuit of technological and scientific innovation. Just five years after American and Israeli officials provided the seed funding for the BSF, the two countries established the US-Israel Binational Research Development Foundation (BIRD). Unlike the BSF, the goal of the new foundation was "to stimulate, promote, and support industrial R&D" that would help the American and Israeli agricultural, communications, construction, electronics, electro-optics, life sciences, software, homeland security, and alternative energy sectors. A long list of major companies have taken part in the one thousand projects the foundation has supported since 1977, including Applied Materials, Dell, Eastman Kodak, EMC, General Dynamics, General Electric, Johnson & Johnson, and Whirlpool.

Efforts to promote collaboration among American and Israeli scientists and tech companies continued in 1994, when President Bill Clinton and Israeli prime minister Yitzhak Rabin established the US-Israel Science and

Technology Commission (USISTC). A year later, the two countries established the US-Israel Science and Technology Foundation (USISTF), which was charged with funding and managing USISTC efforts. The underlying assumption for the creation of the organization was that the United States and Israel had unique, yet complementary, expertise in the high-technology and biotechnology sectors that could drive economic progress to benefit Americans, Israelis, and the world.

The BSF, BIRD, and USISTC/USISTF are the primary examples of a broad American effort that has contributed to the development of Israel's economy, which, in turn, is critical to Israel's security both directly and indirectly. Included in this effort is the 1985 US-Israel Free Trade Agreement (FTA), which was the United States' first bilateral FTA and has facilitated business development and investment between both countries. The collaboration has reaped rewards for both countries, but especially Israel, which has become a critical component of the global high-technology ecosystem. Major global tech behemoths like Microsoft, Intel, Apple, Facebook (now Meta), and Amazon either have purchased Israeli firms or have research centers in Israel. For example, Israel does not produce any cars, but General Motors employs Israelis to write computer code for the company's vehicles. The future of autonomous vehicles is located in an office building in Jerusalem at the headquarters of a firm called Mobileye. The Israeli government reported that in 2021 alone, the country produced eleven new cybertechnology "unicorns"—companies valued at more than $1 billion. A third of the globe's cyber unicorns are Israeli firms, and 40 percent of all private cybersecurity investment is in Israel.[37] The country's success as an innovator is also reflected in the fact that as of the early 2020s, there were seventy-nine Israeli firms—including thirty-eight health care companies, twenty-four tech firms, and seven consumer-goods companies—listed on the NASDAQ exchange with a total market capitalization of $88 billion.

It is possible that Israel's thriving tech sector could have developed without the help it received from joint US-Israeli scientific research and development programs. Some analysts trace at least part of the country's blossoming tech sector to the failed 1980s-era effort to build an indigenous fighter plane, the Lavi.[38] Large numbers of engineering experts with various specializations, having been released from the ill-fated project, went on to found innovative companies, supporting the view that the Lavi's failure planted the seeds of Israel's high-tech and entrepreneurial culture. It is a compelling story, though it is important to recognize that the plane was being developed with the help of American military assistance, which is germane to a theme of this book: Washington's effort to help ensure Israel's sovereignty and security has had knock-on effects economically and diplomatically. The Jewish state's global integration is a manifestation of overall US efforts to forestall challenges to Israel's survival.

Israel and the World

Israel's status as a regional power, global high-tech innovator, and strategic partner of the United States has, over the years, contributed to the Israeli government's ability to break out of the global isolation the country once endured. During the late summer of 2020, analysts inside the Washington Beltway were handicapping which Arab country would be the next one to recognize Israel—an extraordinary transformation of Israel's place in global politics. This enthusiasm stemmed from the Abraham Accords, a multicountry agreement announced that August, which paved the way for normal relations between Israel and the United Arab Emirates, Bahrain, Morocco, and Sudan. The agreement was met with a fair amount of criticism among Palestinians and their international supporters because the normalization did not require resolution of the Palestine problem. Since the 2001 Arab Peace Initiative, Israel's neighbors maintained that they would establish relations with the Jewish State only after its conflict with the Palestinians was resolved, but not before then. The Abraham Accords violated that principle. It was a sign of how far Israel had come in the world.

For most of Israel's history—from the country's establishment to the early 1990s—Israel was not quite a pariah state, but it was close. In 1949, Israel only had diplomatic relations with a handful of states. By the early 2020s, it had diplomatic relations with 166 out of 195 countries, including with every member of the European Union; major global powers like China, Russia, India, South Korea, Japan, and Brazil; along with six members of the Arab League. Some of this progress is attributable to Israel's domestic achievements, making partnerships and investment attractive. For example, part of the impetus for the normalization of ties between the United Arab Emirates and Israel was the mutual benefit that Israeli and Emirati officials believed would be realized from cooperation in the tourism, health care, communications, technology, and other important economic areas, as well as the security sector.[39]

Israel's diplomatic achievements are its own, but there is no denying the role the United States has played helping to expand Jerusalem's relations with Middle Eastern states and beyond, thereby helping to prevent challenges to the country's security. Washington has, for example, underwritten peace agreements (notably the one between Egypt and Israel); spearheaded the effort, completed in 1991, to repeal UN General Assembly Resolution 3379, which called "Zionism a form of racism and racial discrimination"; and demonstrated to countries the advantages that would accrue in their relations with Washington as a result of normal ties with Israel. Sometimes this has included strong-arming governments in countries such as Sudan, which the Trump administration pressured to pay $335 million to American victims of terrorism and recognize Israel in order to be stricken from the list of state sponsors of terrorism. This paved the way for much-needed aid and investment in the country.

At other times, the United States has offered diplomatic, economic, and security incentives for improved relations with Israel. President Trump, for instance, offered to change long-standing US policy and recognize Moroccan sovereignty over the Western Sahara to encourage the establishment of ties between Rabat and Jerusalem. Following the Abraham Accords, Washington agreed to supply the UAE with a $23 billion arms package, including the most advanced warplane in the American inventory, the F-35 Joint Strike Fighter. In the mid-1990s, the Clinton administration promised to forgive Jordan's $702 million debt after it signed a peace treaty with Israel. And Egypt has also enjoyed an annual allotment of military assistance—totaling about $50 billion—from the United States (as well as varying amounts of economic aid) since it came to terms with Israel in 1979.[40] The tactics that American presidents have employed may differ, but the result has been the same: the expansion of Israel's diplomatic relations with other Middle Eastern countries. Of course, countries that have signed peace treaties and normalized their relations with Israel have not done so only because the United States has advocated for these ties, but the incentives that Washington has offered have made it easier to take these politically difficult steps.

For all the Israeli and American success breaking Israel's international isolation, the country remains the target of international opprobrium and censure because of its mistreatment of Palestinians and its creeping annexation of West Bank territory (discussed below). This criticism is best reflected in the decades-long campaign that Israel's opponents have waged in the UN General Assembly, the UN Human Rights Council, and the World

Conference Against Racism, Racial Discrimination, Xenophobia and Related Intolerance, and even the seemingly nonpolitical UN Educational, Social, and Cultural Organization to delegitimize the country's existence and cast doubt on the incontrovertible historical linkages between the land that is now Israel and Judaism.[41]

Yet despite the heated controversies over Israel at the UN and the determined efforts on university campuses as well as among human-rights groups to cast Israel as an outlaw, the US government has maintained extensive diplomatic, security, and economic links with the country. In the meantime, as noted above, Israel has become well integrated into the global economy and is too important in its region for projects like the Boycott, Divestment, and Sanctions (BDS) movement to gain significant traction in the halls of government and corporate boardrooms.[42] Investment from all over the world continues to pour into Israel's high-tech sector. No major power has taken steps to abide by the demands of BDS. And in March 2022, four Arab foreign ministers—from Egypt, the United Arab Emirates, Bahrain, and Morocco, as well as the American secretary of state—took part in a first-ever summit at Sde Boker, the resting place of Israel's founding father, David Ben-Gurion, in the Negev region. The final communiqué of the meeting indicated the summit would become an annual gathering. Although political and economic calculations can change, the overall trend at the time of that historic meeting was in the opposite direction of boycott, divestment, and sanctions.

The Emiratis may have been out front in developing ties with Israelis, but their neighbors were not that far behind. The Saudis continued to resist formal normalization with Israel because of its conflict with the Palestinians, but they permitted Israeli airliners to traverse Saudi Arabia's airspace and were also not-so-secretly issuing special visas for Israeli business executives.[43] The Qataris allowed Israel's diamond traders to set up shop in Doha and had established good working ties with Jerusalem in the effort to distribute relief and reconstruction funds in the Gaza Strip.[44] In the Bahraini capital of Manama, the Israelis planned to post a defense attaché at their new embassy with the apparent assent of the Saudis. Even after the war between Israel and Hamas exploded in October 2023, no government had—at least during the early weeks of the conflict—broken diplomatic relations with the Jewish state despite an outpouring of global criticism over the Israeli military's assault on the Gaza strip.

Israel's place in the world on the seventy-fifth anniversary of its independence is assured. This has much to do with US predominance in the Middle

East. It is not just that the United States has provided copious economic assistance, a steady supply of high-tech weapons, and diplomatic support, but also the way that America has, over time, shaped the geopolitics of the region that has not only made it harder for Israel's adversaries to achieve their goals but has also forced a change in outlook.

Although gauging public opinion in Arab countries presents unique challenges, it is abundantly clear that Palestine remains a critical and symbolic issue for many in the Middle East and large majorities remain opposed to normalization with Israel. At the same time, the data also reveal that the conflict between Israel and the Palestinians is not as much a factor in Arab politics as other issues of more immediate importance.[45] Overall, the polling suggests that Arabs remain opposed to normalization but have also come to terms—albeit regretfully and resentfully—with the reality of Israel in the region. This reflects conditions within Arab societies, but it is also a manifestation of America's Middle East, in which the US commitment to Israel's sovereignty and security has given the country the opportunity to thrive. Despite generalized opposition to decades of critical support that Washington has afforded the Jewish state, regional governments—with the notable exception of the Islamic Republic of Iran—have come to understand there is nothing that they can do about it. Indeed, despite the large number of casualties and heavy damage that Hamas inflicted on Israel in late 2023, the days when liberating Palestine seemed even remotely possible are long gone.

The Costs of Success

The United States benefited from helping secure Israel's future. Strategic cooperation, intelligence sharing, and the way "Silicon Wadi" plugged into Silicon Valley contributed to the development of a range of advances in high-tech fields. It also benefited American politicians because being pro-Israel has long been good politics in the United States. Yet there was a price to this success. Washington's broad-based efforts aimed at preventing challenges to Israeli security came at great material cost to Palestinians—who have been dispossessed, scattered, and dehumanized along the way—and moral cost for the United States.[46]

Indeed, the triumph of Zionism had a dark underside known to Palestinians and Arabs more generally as the *nakba*—or catastrophe—which is ongoing. As Israelis continue to occupy the West Bank, in a slow process of de facto annexation, and maintain their cordon around the Gaza Strip since 2007, the possibility of Palestinians achieving a measure of justice through a state of their own diminishes. In the West Bank, there are more than 400,000 Jewish settlers scattered across 132 settlements and 140 "settlement outposts." As with everything related to the conflict between Israelis and Palestinians, there is a dispute as to whether the establishment of these communities violates international law. Article 49 of the Fourth Geneva Convention (1949) states that an "Occupying Power shall not deport or transfer parts of its own civilian population into the territory it occupies." That seems straightforward, but Israelis and their supporters have raised questions about whether the convention applies because Jordan previously occupied the West Bank and illegally annexed the area in 1950. Thus, Israelis argue, if Jordan has no legal claim to sovereignty over the West Bank, Israel is not in violation of the convention.[47] When it comes to the outposts, there is no controversy that, at the very least, they contravene Israeli law.[48] In East Jerusalem, which Israel annexed in 1980—but which most of the world regards as disputed—there are approximately another 215,000 Israelis.

The combination of settlements, population, and infrastructure development devoted to sustaining these communities makes it hard to imagine that the Israelis will ever be willing to end their occupation of the West Bank. Israeli leaders have affirmed their willingness to resolve the conflict with the Palestinians and they have, in fact, engaged in negotiations. Yet Israel's minimum demands for peace—a quasi-sovereign, demilitarized Palestinian state; retaining Jerusalem as the undisputed capital of Israel; and abandonment of refugees' "right of return"—are impossible for any Palestinian leader to accept. The Palestinians' minimum demands for peace are a mirror image of Israel's, including its own capital in Jerusalem, the right of return for refugees, and a territorially contiguous state with full sovereignty. The United States has only been willing to try to use its political, diplomatic, and financial power to alter Palestinian demands, preferring to operate as "Israel's lawyer," in the words of one American diplomat.[49]

On the occasion when an Israeli leader has demonstrated the political courage to offer Palestinians a far-reaching, conflict-ending deal, their leaders have balked. In 2008, for instance, then Israeli prime minister Ehud Olmert offered to withdraw from all but about 6 percent of West Bank territory, establish joint Israeli-Palestinian-Saudi-Jordanian-American sovereignty over the Old City of Jerusalem, and accept thousands of Palestinian refugees, but Palestinian Authority president Mahmoud Abbas rejected the deal.[50] Why? Israelis and American officials often portray Abbas as need-lessly obstreperous, but Olmert's offer fell short of what Palestinians could ac-cept. Specifically, Abbas feared his opponents would attack him on refugees and borders, and especially on what were likely to be Israel's onerous security conditions that compromised Palestinian sovereignty. There was also a fair amount of Israeli politicking around Olmert's offer that convinced Abbas to rebuff it.

This is not to dismiss the significant problem of Palestinian rejectionism. Hamas—the Arabic acronym for the Islamic Resistance Movement—prevailed in Palestinian elections in 2006. The group controls the Gaza Strip and retains a substantial following in the West Bank. Unlike its main rival, Fatah, which Abbas leads, Hamas's 1988 charter calls specifically for Israel's destruction.[51] A revised version of the charter promulgated in 2017 was supposed to indicate a softening of the group's position, but actually does nothing of the sort. For example, Article 18 states:

> The following are considered null and void: the Balfour Declaration, the British Mandate Document, the UN Palestine Partition Resolution, and whatever resolutions and measures that derive from them or are similar to them. The establishment of "Israel" is entirely illegal and contravenes the inalienable rights of the Palestinian people and goes against their will and the will of the Ummah; it is also in violation of human rights that are guaranteed by international conventions, foremost among them is the right to self-determination.[52]

Notwithstanding the above passage, Palestine's supporters argue that the updated covenant does include important changes. For example, it declares the establishment of a Palestinian state with Jerusalem as its capital and the return of refugees along the lines of the June 4, 1967, borders to be "a for-mula of national consensus."[53] Yet it is not clear whether Hamas's authors meant that a national consensus had been reached or that the idea of a state east of the 1967 lines remained subject to debate. It does not matter much, for three reasons. First, the Israelis reject a withdrawal to those borders. Second, they will not agree to a Palestinian capital in Jerusalem. Third, Hamas's revised charter brooks no compromise on the legitimacy of vio-lence, declaring: "Resisting the occupation with all means and methods is a legitimate right guaranteed by divine laws and by international norms and laws. At the heart of these lies armed resistance, which is regarded as the strategic choice for protecting the principles and the rights of the Palestinian people."[54]

Many Israelis and their supporters, including American politicians, emphasize Palestinian miscalculations like Abbas's in 2008 and Hamas's violent objectives to absolve Israel of its responsibility for, and to minimize the American role in, the condition of the approximately five million Arab inhabitants of the West Bank and the Gaza Strip.[55] There is truth to this, but it is also part of a collective effort to avoid an uncomfortable reality to which Washington has long contributed. World Bank data reveal that a quarter or more of the Palestinian population is consistently unemployed; unemployment in the West Bank and Gaza last dipped below 20 percent in the early 2000s. Palestinian per-capita GDP is $5,400 (in 2020), which is about $37,600 less than that of Israelis.[56] The national poverty rate in 2016 (the most recent year for which these data are available) was 29.2 percent. Life expectancy in the West Bank and Gaza Strip is about seventy-four years, which sounds good, but is a decade short of that in Israel. These data do not include the millions of refugees scattered in neighboring countries, many of whom live in thirty-four refugee camps.

The statistics derived from the World Bank and the Palestinian Authority, moreover, do not fully capture the enduring hardship of Palestinians. Their statelessness has left them with few, if any, rights under an Israeli military occupation that is alternately brutal and indifferent. Gaza has been under a blockade, imposed by Israel—and enforced jointly with Egypt—since shortly after Israel's 2005 withdrawal from the area because Palestinian terrorist groups rained rocket fire on nearby Israeli towns. As a result, the cordon around Gaza has, in the almost two decades since its imposition, taken on an air of permanence. Within what Palestine's supporters regard as an open-air prison, public services like reliable electricity and potable water have deteriorated over the years. To make matters worse, the Israel-Hamas war that began in late 2023 destroyed much of Gaza's civilian infrastructure, promising to further immiserate Gazans.

In the West Bank, the occupation looks increasingly like annexation, even if that is not the declared policy of successive Israeli governments.[57] The Israeli towns and cities that the world refers to euphemistically as "settlements" have divided the land, leaving Palestinians in tenuously connected atolls of self-government. An enormous wall and fence cuts through Palestinian territory. It was a brainchild of Israel's center-left during the darkest days of the Second Intifada, a mini-war Israel and Palestinian militias waged against each other in the early 2000s. Yet far from achieving "separation," the wall's eventual route instead indicated an intention to fragment the Palestinians further and more deeply entrench control over them.

Palestinians are forced to traverse this landscape under the watchful eyes of the IDF and the General Security Service, also known as *Shabak* (or *Shin Bet*), which have worked continuously over six decades to refine and perfect their means of surveillance and political control. This is the dark side of "innovation nation." The security apparatus built around the settlement project has robbed Palestinians of their personal autonomy and dignity.

The dispossession and continuing statelessness of the Palestinian people has another cost: Extremist groups use it as a mechanism for mobilization. In the immediate aftermath of the attacks on the World Trade Center and the Pentagon in 2001, Israel's supporters argued that al-Qaeda's motives and objectives had little to do with American support for Israel. That is partially true. The attacks were orchestrated to undermine American support for Arab regimes—notably Egypt and Saudi Arabia—thereby facilitating their overthrow and allowing for the establishment of Islamist governments. That said, there was a certain amount of willful ignorance among Americans concerning the broader context of Osama bin Laden's extremism. At various times, bin Laden had been clear that American support for Israel contributed to his "political awakening."[58] It is worth quoting, at some length, the fatwa that bin Laden issued in early 1998 that dealt with "Jihad Against Jews and Crusaders":

If the Americans' aims behind these wars [against Iraq and the people of the Arabian Peninsula] are religious and economic, the aim is also to serve the Jews' petty state and divert attention from its occupation of Jerusalem and murder of Muslims there. The best proof of this is their eagerness to destroy Iraq, the strongest neighboring Arab state, and their endeavor to fragment all the states of the region such as Iraq, Saudi Arabia, Egypt, and Sudan into paper statelets and through their disunion and weakness to guarantee Israel's survival and the continuation of the brutal crusade occupation of the Peninsula.

All these crimes and sins committed by the Americans are a clear declaration of war on Allah, his Messenger, and Muslims. And ulema [clerical scholars] have, throughout Islamic history, unanimously agreed that the jihad is an individual duty if the enemy destroys the Muslim countries. . . .

On that basis, and in compliance with Allah's order, we issue the following fatwa to all Muslims:

The ruling to kill the Americans and their allies—civilians and military—is an individual duty for every Muslim who can do it, in any country in which it is possible to do it, in order to liberate the al-Aqsa Mosque and the holy mosque [Mecca] from their grip.[59]

The connection between America's ties with Israel and the rationale for jihad could not be clearer.

Bin Laden was not the only extremist to make this link. In the decades before his fatwa, extremist theoreticians believed that by defeating "apostate" Arab regimes, the liberation of Palestine would be possible.[60] Among the reasons that Egyptian president Anwar el-Sadat was in the crosshairs of the jihadists who assassinated him (including bin Laden's deputy and later his successor, Ayman al-Zawahiri) was the Egyptian leader's willingness to come to terms with Israel. In this worldview, Israel was a critical component of an inherently debased regional order that also included America's Arab partners, all of which colluded to undermine the emergence of societies based on God's law. Israel was a colonial outpost of America—known in jihadist parlance as the *Far Enemy*—and Palestine was sacralized as an "Islamic" cause. The impunity with which Israel repressed Palestinians was a clear indication of the perfidy of the United States and its Arab clients.

Critics have made the case that Washington's effort to reduce the costs to Israel over its treatment of the Palestinians has left the United States and its regional allies open to threat and occasional attack.[61] It could be that Israel is the principal reason that the United States found itself in global conflict with extremists even before terrorists rammed planes into the World Trade Center and the Pentagon, but a further thought experiment is required: if Washington were to lift the "cocoon of immunity" in which it has wrapped Israel and became an actual arbiter of the conflict between Israelis and Palestinians, would that resolve or at least mitigate the problem of extremism?[62] This seems unlikely, given how extremists frame the struggle with the West and Israel. That is to say, from the jihadist perspective, the repression of the Palestinians is not the problem per se. Israel (which represents the West) is. If that is the case, the logical way to reduce America's costs in support of the Jewish state would be Israel's destruction. No American leader would accept this argument given the moral and political costs associated with it. After all, the world as it is includes Israel.

Beyond the moral price and potential physical costs to the United States because of its support for Israeli well-being, there are domestic political distortions associated with America's long-term efforts to help ensure Israeli security. At first blush, it might seem odd to explore how Israel affects politics within the United States. What, after all, does this have to do with helping to ensure Israeli security, especially in a work that draws analytic inspiration from a school of thought that specifically rejects the idea that domestic politics explains the behavior of states? As noted in the first chapter, realism cannot explain everything—a point that two leading realists implicitly acknowledge in their book *The Israel Lobby*.[63] In the world as it exists there is a country called Israel and there are people in the United States who care a lot about its continued existence. This has fused US policy toward the Jewish state with American domestic politics.

American citizens who strongly support Israel and close US-Israel relations have come together to press their case directly to elected officials. To its critics, the group's demonstration of organizational and financial power has narrowed the policy choices of American officials in the Middle East to essentially one—maintaining the special US-Israel relationship. And in the judgment of its most prominent and well-respected detractors, these close ties are not in the American national interest.[64] In other words, without pro-Israel groups, the Jewish state would not enjoy the generous support of the American taxpayer or at least nowhere near the amount of assistance the Jewish state has long enjoyed.

Perhaps the most prominent pro-Israel organization is the American Israel Public Affairs Committee (AIPAC). For decades, US presidents, vice presidents, congressional leaders, and presidential candidates blocked the dates of AIPAC's annual policy conference on their calendars. Like John F. Kennedy's address to the ZOA at the Statler Hilton Hotel in 1960, politicians came to the AIPAC meeting to burnish their pro-Israel credentials. Although AIPAC did not, until 2022, endorse any candidates, an appearance at the meeting could earn candidates the political and financial support of other pro-Israel groups and individuals. Before the policy conference was discontinued in favor of direct support for candidates, it culminated in a "lobby day" in which attendees visited congressional offices to make the case to their elected leaders why support for Israel was in America's interest. It was an awesome demonstration of AIPAC's organizational capacity and the commitment of thousands of Israel's supporters. In this, it is hard not to see how AIPAC and other pro-Israel groups can influence the thinking of America's elected representatives.

Yet for all of the Israel lobby's prominence and influence, its record is actually mixed.[65] There is not a single contemporary case in which pro-Israel groups defeated an American president. In 1981, for example, the Reagan administration sold Airborne Warning and Control System aircraft to Saudi Arabia over the Israel lobby's objections. It lost to President George H W. Bush a decade later when he decided to delay loan guarantees to Israel over its settlements policy.[66] And Israel's friends in the United States were also unable to derail President Obama's 2015 nuclear deal with Iran—the Joint Comprehensive Plan of Action.

Although pro-Israel groups have at important moments failed to sway the White House, the unique attributes of the American political system with its divided and open system of government have helped make the Israel lobby quite effective on Capitol Hill. Despite increasing scrutiny of Israel's treatment of the Palestinians in the West Bank and the Gaza Strip among members of the Democratic Caucus, Congress has never penalized the country. Lopsided votes on Capitol Hill in favor of Israel are typical.[67] It may very well be that members of Congress believe that, by casting pro-Israel votes, they are best serving the interests of the United States. It is also true that supporters of Israel pay careful attention to how members of Congress vote on issues about which they care, creating an environment in which politicians engage in self-censorship and self-limiting behavior out of fear they will be targeted for being "anti-Israel."

At the same time, there is nothing unusual about the way the pro-Israel interest groups operate. There are many organizations that maneuver for influence within the Congress by backing candidates who support their issues and seeking to punish those who do not. That is the way the American political system works, which helps to underline that while pro-Israel groups may have at times failed to sway American presidents, they have remained influential on Capitol Hill. And because the politics of Israel is often brutal and, for its protagonists, high stakes, it can be distorting.

Consider, for example, the 2022 Democratic primary to fill the congressional seat in Maryland's fourth district. Donna Edwards sought to win back the seat she held between 2008 and 2017 but lost to a former state's attorney named Glenn Ivey. After her loss, Edwards's supporters highlighted how much of AIPAC's money twisted the outcome. That is a provocative claim, especially since Ivey only outraised Edwards by $220,000.[68] In the context of contemporary campaign spending, that is not a significant sum and effective candidates with far greater fundraising deficits have prevailed in the past. If the impact of outside financing was an overstated factor, the race nevertheless brought into sharp relief the intersection of foreign policy and parochial politics where Israel is concerned. According to news reports, the economy, public safety, and gun violence were most important to voters in Prince George's County, yet the primary turned out to be a proxy battle between AIPAC and another leading pro-Israel organization, its liberal competitor, J Street, which backed Edwards.[69] Both groups were heavily invested in the race, but neither seemed much interested in the preferences of Prince George's County voters, who, like most Americans, tend to rank foreign-policy issues as secondary concerns. Any objective view of the two Democratic competitors suggests that on the issues, the two were not all that indistinguishable; thus it was reasonable to surmise their positions on Israel could have made the difference in the race.

It is important to note, however, that Edwards ran a bad campaign and, according to a *Washington Post* editorial endorsing her opponent, during her previous stint in Congress, she developed a reputation for "spurning hard fought compromises" and poor constituent services.[70] Of course, AIPAC used its resources to highlight these flaws and, in turn, helped secure the primary victory for Ivey, who it hoped would be a reliable pro-Israel vote in the House of Representatives, which turned out to be the case.[71] Edwards may or may not have lost because AIPAC supported her rival, but the fact that the race became a slugfest between two different Israel-related special interest groups highlights the potency of Israel in American politics, leaving it ripe for distortion. It is a price Americans agree to pay for living in an open political system, however.

The willingness of American policymakers to support Israel and help prevent challenges to the country's security has long been bound up in a complicated mix of historical, religious, political, and geopolitical factors that have shaped the way they view the world. It was not always the case that the American political elites prioritized Israel. As they understood the world, presidents Truman and Eisenhower believed the best way to help Israel was through economic assistance in the form of loans while they sought to ensure the free flow of energy resources and build an anti-Soviet coalition in the region. Since the 1960s, however, with President Kennedy's assertion of a "special relationship" between Washington and Jerusalem, precluding threats to its security has been a core national interest of the United States. Even at a moment of crisis in October 1973, when America's two interests in the Middle East collided on the battlefields of the Sinai Peninsula and Golan Heights, policymakers chose Israel over oil. Since then, the United States has

used its power in multidimensional ways to shape a geostrategic environment in which a given country or group of countries cannot threaten Israel.

By the measure of what American officials across administrations wanted
to accomplish, the policy aimed at preventing threats to Israel's existence
was a success, though that accomplishment came with considerable moral
costs to the United States. For many in the Middle East, the dispossession
of Palestine and US support for Israel are an enduring symbol of American
hypocrisy. Yet for US policymakers, the world as it is (or perhaps as it was)
entailed support for Israel that also provided benefits to themselves and the
United States. The question now before the American foreign policy community as it debates what kind of role Washington should have in the Middle East
is, Are there any lessons to be learned from the US experience with Israel?
Like Washington's interest in preventing the disruption of energy exports
from the region, the policy toward Israel offers insight for a way forward for
the United States in the region. But before exploring how US policymakers
should approach the Middle East and the role of the United States there, it is
important to understand how Washington went from success to failure.

4

The Great Transformation

On June 8, 1991, General Norman Schwarzkopf led eight thousand soldiers down Washington's Constitution Avenue, past the White House, and across the Memorial Bridge. The military parade, marking the victorious end of Operation Desert Storm, was the largest of its kind since the end of World War II. There were impressive flybys of helicopters, fighter jets, and transport aircraft, while M1A1 tanks, Harrier jets, Black Hawk helicopters, and Humvees were placed on the National Mall for the public to view. The Washington Metropolitan Area Transit Authority reported that DC's subway system, the Metro, served a record number of riders that day, as hundreds of thousands poured into the nation's capital to support the troops. Not everyone was so enthusiastic, however. In the days leading up to the parade, flyers appeared on lampposts, bus shelters, and pretty much anywhere something could stick, declaring opposition to the Bush administration's "National Victory Celebration," which its opponents dubbed a "Wargasm."

The provocative handbills expressed a minority view. Most Americans seemed to agree that pushing the Iraqis out of Kuwait was a "war of necessity," as one senior American official famously put it years after the fact.[1] The phrase aptly captured the character and worldview of the administration's leadership—President George H. W. Bush himself, National Security Advisor Brent Scowcroft, and Secretary of State James Baker. Yet even before he gave the order to commence military operations, the president began to talk about the coming conflict and his goals for it in ways that betrayed his well-deserved reputation as a sober statesman. In the memoir he coauthored with Scowcroft, President Bush revealed that as the crisis wore on, he came to regard driving Iraq from Kuwait not just as a strategic challenge, but as a "moral crusade."[2]

In a speech before a joint session of Congress on September 11, 1990, to update the American people on the situation in the Gulf and on US-Soviet relations, Bush outlined a soaring vision for the future:

We stand today at a unique and extraordinary moment. The crisis in the Persian Gulf, as grave as it is, also offers a rare opportunity to move toward an historic period of cooperation. Out of these troubled times, our fifth objective—a new world order—can emerge: a new era—freer from the threat of terror, stronger in the pursuit of justice, and more secure in the quest for peace. An era in which the nations of the world, East and West, North and South, can prosper and live in harmony. A hundred generations have searched for this elusive path to peace, while a thousand wars raged across the span of human endeavor. Today that new world is struggling to be born, a world quite different from the one we've known. A world where the rule of law supplants the rule of the jungle. A world in which nations recognize the shared responsibility for freedom and justice. A world where the strong respect the rights of the weak.[3]

The "new world order" was neither specific to the Middle East nor was it an endorsement of transformation, but in an unintended way, it helped set the stage for a new direction in American foreign policy. After the victory over Iraq, policy entrepreneurs used the phrase to advance their transformative agenda. Whereas the United States had previously focused its actions on prevention—preventing the disruption of energy supplies, preventing challenges to Israeli security, and preventing the Soviets from challenging the American led order in the region—the easy victory over Saddam Hussein encouraged policymakers, analysts, journalists, and editors that made up the foreign-policy community to think in more ambitious terms: using American power to drive positive change.[4]

The narrative and analysis that follows traces the arc of America's outsized ambition in the Middle East after the end of the Cold War. It locates the roots of the American effort to transform societies in assumptions and ideas about the world, the region, and the ostensibly exceptional nature of the United States that departed from objective reality yet became the basis for US policy. During this period, officials and analysts lost focus on historical American priorities, such as the flow of oil and Israeli security, adding a long list of new issues to be in the national interest. Like the Greek mythological figure Icarus, who flew too close to the sun, the United States crashed in the Middle East as failures piled atop failures. This chapter critically examines the overly ambitious and necessarily flawed way the United States sought to transform the world, the Middle East included.

Redeeming the World

Just ten months after Iraqi forces waved the white flag of surrender, two men appeared atop the dome of the Kremlin. With little ceremony, fighting a stiff breeze, they lowered the enormous red flag with its iconic gold hammer and sickle. In its place, they raised the Russian red, white, and blue tricolor. In the minute or so it took to exchange the standards, the Soviet Union ceased to exist. And in that death, the new world order that President Bush declared seemed to come to life.

The collapse of communist dictatorships in Eastern and Central Europe and the sputtering dissolution of the Soviet Union were alleged to be some sort of historical endpoint, proving the strength of once-popular social science theories averring that societies will ultimately "converge." The apparent victory of the liberal democratic order was, however, just the beginning of a grand American project. By encouraging and guiding reforms to help transform countries in ways that would resemble the politics, economics, and sensibilities of the West, the American foreign-policy community believed that Washington could diminish the threat of future war, conflict, and ideological struggle on a global scale.

President Bush was determined not to gloat about the West's Cold War triumph, out of fear of stoking a backlash in Moscow. Surveying the radically changed world before them, however, both the president and his national security advisor allowed themselves to think out loud about the "possibilities" that lay before the United States in shaping a peaceful, democratic, and prosperous order.[5] That message seemed to resonate with Americans. Some of them, including college students, academics, consultants, and faith groups, got to work making these ideas reality. Generation X fanned out across what was once the Eastern Bloc to teach English, help newly established political parties, support student journalism, promote the rule of law, and keep the winds of change that had been sweeping through Eastern Europe and the Soviet Union blowing until democracy was firmly established. Business executives surveyed potential new markets with millions of consumers. General Electric (GE) produced a memorable television commercial of the lights coming on across Eastern European cities, culminating in a proud Hungarian woman declaring, "Freedom is breaking out everywhere!" The political metaphor was as hard to miss as the commercial one: GE and others were ready to sell lightbulbs, power plants, airplanes, sneakers, music, burgers, and whatever else American multinationals had to offer.

But before Western firms could sell their wares, economies that had been centralized to achieve a workers' paradise had to be fixed. Economists like Columbia University's Jeffrey Sachs and his former student David Lipton became consultants to the governments of the region and advised them to pursue "economic shock therapy." Pioneered in the mid-1970s in Chile and a decade later in Bolivia, the program entailed privatization of state-owned enterprises, ending price controls, floating the currency, and liberalizing trade simultaneously and quickly. The underlying assumption was that the best path to prosperity was the application of regrettable but necessary pain on a society all at once to force lasting economic change. Advocates of this rip-off-the-bandage approach argued that gradual transitions from central planning would likely fail because the vicissitudes of politics posed a threat to drawn-out reforms. The faster the post-communist economies could plug into American-style globalization, the better.

The United States also pushed to erase old political fault lines in pursuit of a Europe that was whole and free. One of the ways this was to be accomplished was the enlargement of NATO. The idea first surfaced among mid-level analysts and political appointees at Bush's State Department, but it did not die when the president lost his re-election bid to Bill Clinton in 1992. With only a residual Russian threat to Europe—at least at the time—the extension of the alliance eastward became a way for the United States and its allies to advance the political and economic transformation of Eastern and Central Europe.[6] NATO would thus extend security to those countries that also embraced democracy and market economics.[7]

Democratic Deficits

With the countries of Eastern and Central Europe on their way to joining the ranks of liberal democracies, only the Middle East seemed to defy global trends toward greater openness and prosperity. Of the eighteen countries in the region, only Israel and Turkey were democracies and they were imperfect, unable to cope with the contradictions between democratic politics and ethno-religious nationalism and ethno-nationalism, respectively. Gulf monarchies leveraged oil wealth, sparse populations, and coercion to ensure stability. Leaders in Egypt, Yemen, Jordan, Lebanon, Syria, Morocco, and Tunisia cared less about the well-being of their vast reservoirs of poor people than they did about maintaining their grip on power. Of course, a significant number of these countries were American partners and thus could count on Washington's support for these autocracies.

Iraqis, Libyans, and Algerians should have been better off, given the enormous oil and gas reserves in these countries, but strongmen wasted the proceeds on misbegotten economic schemes, vanity projects, wars, and conflicts that, in the cases of Baghdad and Tripoli, invited international sanctions, making the lives of citizens worse. Living among them all were the Palestinian refugees, numbering 8.5 million, scattered across the region and beyond in permanent statelessness and widely varying economic conditions.

A *New York Times* journalist once wrote that the Middle East was "democracy's desert," which was true, but the region's deficit in democratic politics was not its only problem.[8] As a whole, the Arab world lagged behind all others except Africa along a range of socioeconomic indicators. Opportunity for economic advancement was limited, women and minorities remained vulnerable to harassment and social exclusion, and even literacy was low in many places, especially Egypt, home to a quarter of the Middle East's population. Countries in the region squandered vast resources on big armies and oversized internal security forces whose missions were less concerned with defending the country than defending regimes and ensuring social control.

These challenges had long been clear in the Middle East, of course, but as the last decade of the twentieth century got underway, the United States stood alone for the first time. With no peer competitor in the world and a surplus of power, Washington sought to use that power to promote positive change. And it would do so based on a set of ideas about the Middle East that was deeply appealing to Americans. These assumptions placed a premium on economic development, averred that culture did not matter, claimed that democracy did not require democrats, and understood that Israeli-Palestinian peace correlated with democracy and prosperity. To suggest that this was paternalistic and smacked of "white man's burden" is an understatement, but Americans did not see it that way. They had an opportunity to remake the world.

As a presidential candidate, Bill Clinton professed more interest in domestic policy than in foreign affairs, but there were several foreign-policy issues that captured his attention: human rights, promoting democracy, and, in particular, Middle East peace.[9] Efforts to resolve the conflict between Israelis and the Arab states long preceded Clinton's presidency, but he arrived in the Oval Office at what seemed to be an auspicious moment. A little more than a year before Clinton was elected, President Bush and Soviet president Mikhail Gorbachev had welcomed Israeli, Syrian, Lebanese, Jordanian, and Palestinian delegations (the latter two appeared as one group) to the Royal Palace in Madrid for face-to-face negotiations. The Madrid Peace Conference launched bilateral talks between Israel and its neighbors aimed at finding a resolution to the Arab-Israeli conflict.

During the last year of the Bush administration, the "Madrid process" proceeded in fits and starts with few concrete accomplishments beyond the perpetuation of dialogue. To be fair, the fact that the parties were participating in direct discussions about peace could in and of itself be counted as a significant achievement, given long-standing Arab resistance to acknowledging Israel's existence. When President Clinton took office, he and his advisors continued to shepherd these talks, emphasizing different tracks—Israeli-Syrian, Israeli-Palestinian, Israeli-Jordanian—as conditions and the thinking of Israel's prime minister permitted.[10]

That is where things stood until the late summer of 1993, when reports surfaced that several Israeli academics—with the blessing of Israel's foreign minister, Shimon Peres—had been meeting with Palestinian officials far away from the spotlight at various locations in Norway. In about a dozen secret meetings, the Israelis and Palestinians hammered out an agreement that they hoped would finally bring the conflict over Palestine to an end. Subsequent events moved quickly. In an exchange of letters on September 12, Israel recognized the Palestinian Liberation Organization (PLO), a group Israelis had long called a terrorist organization, as the "sole representative of the Palestinian people." The PLO, in turn, recognized Israel's right to exist. A day later, under a blazing September sun on the White House lawn, Israel's prime minister, Yitzhak Rabin, and PLO chairman Yasir Arafat signed the "Declaration of Principles on Interim Self-Government Arrangements." As the gathered dignitaries showered Rabin, Arafat, and Peres with applause, President Clinton gently prodded the Israeli prime minister and Palestinian leader—two sworn enemies—to shake hands. It was a remarkable development after decades of unremitting hostility, captured in a now-iconic photo that seemed to vindicate Clinton's interest in Middle East peacemaking.

A little more than a week after the signing of the Declaration of Principles, President Clinton's National Security Advisor, Anthony A. Lake, gave a major foreign-policy speech called "From Containment to Enlargement" at the Paul H. Nitze School of Advanced International Studies, an outpost of the Johns Hopkins University in Washington, DC. For all of Lake's effort to be stirring, the speech mostly fell flat. There was, however, one section of the address that stood out:

> Democracy and market economics are ascendant in this new era, but they are not everywhere triumphant. There remain vast areas in Asia, Africa, the Middle East and elsewhere where democracy and market economics are at best new arrivals—most likely unfamiliar, sometimes vilified, often fragile.
>
> But it is wrong to assume these ideas will be embraced only by the West and rejected by the rest. Culture does shape politics and economics. But the idea of freedom has universal appeal. Thus, we have arrived at neither the end of history nor a clash of civilizations, but a moment of immense democratic and entrepreneurial opportunity. We must not waste it. . . .
>
> Throughout the Cold War, we contained a global threat to market democracies; now we should seek to enlarge their reach, particularly in places of special significance to us.
>
> *The successor to a doctrine of containment must be a strategy of enlargement—enlargement of the world's free community of market democracies.*[11] (italics original)

Even though the national security advisor made only passing reference to Middle East peace in his address, the agreement between Israel and the Palestinians was intertwined with Clinton's vision of America's role in the democratic transformation to come. In the administration's thinking, Israeli-Palestinian peace was an essential precursor to regional democracy. In his memoir of his years trying forge a solution to the question of Palestine, Martin Indyk writes: "We calculated that once we had put an end to the Arab-Israeli conflict, these Arab authoritarians would be deprived of their excuse for delaying much-needed domestic reforms. And once peace was established, resources that had previously been devoted to war could be freed up for that process."[12]

There was a certain elegance to this policy sequencing, but it was naïve to believe that the road to democratic polities in the Middle East ran through Jerusalem. It had also never been a priority of the United States to promote democracy in the region. The authoritarians in the region indisputably used the conflict between Israelis and Palestinians to justify all kinds of predatory policies, but it did not necessarily follow that peace would compel leaders to pursue reforms. In fact, all the political incentives facing these leaders encouraged more political control and coercion of their populations. And it was overly ambitious to believe that the United States could fashion an agreement between Israelis and Palestinians in the span of a presidential term (or two) that would trigger the dynamic change that the Clinton team imagined. In embarking on this project, American officials believed they could alter the interests and political constraints of the parties who were in an existential struggle involving complex layers of competing nationalisms, identities, and historical memories. Despite this daunting reality, President Clinton was determined, in his words, "to move the Middle East into the twenty-first century by ending the Arab-Israeli conflict."[13]

Over eight years, the administration pushed the peace process despite the massacre of Palestinians at dawn prayer in Hebron; waves of Palestinian terrorist attacks that took the lives of Israeli civilians on buses, cafés, and clubs; bloody IDF reprisals; the assassination of Yitzhak Rabin; and a change in the Israeli government that brought an avowed opponent of the Oslo Accords, Benjamin Netanyahu, to power. Even with the blood of innocents running in the streets, the Clinton team argued that peace would undermine extremists and that, with enough diplomacy and creativity, Netanyahu could be cajoled into accepting what he insisted he could never accept: Palestinian sovereignty in the West Bank and Gaza Strip. The reality was just the opposite. The prospect of peace stirred Israeli and Palestinian extremists to action precisely because compromise threatened their unbending worldviews. When it came to actual negotiations, American diplomats made little headway despite considerable effort because the "peace processers" seemed to want a deal more than the recalcitrant parties.

Almost exactly seven frustrating years after Israelis and Palestinians revealed their secret Norway negotiations to the world, President Clinton made a last-ditch effort to realize the peace that had animated him as a candidate and that he had worked so hard to achieve as president. He convened a summit at Camp David with Arafat and a new Israeli prime minister, Ehud Barak, a former army chief of staff who vowed to conclude a peace agreement with the Palestinians quickly. The symbolism of the venue was intended to remind Israelis and Palestinians of the courageous steps Menachem Begin and Anwar el-Sadat took to make peace between Israel and Egypt twenty-two years earlier. It was not to be. After two and a half weeks in which he devoted considerable attention to ending the conflict, Clinton left the presidential retreat in western Maryland empty-handed.

The denouement of the Clinton-era peace process came not long after the delegations cleared out of their cabins in the Catoctin Mountains. In

September 2000, the Israeli politician Ariel Sharon visited the plateau where the Jewish temple in Jerusalem once stood and where the al-Aqsa Mosque and Dome of the Rock stand. Sharon was a complicated and controversial character. His exploits in the Sinai theater during the October 1973 War earned him plaudits from military strategists around the world, but he also planned Israel's invasion of Lebanon in 1982 and its bloody aftermath. An Israeli commission of inquiry found him at least indirectly responsible for the Sabra and Shatila massacre that killed anywhere from 450 to 3,500 Palestinians. For those and other reasons, including his role in the expansion of Israeli settlements in the West Bank and Gaza Strip, Palestinians and Arabs more generally vilified him. His visit to Judaism's holiest site, which is also sacred for Muslims, sparked protests among Palestinians that spiraled into the violent and bloody Second Intifada. When Clinton left office in January 2001, the transformation he envisioned had come to naught. Israelis and Palestinians were further from peace than at any time during the president's two terms and regional authoritarians remained in power.

Meanwhile in Baghdad

Against the backdrop of the American push to settle the Arab-Israeli conflict and transform the Middle East was an ongoing confrontation over Iraq. In the years after his military defeat in Kuwait, Saddam Hussein continued the confrontational approach that had been a hallmark of his rule. He regularly challenged the no-fly zones the United States established over the northern and southern tiers of his country in the aftermath of Operation Desert Storm to protect the country's Kurds and Shia from the predations of the regime in Baghdad. The Iraqis also sought to subvert international sanctions and only cooperated with UN weapons inspectors intermittently. In April 1993, Saddam sent a hit squad to kill President George H. W. Bush during his visit to Kuwait.

While Saddam Hussein was testing Washington's resolve to contain him, there was a political battle over Iraq being waged in Washington. Republican members of Congress accused the administration of being insufficiently tough on Saddam. At the same time, veterans of the Bush administration, right-leaning analysts, and neoconservative pundits were setting their sights higher than simple political advantage. Over the course of the 1990s, they mounted an effort to convince Americans that the limited aims of Operation

Desert Storm only temporarily mitigated the threat that Saddam Hussein posed to the United States, its interests, and its partners in the region. More permanent action, they argued, was necessary.

This group of pundits, intellectuals, analysts, and former officials, which included noted figures like William Kristol, Robert Kagan, Paul Wolfowitz, Charles Krauthammer, Fouad Ajami, Richard Perle, and others, believed that efforts to "keep Saddam in a box" were untenable. And, coinciding with President Clinton's second term, they became increasingly vocal in demanding regime change. Emblematic of this worldview was a November 1997 editorial in the *Weekly Standard*—a neoconservative weekly opinion magazine. It decried America's "humiliation" at the hands of Saddam Hussein, who was defying UN weapons inspectors and making a set of demands on the United States including the suspension of surveillance flights over Iraq.[14] In the estimation of the editorial writers, it was time to take "the next step of finishing the job [President George H. W.] Bush started" with a ground invasion that would drive to Baghdad and overthrow the Iraqi regime.[15] The call to arms was couched in terms of America's apparently tattered credibility and the threat to Israel and US forces in the region from Saddam's arsenal of weapons of mass destruction.

Not long after the *Weekly Standard*'s editorial appeared, a group called the Project for the Next American Century (PNAC) sent a letter to President Clinton echoing and expanding the same themes, but with an ever-greater sense of urgency. For the eighteen signatories of the letter to the president, Saddam and his putative weapons program posed a threat "more serious than any we have known since the end of the Cold War." They implored Clinton to remove Saddam from power because "the security of the world in the first part of the 21st century will be determined largely by how we handle this threat."[16] Although the letter acknowledged the difficulty of its policy prescription, the melodramatic prose about the danger of Saddam's Iraq overshadowed any sense of the consequences of overthrowing the Iraqi regime. And, conveniently, advocates had a ready-made alternative to Saddam's "republic of fear."[17]

In the spring of 1991, President Bush had given the CIA secret authority to topple Saddam Hussein. The plan was channeled in part through a US government-funded group called the Iraqi National Congress (INC). Composed of Iraq's major Kurdish parties and a broad swath of regime opponents in exile, the INC purported to be a multiethnic and multireligious coalition of regime opponents who supported democracy and human rights—an apparently compelling substitute to the Iraqi government. The group was led by an MIT- and University of Chicago–educated mathematician and banker named Ahmed Chalabi, who was an urbane and cosmopolitan contrast to the thinly educated and vicious Saddam. He was also a con man whose financial chicanery had led to the collapse of a number of banks, and under his leadership, the INC proved to be mostly dysfunctional and rife with infighting.[18]

Chalabi and the INC had a fair number of detractors in Washington, especially within the permanent foreign-policy bureaucracy, but they also had powerful supporters and a compelling, politically effective narrative that made it hard, especially for members of Congress, to oppose. The triumphant zeitgeist of the 1990s, with the United States at the zenith of its power and democracy breaking out in the former East Bloc, added potency to the politics of Iraq in Washington. Could American politicians publicly oppose an Iraqi who claimed to represent a multiethnic, democratic future after Saddam? That is precisely the political calculation that Chalabi was counting on as he made his way through congressional office buildings, lobbying on behalf of his organization. And it is how the INC, despite its many deficits, became an important element in building the case for what would be the most audacious American foreign undertaking since the Vietnam War: regime change in Iraq.

The Clinton administration had been pursuing an official policy of containment in Iraq since 1993, with the goal of minimizing Baghdad's regional influence while it focused on Arab-Israeli peace. In response to pressure from groups like PNAC, the *Weekly Standard*, and Republican members of Congress, however, Clinton triangulated. Consistent with his own policy to limit the Iraqi government's capacity to sow instability, he continued the no-fly operations over northern and southern Iraq, maintained sanctions on Saddam's regime, and sought to pressure Baghdad via the UN Security Council. But he also devoted financial resources to the INC, and, in October 1998, he signed the Iraq Liberation Act.[19] The legislation stated: "It should be the policy of the United States to support efforts to remove the regime headed by Saddam Hussein from power in Iraq and to promote the emergence of a democratic government to replace that regime."[20] This enabled Clinton to demonstrate that he took Iraq seriously without ever intending to launch a land war or get himself into a Bay of Pigs–like operation on the Euphrates. Instead, the president remained committed to the idea that peace between Israelis and Palestinians was both "within reach" and that it could catalyze the transformation of the region. Yet by the end of the Clinton presidency, Israelis and Palestinians were engaged in a low-level war, Saddam Hussein remained in power, and the political systems of the region remained authoritarian.

The Hinge Moment

A little more than a week after terrorists brandishing civilian airliners destroyed the two (almost) identical buildings at 285 Fulton Street in New York City, President George W. Bush spoke to a joint session of Congress. In his address, he reviewed the events of September 11, 2001, offered an explanation as to why the attacks occurred, and previewed the American response—a "war on terror." He averred that the United States was attacked because "They [al-Qaeda and other jihadist groups] hate our freedoms: our freedom of religion, our freedom of speech, our freedom to vote and assemble and disagree with each other."[21] Bush and his speechwriters were laying the ground for the next great ideological struggle. It was a grim opportunity for a radical change.

In the years since, experts have disparaged the speech, but Bush was not entirely wrong. Al-Qaeda and other groups have a different conception of the way societies should be organized. The ideals and principles upon which the American political system is based have no place in the Islamic societies that the theoreticians of transnational jihad envision. Still, the very existence of America's democratic and liberal system of government is not why nineteen young men hijacked four planes, intent on mass murder. Instead, the plot was part of a broad effort that al-Qaeda had begun in 1996 with Osama bin Laden's "Declaration of Jihad on the Americans Occupying the Land of the Two Holiest Sites" to force the United States out of the Middle East, thus leaving "apostate" regimes like those in Egypt and Saudi Arabia vulnerable to overthrow.[22]

No matter; the idea that the terrorist attacks in September 2001 were linked to freedom (or lack thereof), and that the antidote to the problem was democracy, became a centerpiece of the Bush administration's effort to transform the Middle East. In the confusing days, weeks, and months after 9/11, the Washington policy apparatus kicked into high gear seeking an explanation for what happened and, importantly, how to protect the American people. Within government, a certain amount of intellectual improvisation took over alongside bureaucratic opportunism, reflected in the fact that Europeanists (especially at the State Department) played a significant role in crafting the American response to the attacks. Outside the machinery of government, everyone seemed to transform themselves into experts on the Middle East and transnational terrorism, and they all seemed to latch on to the idea that the region produced terrorists because the countries there were neither democratic nor prosperous. It quickly became prevailing wisdom that political and economic dysfunction of Arab states drove mostly young men into the arms of religious extremists who justified their grievances and provided the disaffected an opportunity to redress them through violence.[23]

These ideas were not outside mainstream thinking, though. In the hectic aftermath of the attacks, administration officials and government analysts scanned their bookshelves for insight into the Middle East's pathologies and ways to ensure that terrorists from the region could not threaten the security of the United States again. They embraced a constellation of ideas from disparate books and articles that they thought might help them and, in the process, cobbled together a mental map linking the Arab world's democratic deficit and weak economies to extremism and violence, even though the phenomena are not causally linked.[24]

Although advancing political change in the region was already well underway, President Bush did not officially articulate the policy until two years after the 9/11 attacks when he announced his "forward strategy of freedom" in a major address at the US Chamber of Commerce.[25] The time lag reflected the fact that wheels of the American bureaucracy turn slowly, but it also gave the Bush administration an opportunity to build an argument that its operation in Iraq was about both proliferation and freedom. Promoting open and democratic political systems in Iraq and other Middle Eastern countries would, the White House posited, give people an opportunity to hold their leaders accountable, make for a more peaceful region because democracies do not fight each other, and "drain the swamp" of terrorists. Democratic transformation thus became the organizing principle for the US government's approach to the region.

As such, the president made a point of speaking out forcefully for reform in the Middle East. The examples are too numerous to quote, but many of them emphasized a set of themes that Bush articulated at the University of South Carolina in May 2003:

Our nation is strong. Our greatest strength is that we serve the cause of liberty. We support the advance of freedom in the Middle East because it is our founding principle, and because it is in our national interest. The hateful ideology of terrorism is shaped and nurtured and protected by oppressive regimes. Free nations, in contrast, encourage creativity and tolerance and enterprise.[26]

So did his senior advisors, none more so than Condoleezza Rice. She played a critical role in crystallizing the administration's democracy-promotion policies as national security advisor; then, as secretary of state, she sought to carry them out. Her speech at the American University in Cairo in 2005 was in many ways the lodestar of the administration's democratic push in the region and included these memorable lines: "For sixty years, my country, the United States, pursued stability at the expense of democracy in this region here in the Middle East—and we achieved neither. Now, we are taking a different course. We are supporting the democratic aspirations of all people." This was a bold statement highlighting a significant change in US policy, but subsequent passages are even more revealing of the transformational goals of the Bush administration:

There are those who say that democracy leads to chaos, or conflict, or terror. In fact, the opposite is true: Freedom and democracy are the only ideas powerful enough to overcome hatred, and division, and violence. For people of diverse races and religions, the inclusive nature of democracy can lift the fear of difference that some believe is a license to kill. But people of goodwill must choose to embrace the challenge of listening, and debating, and cooperating with one another.

For neighboring countries with turbulent histories, democracy can help to build trust and settle old disputes with dignity. But leaders of vision and character must commit themselves to the difficult work that nurtures the hope of peace. And for all citizens with grievances, democracy can be a path to lasting justice. But the democratic system cannot function if certain groups have one foot in the realm of politics and one foot in the camp of terror.

There are those who say that democracy destroys social institutions and erodes moral standards. In fact, the opposite is true: The success of democracy depends on public character and private virtue. For democracy to thrive, free citizens must work every day to strengthen their families, to care for their neighbors, and to support their communities.

There are those who say that long-term economic and social progress can be achieved without free minds and free markets. In fact, human potential and creativity are only fully released when governments trust their people's decisions and invest in their people's future. And the key investment is in those people's education. Because education—for men and for women—transforms their dreams into reality and enables them to overcome poverty.[27]

It is easy to forget, due to the partisan divides that have hampered policymaking both before and since, that promoting democracy in the Middle East was not controversial in post-9/11 Washington. Most policymakers at the time had been shaped by the post–World War II and Cold War eras, in which liberal internationalism dominated American foreign-policy thinking. Encouraging positive political change and reform in the Middle East was appealing—aligned with American mythology, if not with its policies in the region to date. After the attacks, the values upon which the United States was founded could be leveraged in pursuit of national security, transforming politics in the Middle East in the process.

The murder of 2,996 people did not just enable America's effort to bring democracy to the Middle East, it also made regime change in Iraq possible. The weekend after the attacks, President Bush repaired to Camp David with members of his cabinet, his national security advisor, and other senior officials to consider the best options to respond to al-Qaeda. The official photos from that retreat feature grim-faced and haggard-looking officials still reeling from the shock of 9/11 and wrestling with the awesome responsibility of determining the best way forward.

An attack on al-Qaeda and its Taliban protectors in Afghanistan was a given; that war would begin just weeks later. But Paul Wolfowitz—the deputy secretary of defense and a long-standing, vocal advocate for regime change in Baghdad—advocated for going to war against Iraq, as well. Critics of the Bush administration have often held up his relentless pursuit of regime change in Iraq with particular scorn, but Iraq was already on the minds of other senior officials, including the president. On September 11, Secretary of Defense Donald Rumsfeld told Vice Chairman of the Joint Chiefs of Staff General Richard B. Myers that "his instinct was to hit Saddam Hussein at the same time—not only bin Laden." Also, on the day of the attacks, the president himself asked Richard Clarke, his counterterrorism advisor, to determine whether the Iraqis were responsible. That is why, when Bush's "war cabinet" arrived at Camp David, their briefing materials included information about Iraq and preliminary intelligence assessments of Saddam Hussein's culpability. The intelligence agencies assessed that Iraq was likely not to blame for the destruction of the World Trade Center and the damage to the Pentagon.

To supporters of removing Saddam from power, the fact that he was not responsible for the attacks was to have "miss[ed] the point." In a now infamous October 2001 column for the *Weekly Standard*, Max Boot of the Council on Foreign Relations thundered:

> Once we have deposed Saddam, we can impose an American-led, international regency in Baghdad, to go along with the one in Kabul. With American seriousness and credibility thus restored, we will enjoy fruitful cooperation from the region's many opportunists, who will show a newfound eagerness to be helpful in our larger task of rolling up the international terror network that threatens us.
>
> Over the years, America has earned opprobrium in the Arab world for its realpolitik backing of repressive dictators like Hosni Mubarak and the Saudi royal family. This could be the chance to right the scales, to establish the first Arab democracy, and to show the Arab people that America is as committed to freedom for them as we were for the people of Eastern Europe. To turn Iraq into a beacon of hope for the oppressed peoples of the Middle East: Now that would be a historic war aim. Is this an ambitious agenda? Without a doubt.[28]

Despite the forceful eloquence that Boot, who years later disavowed his support for regime change in Iraq, brought to bear on the transformational promise of bringing down Saddam Hussein, the Bush administration's most politically potent argument connected Iraq's apparent nuclear- and biological-weapons program to the issue of terrorism.[29] To frightened Americans, another attack on the United States seemed both plausible and imminent. A series of anthrax attacks in the weeks following the carnage in New York City and Washington added to the sense of dread. On the one-year anniversary of the invasion of Afghanistan, President Bush outlined these dangers to the American people:

> Some have argued that confronting the threat from Iraq could detract from the war against terror. To the contrary; confronting the threat posed by Iraq is crucial to winning the war on terror. When I spoke to Congress

more than a year ago, I said that those who harbor terrorists are as guilty as the terrorists themselves. Saddam Hussein is harboring terrorists and the instruments of terror, the instruments of mass death and destruction. And he cannot be trusted. The risk is simply too great that he will use them or provide them to a terror network . . . Terror cells and outlaw regimes building weapons of mass destruction are different faces of the same evil. Our security requires that we confront both.[30]

Over the years, Saddam had offered support to a variety of Palestinian organizations that had attacked Israelis, including the Popular Front for the Liberation of Palestine, the Democratic Front for the Liberation of Palestine, and the Abu Nidal Organization. And during the Second Intifada, he sent $25,000 to the families of Palestinian suicide bombers.[31] Despite this bloody trail, there was—as the intelligence agencies reported the weekend after the attacks—a paucity of evidence linking Iraq to the destruction of the World Trade Center and the damage at the Pentagon. This mattered little to the Bush team, which continued to hammer away at the terrifying nexus of Iraq, its alleged weapons of mass destruction, and terrorism.

The administration also attempted to link the war against Iraq with its heretofore uncontroversial democracy-promotion agenda. As Wolfowitz claimed in a May 2003 interview with *Vanity Fair*, Saddam's "criminal treatment of the Iraqi people" played a critical role in the decision to launch Operation Iraqi Freedom. Even the invasion's moniker itself reflected broader American goals beyond mere disarmament. Wolfowitz's reference to the brutality of Iraq's regime dovetailed with Boot's earlier call for American empire and the democratic transformation of Iraq as well as the Middle East. Reflecting on the decision to invade Iraq in her book *Democracy: Stories from the Long Road to Freedom* (2017), Secretary Rice argues that the decision to overthrow Saddam was linked primarily to global security, but she also emphasizes that Iraq's democratic transformation was central to the entire enterprise:

The decision to give Iraqis a chance at a democratic future was a separate one—and driven by a different logic. Some within the administration, including Don Rumsfeld, argued that we might be better off to install another strongman once Saddam was gone. Just find a general who wasn't implicated in his war crimes and let the Iraqis sort it out. It was a reasonable idea, but the president believed that America had done enough of that in the Middle East, with unacceptable outcomes. The freedom gap was in part to blame for terrorism and instability in the region.[32]

This was a significant shift. Previously, advocates for overthrowing Saddam Hussein rested their arguments on regional stability, his alleged drive to develop nuclear weapons, and protection of US partners and interests. Yet in the eighteen months between 9/11 and the beginning of the invasion, the administration officials, their allies within the media, and sympathetic analysts made the case that regime change in Iraq and the country's transformation into a democracy would diminish the terrorist threat, intimidate troublesome countries, and mitigate regional instability.[33] Toppling the Iraqi government would thus be the fulfillment of the benevolent hegemon that neoconservatives had been postulating ever since the successful conclusion of Operation Desert Storm and the end of the Cold War.

They were far from alone, however. The Bush administration's narrative about the power of American arms to force change was the mirror image—in which objects are inverted—of the Clinton team's approach, which also sought regional transformation. Yet rather than Israeli-Palestinian peace as the catalyst, bringing down Saddam and installing a new government that reflected the will of the Iraqi people—who would welcome American liberation—would make for a more democratic and peaceful region overall. Whereas analysts and officials once believed that a new Middle East would run through Jerusalem, they now averred that this transformation would run through Baghdad.

Palestine

President Bush and his advisors entered the White House wanting to steer clear of the kind of investment their predecessors had made in the conflict between Israelis and Palestinians. Yet the circumstances the summer before the 9/11 attacks forced the administration's hand. Unlike the first Palestinian uprising in the late 1980s, which pitted Palestinian teenagers throwing rocks and the occasional Molotov cocktail at Israeli soldiers, the Second Intifada was far more violent and lethal. It was also broadcast live on television. The footage of a Palestinian boy named Mohammed al-Dura dying in his father's arms after being shot by Israeli soldiers immediately became iconic, his name a rallying cry for supporters of Palestinians around the world. Among those watching events unfold in the West Bank, the Gaza Strip, and the streets of Jerusalem was the de facto ruler of Saudi Arabia, Crown Prince Abdallah bin Abdulaziz Al Saud. The Saudi leader was outraged at the force the Israelis were employing and angry at the Bush administration's hands-off approach to the violence.

In late August 2001, the Crown Prince ordered his nephew, Prince Bandar bin Sultan—the longtime Saudi ambassador in Washington—to decamp from his compound in Aspen, Colorado, and communicate Riyadh's displeasure directly to the White House. According to news reports, Prince Bandar told National Security Advisor Condoleezza Rice and Secretary of State Colin Powell: "We believe there has been a strategic decision by the United States that its national interest in the Middle East is 100 percent based on [Israeli Prime Minister Ariel] Sharon. . . . From now on, we will protect our national interests, regardless of where America's interests lie in the region."[34] Then, in March 2002, during a visit to President Bush's ranch in Crawford, Texas, Crown Prince Abdallah took the opportunity to warn the president of "grave consequences" should the United States continue to support fully the Israeli response to the Second Intifada. The Saudi leader wanted a visible American commitment to address the Palestinian issue and demanded that the White House restrain the IDF.[35]

What the Saudis did not know was that there had been a fierce debate underway within the Bush administration about how best to approach the conflict between Israelis and Palestinians. Secretary of State Powell and the diplomats in his Bureau of Near Eastern Affairs favored an approach for reducing the violence that, in its basic principles, did not differ substantially from the Clinton administration's efforts. For their part, a group of officials clustered around the National Security Council, the Office of the Secretary of Defense for Policy, and the Office of the Vice President did not believe that more diplomacy would yield better results. Instead, they zeroed in on Palestinian leader Yasir Arafat as the primary obstacle to ending the conflict, arguing that he was an unreconstructed terrorist and that there would never be peace as long as he remained in power. They seemed to be vindicated when, in January 2002, Israeli forces intercepted a freighter in the Red Sea linked to Arafat's Palestinian Authority (PA) called the *Karine A*. In its hold were fifty tons of high explosives, Katyusha rockets, antitank missiles, and other armaments destined for Palestinian forces from Iran. The uproar over the *Karine A*, plus Saudi anger, combined with the ongoing battle within the administration over how best to deal with the second intifada, led to the Bush administration's Arab-Israeli framework, the "Roadmap for Peace."

According to one former US official, the roadmap was the one policy proposal that everyone in the administration could agree on because it gave each
faction something it wanted. That may have been so, but it also launched the
administration on a similar transformative project that occupied so much of
President Clinton's time and energy. The roadmap obliged the United States
to change the Palestinian leadership and mandated democratic reform of
the Palestinian political system. It also provided Palestinians a political horizon for statehood by way of a first ever public American commitment to
Palestinian statehood.[36]

In President Bush's estimation, transforming Palestinian politics was
critical to making long-elusive Middle East peace possible. If Clinton's approach put faith in the idea that reform would flow from peace, President
Bush believed the inverse: that sweeping away a corrupt, cynical, and violent
leadership would empower new leaders who would be responsive to and re-
flect the will of the Palestinian people, and who would thus pursue peace. In
the abstract, the idea was compelling. If democracies do not fight each other,
and if Israel's utmost concern is security, then what better assurance of Israeli
safety than a democratic Palestine?[37] This approach to peace also fit neatly
into the larger transformative American strategy of democracy promotion
that was taking shape in Washington.

Yet the policy, which essentially sought revolutionary changes in
Palestinian politics, was overly ambitious. This is not to suggest that
Palestinians themselves were incapable of changing their own political
circumstances, but it was unclear how the United States was supposed to
accomplish such a task. Washington had few, if any, policy instruments to
redeem Palestine other than persuasion, proposals for economic reform,
and anti-corruption initiatives, all of which Palestinian leaders resisted.
Democratic change was also beside the point. Had Arafat given way to a new
reform-minded leadership and Palestinian politics become democratic, it
would have been good for Palestinians, but it would not likely have altered
hard realities of their conflict with Israel. As noted in earlier chapters, the
Palestinian problem was intertwined with competing claims over land, nationalism, historical memory, identity, and religion—issues with which
American diplomacy was ill-suited to resolve. A democratic Palestine would
not have fundamentally changed this reality and may have even made it
more difficult for Palestinian leaders to compromise for peace because of the
importance of public opinion and the exigency for politicians to remain in
office.

By the fall of 2003, with the president's formal announcement of his "forward strategy of freedom" in the Middle East, the three primary components of the Bush administration's ambitious effort at international social engineering were in place: regime change in Iraq, regional democracy promotion, and the establishment of a Palestinian state. By the time he left the White House in January 2009, each of these three components was a failure.

Iraq, it turned out, was not an urgent threat to global peace. It did not have nuclear, biological, and chemical weapons for its own use or the use of terrorists. Instead of becoming a bellwether of democracy and decency in the region, dysfunction, violence, and instability were the salient features of a country that had been liberated from Saddam only to find itself under foreign occupation. This, despite the anywhere from $815 billion to $8 trillion that Americans are estimated to have spent on the war, as well as the sacrifice of 4,300 American lives and 32,000 wounded or the untold number of Iraqis killed and maimed.[38] Iraq had also become a satellite of Iran—a member of what President Bush had called the "axis of evil"—and a breeding ground for terrorists.[39] The cakewalk that the administration and its supporters so confidently predicted had become a quagmire.

Many miscalculations plagued Operation Iraqi Freedom and its aftermath, but at a fundamental level, the Bush administration's disregard for the political, economic, and social realities of Iraq is what made it possible to believe that the United States could transform that country. On the eve of the American operation, decades of war and international sanctions had pummeled the Iraqi economy and infrastructure, and dictatorship, state violence, and corruption were the norms. The people recruited to lead the country into a democratic future knew very little about it, having spent so much of their lives in exile. These were realities that US officials chose to ignore, hoping against hope that through the iron of American arms, the United States could forge a democracy in Iraq.

When it came to democracy promotion, US efforts did little, if anything, to break the authoritarian syndrome that characterized the region's politics. There were some cosmetic changes, of course. Egyptian president Hosni Mubarak ran for re-election in 2005 against two opponents—previously there had been none—but still garnered an improbable 88.6 percent of the vote. And Saudi Arabia held partial elections of municipal councils—women were not permitted to run or vote—and legalized some civil-society groups. Yet the fundamentally authoritarian nature of the Egyptian, Saudi, and other political systems in the region remained intact. Indeed, the American officials who developed the Freedom Agenda vastly underestimated the durability of the Middle East's authoritarians and their ability to deflect external pressure for change. Supporting civil society, women's empowerment, literacy, and the development of small and medium businesses was noble, as were the forthright statements about democracy and freedom from President Bush, but they were also no match for the national security states of the Middle East. After initially pushing Arab leaders back on their heels, the kings, presidents, generals, and prime ministers of the region regained their balance and continued to repress opponents, institutionalize their power, and oversee spectacular levels of corruption.

In addition, US officials—many of whom had cut their teeth in Europe after the Cold War—overlooked or did not fully grasp the way the commercial, but not market, economies worked in the region. Rather than potential allies and supporters of democratic change, the interests of crony capitalists lay firmly with authoritarian leaders. And finally, the very fact that the United States was purveying democracy while occupying Iraq and underwriting Israel's repression of Palestinian rights rendered the Freedom Agenda just another—among many—of American hypocrisies in the Middle East. An appreciation of these political, economic, and social realities, along with the obstacles to change they represented, was mostly lost in Washington's zeal to promote democracy in the Arab world.

In Palestine, the Bush administration encouraged democratic change based on its belief that democracy was an antidote to terrorism and that political reform would, in turn, contribute to peace, but Hamas won elections in 2006. Instead of democratic politics diminishing the terrorist threat, Palestinian terrorists used the elections to accumulate political power. It was a stunning irony and underlined the faulty assumptions about politics and society that were the foundations of the American effort to foster a democratic Palestine. To make matters worse, when the Bush administration refused to recognize the group's victory, it vindicated those in the region who regarded Washington's democracy promotion as little more than a cynical neo-colonial project and led to a violent showdown between Hamas and the Palestinian Authority. The former prevailed—expelling PA troops and officials from the Gaza Strip in the process—producing a schism in Palestinian politics that has never been resolved. The collapse of the administration's effort to forge a Palestinian state by way of democracy promotion did not mean that it pulled back from promoting peace, however. The president, who had wanted people to think in novel ways about how to resolve the conflict between Israelis and

Palestinians, found himself engaged in more traditional peace-process diplomacy when he convened a peace conference in Annapolis, Maryland, in late 2007. It, too, was a failure.

The yawning gap between President Bush's ambition to transform the region and his achievements was so great that, after they left office, administration officials were left pointing to Libya as a mark of the administration's success. Libyan leader Muammar al-Qaddafi's decision to give up his weapons of mass destruction was surely important and good news. But it was hardly the region-wide embrace of liberty and freedom that the president's rhetoric had led Americans to expect throughout his two terms in office. When Bush limped away from office with 34 percent approval ratings, Americans had grown weary of the effort to change the Middle East.[40] In the next three presidential elections, they sought candidates who said they would bring an end to Washington's transformational impulses.

5

The Aborted Revolution

When Barack Obama became president in 2009, he made it clear that he would avoid unnecessary wars in the Middle East and ambitious efforts to remake the region. Informally, he summarized this new approach as "Don't do stupid stuff," though he is widely believed to have used another s-word for "stuff." More formally, six months after he took the oath of office, the new president laid out his vision for US relations with the Middle East and the Islamic world in a speech before three thousand guests at Cairo University, Egypt's flagship public university. He emphasized America's right to defend itself against violent extremists; criticized the invasion of Iraq; underscored an American commitment to Palestinian statehood while reaffirming the "unbreakable bond" between the United States and Israel; eschewed democracy promotion, though he made clear that wherever democracies emerged, America stood ready to help them; underscored the importance of women's rights; promoted innovation and education as sources of economic development; and extended a hand to Iran.[1] Whereas his predecessor had pursued regional transformation with moral certainty, President Obama harbored a more limited sense of American objectives in the region and promised to use American power judiciously.[2]

There were a few issues that Obama listed that were not, strictly speaking, departures from his predecessors. For example, the new American president also supported Palestinian statehood. Yet beyond a brief moment early in his administration when he applied pressure on the Israeli government to accept a two-state solution, Obama never invested his own political capital in negotiations between Israelis and Palestinians. When it came to democracy promotion, he did not dismantle the State Department's Middle East Partnership Initiative, which had begun under Bush, or other government initiatives with similar goals despite Obama's apparent skepticism of the Freedom Agenda.

Even with these few continuities, the president's pragmatic tone reflected his intention to rein in the most ambitious aspects of the Bush administration's approach to the region. Toward that end, he sought to repair relations with Egypt and Saudi Arabia, damaged by the Bush administration's effort to promote political change. He also sought to improve ties with Turkey, a NATO ally whose security had been compromised as a result of the invasion of Iraq. And, as he had promised during his first year in office, Obama made sure that all American combat forces were withdrawn from Iraq by December 2011.

Events sidetracked the Obama administration's intentions to de-emphasize democracy promotion and disentangle the United States from the politics of Middle Eastern countries, though. A year before the president brought America's occupation of Iraq to an end, a young Tunisian man named Mohamed Bouazizi set himself alight in the central square of his small town, Sidi Bouzid. The proximate cause for Bouazizi's self-immolation was the abuse he had suffered at the hands of the police, who had confiscated his fruit and vegetable cart for lack of a permit. His death quickly became a rallying cry—a symbol of resistance to the arrogance of power, corruption, crony capitalism, and police brutality—for Tunisians from all walks of life. Within a month, the ensuing popular uprising brought down the country's longtime dictator, the fearsome and loathsome Zine al Abidine Ben Ali, and chased him into exile in Saudi Arabia. The story did not end there, however. From tiny Tunisia, popular protests radiated across the region. The uprisings claimed Egypt's Hosni Mubarak, Libya's Muammar al-Qaddafi—the longest-serving leader in the region—and Yemen's president, Ali Abdallah Saleh. Among the most determined protesters were those in the tiny Persian Gulf country of Bahrain, where the royal family was forced to call on Saudi and Emirati troops to restore order. Of the twenty-one members of the Arab League, only Qatar and the UAE remained quiet.

The Arab uprisings were extraordinary and mostly unexpected events. In the span of just a few months, analysts and government officials shifted their expectations from the continuation of what they called "authoritarian stability" to democratization.[3] Consistent with his Cairo address, in which he committed the United States to supporting democratic transitions, President Obama put Washington back in the democracy-promotion business. At the State Department in May 2011, he told diplomats and civil servants that the United States now had "a chance to pursue the world as it should be."[4] Despite the "seeing the world as it is" quality of Obama's Cairo University address, the president implied that the United States had enough wisdom and resources to influence the domestic politics of Middle Eastern societies in ways that made democracy more likely.

Instead of transitions to democracy, it was Syria and Libya that defined the Obama administration's response to the so-called Arab Spring. In Syria, Bashar al-Assad's military response to peaceful demonstrations against his regime produced horrifying carnage. Notwithstanding copious bloodshed, the displacement of half the Syrian population, the use of chemical weapons, and his soaring rhetoric about shaping politics in the Middle East, the president remained steadfast in his unwillingness to intervene directly to bring Assad down. This reflected the "don't do stupid stuff" principle that was at the core of Obama's corrective foreign policy. To commit American forces to the conflict in Syria, even in response to the death and destruction that Assad visited upon Syrians, would have risked another long and arduous ground war in the Middle East. From the White House's perspective, there was no American interest at stake in Syria's civil war. This was Obama the realist.

In Libya, by contrast, the United States did intervene. President Obama did not, by his own admission, believe that American interests were at stake, but after agonizing debates between him and his advisors, he split the difference between his impulse to avoid military conflict in the region and a potential massacre of civilians, as Qaddafi had promised.[5] This was Obama "the realist who felt bad about it," as one of his advisors once quipped. As such, he ordered air strikes in coordination with NATO and members of the Arab League. And when the president addressed the American people about the Libya operation on March 28, 2011—nine days after it began—Obama stressed the potential humanitarian disaster that would have unfolded had his administration refused to act.[6] Yet it was hard not to see how this mission was intertwined with regime change. To save Libyans, Qaddafi had to go.[7]

Why did Libyans deserve protection and not Syrians? How was it that regime change in Syria was "stupid stuff," but it was not the same in Libya? One reason may have had to do with the fact that the United States' NATO allies, notably France and the United Kingdom, applied significant pressure on the White House to act in Libya and there were willing participants among members of the Arab League. Also, as President Obama's May 2011 speech indicated, the Arab uprisings also fed into the transformational impulses of the American foreign-policy community.[8] At the time, there was an odd belief in Washington that, among the countries that had uprisings, Libya would be in the best position to make the transition to democracy. After Qaddafi's long rule, this theory went, Libya's "blank slate" would provide an opportunity to build democratic institutions where there had been none before. It was the kind of claim that had no connection to Libya's reality, yet policymakers and analysts maintained faith in their ability to remake the world in America's image. That is how a president who pledged to avoid being sucked into the Middle East became part of an ambitious effort to transform Libya.

President Obama's instincts about the limits of American power were better than his record fostering democratic change in the region. Although its mistakes were orders of magnitude less than those of the Bush administration, the Obama team had its fair share of failures that were the result of bad assumptions about what the United States could achieve after the uprisings.[9] With the exception of Tunisia, the countries that experienced upheaval in 2011 and 2012 were either experiencing resurgent authoritarianism or collapsing in violence when President Obama left office in early 2017. The fault, of course, lay with local and regional actors. In the years that followed the uprisings, it became clear that the American efforts to stabilize regional economies, forgive debt, support small and medium-sized enterprises, spur trade and investment, and help stand up democratic institutions made little, if any, impact.

Unlike his part in promoting democracy in the Arab world, Obama's determination to change US-Iran relations was no accident of history. From the earliest days of his administration, President Obama offered his outstretched hand to Iranians and their leaders. Not long after his inauguration, the president videotaped a greeting to the Iranian people during Nowruz—the Persian new year—and sent two letters to Iran's Ayatollah Ali Khamenei in the first half of 2009. This correspondence reportedly expressed the president's interest in "regional and bilateral cooperation" with Iran.[10] Although his opponents decried these gestures, there was precedent for President Obama's outreach. President Ronald Reagan's national security advisor landed at Tehran's Mehrabad Airport in 1986, in an unmarked aircraft full of spare military parts, a Bible inscribed by the president, and a chocolate cake—baked in Tel Aviv—in the shape of a key, which was supposed to symbolize the way to unlock new, more productive relations. In his inaugural address, President George H. W. Bush declared, "goodwill begets goodwill" a veiled reference universally believed to have been a message to Iran's leaders. After Mohamed Khatami, an alleged reformist, was elected as Iran's president in 1997, the Clinton administration also signaled its desire for better relations.[11]

Like his predecessors, President Obama quickly discovered that the Iranians were not so eager for his outreach. The supreme leader responded coolly to his entreaties for dialogue and there was no change in Iran's support for groups such as Hamas, Palestinian Islamic Jihad, and Hizballah, or

renunciation of irredentist claims to Kuwaiti, Bahraini, and Emirati territory. The Iranians made clear their intention to remain involved in Iraqi politics, through both the bullet and the ballot box, and to vassalize their former
enemies. So Obama changed his tactics, dropping his friendly outreach in
favor of coercion. He cooperated with the Israelis to sabotage Iran's nuclear
program, established NATO radar facilities on Turkish and Polish territory
that was a layer of regional defense against Iran's missiles, and worked to elicit
enough diplomatic support—including from Russia and China—for comprehensive international sanctions on Iran. The combination of diplomatic
pressure, economic pain, and disruption of the Iranian nuclear program
eventually compelled the Iranian leadership to respond to the United States.

The result was the 2015 Joint Comprehensive Plan of Action (JCPOA),
which is referred to colloquially as the "Iran nuclear deal" and includes
Germany, France, the United Kingdom, China, and Russia as well as
the United States and Iran. To boil the sprawling agreement down to its
essentials, the JCPOA traded sanctions relief for a decade-long pause in Iran's
nuclear-development program. To ensure compliance, the Iranians agreed to
intrusive International Atomic Energy Agency inspections. The JCPOA was
Obama's greatest and most important foreign-policy achievement. Although
the agreement's critics argued—without much evidence—that the administration could have negotiated a "better deal," in reality, the JCPOA was unsustainable for three reasons.

First, the agreement rested, in part, on the idea that other regional actors
would either accede to the deal or could be incentivized to accommodate
themselves to it through the sale of copious amounts of weaponry. Yet the
promise of additional security assistance hardly mollified Gulf leaders. Their
primary objection to the JCPOA had more to do with the sanctions relief it
promised than with its defects constraining Iran's nuclear activity, believing
that the resources made available to the Iranian regime would be used to
support its various proxies and destabilize the region. Moreover, the JCPOA
was the latest and perhaps the most alarming in a growing list of Gulf states'
grievances tallied against the United States. These included all the unofficial
Washington chatter dating back to the later George W. Bush years about the
need for dialogue with Iran, President Obama's early outreach to Tehran,
his administration's willingness to accommodate the Muslim Brotherhood's
accumulation of power in Egypt after Hosni Mubarak's fall, the president's
unwillingness to oppose Iran in Syria, and the withdrawal of American
diplomats from Yemen in February 2015. From this, America's Gulf clients

drew the conclusion that Washington had decided to leave them at the mercy of Tehran.

Then there was Israel. Since the 1979 revolution that resulted in the establishment of the Islamic Republic, Iran threatened Israel across a number of dimensions, including symbolic but harmful campaigns to delegitimize the Jewish connection to Palestine and deny the Holocaust. At the same time, the Iranians have invested heavily in terrorist organizations such as Palestinian Islamic Jihad, Hamas, and Hizballah that have waged war on Israel. And because Tehran made itself a central actor in the "resistance" against the United States and Israel, Israelis had reason to believe that Iran's development of nuclear technology was an existential threat. In the estimation of Israel's leaders and other critics of the agreement, because the JCPOA did not go far enough to constrain Iran's nuclear activity, the Israelis could never accommodate themselves to the deal with Iran, no matter how many billions of dollars' worth of advanced weaponry they were promised.

Second, the JCPOA became a cudgel in America's radicalized domestic politics. It is hard to pinpoint precisely when the political discourse in the United States became so polarized. Scholars know that the civil rights movement; Nixon's southern strategy, which played on white resentment toward advances in civil rights for African Americans; the 1994 Republican "Revolution," whose leaders pursued a strategy aimed at vilifying their political opponents; the 2000 presidential election and the Supreme Court's subsequent decision that determined it in *Bush v. Gore* all had profound impacts on political comity in the United States. Regardless of its origins, deep divisions in domestic politics in America were present when Barack Obama was elected president in November 2008. The depth of opposition to the president and his agenda was so great that the Iran nuclear deal was destined to be weaponized.

There was a debate to be had about the JCPOA, but the agreement became so intensely partisan that those who wanted it were almost immediately overwhelmed. To supporters of the president and the deal, the choice was between either the JCPOA or war, implying that the agreement's opponents were in favor of regime change in Iran. The fact that some of the JCPOA's fiercest critics had been advocates of the invasion of Iraq made this a particularly potent discursive tactic. To the JCPOA's detractors, the president was hopelessly naïve because the agreement preserved Iran's nuclear program and thus made war more likely. In this environment, it was impossible to have a serious discussion of both the pros and cons of the JCPOA, especially if you were an ambitious Democrat or Republican. For the former, the agreement became the holy of holies; for the latter, it was the worst deal ever.

Because the JCPOA became just another political hammer to undermine the president, the Republican leadership in Congress was willing to ignore long-standing norms and protocols to undermine it. Enter Israeli prime minister Benjamin Netanyahu. Since his first turn as Israel's head of government in the mid-1990s, Netanyahu had aligned himself with the Republican Party. Both he and Obama's political antagonists had a confluence of interest in destroying the JCPOA. So, the Israeli leader was granted the high privilege of addressing a joint session of Congress on March 3, 2015, during which he outlined his opposition to the nuclear agreement. This gave the Republicans political cover to claim that in their objections to the JCPOA, they were working to help ensure Israel's security—an issue that both was popular, especially with their constituents, and was a core American interest in the Middle East.

Third—and most germane to the overall themes of this book—although the agreement was nominally limited to Iran's nuclear program, Obama and his team hoped that it would have much broader impacts on Iran's internal politics and international behavior. Implicit in the nuclear agreement was the idea that it could mitigate the threat of conflict, diminish the incentive for mischief-making on the part of all the relevant actors, and break Iran's isolation, leading to a regional balance so that all countries could "share" the region.[12] Reflecting on the JCPOA, Ben Rhodes, who served as deputy national security advisor during two terms in office, told the *New York Times Magazine*:

> We don't have to kind of be in cycles of conflict if we can find other ways to resolve these issues. . . . We can do things that challenge the conventional thinking that, you know, "AIPAC doesn't like this," or "the Israeli government doesn't like this," or "the gulf countries don't like it." It's the possibility of improved relations with adversaries. It's nonproliferation. So all these threads that the president's been spinning—and I mean that not in the press sense—for almost a decade, they kind of all converged around Iran.[13]

Writing after the fact, two of Obama's advisors made this point in an article defending the agreement against its critics, declaring that:

> If, by 2030, Iran has not demonstrated that its nuclear program is exclusively peaceful and that it is willing to live in peace with its neighbors, the

United States and its international partners will have difficult decisions to make about how to handle the issue going forward. . . . But since there is a chance that Iran will have different leaders or policies by then—the current Supreme Leader will almost certainly be gone, and a new generation may have come to power—why make those difficult decisions now?[14]

Embedded within Rhodes's statement and the above passage was the hunch that the JCPOA would render the region stable enough for the United States to relieve itself of the responsibility of being the Middle East's sentry. This would, in turn, allow Washington to shift its attention to Asia, where there was a long list of festering challenges and potential opportunities that had been left unaddressed while Washington remained deeply invested in the politics of Arabs, Israelis, Turks, Kurds, and Iranians.

In reality, the JCPOA had the opposite of its intended effects. The Iranian regime's legitimacy is based in part on hostility to the United States. Its leaders could not make a deal with the country they called the "Great Satan" without demonstrating their continued independence from Washington. This virtually assured that, after signing the agreement, the Iranian government would take some destabilizing action to prove they had not lost their revolutionary mojo. So the Iranians continued their support for Hizballah, Palestinian Islamic Jihad, and Hamas. Iran also provided weapons, training, and funding for Shia militant groups in Bahrain and stepped up its support for the Houthis in Yemen. In Iraq, American forces came under increasing fire from Iranian-backed militias. It is likely that the Iranians would have done much of this anyway, but it belied the notion that coming to terms with Iran through the JCPOA would bring more stability to the region. In addition, the financial relief that the agreement provided for meant more resources for Tehran to fund its proxies—both political parties and militias—throughout the region.

Rather than sharing the region, the Israelis, Emiratis, Saudis, Bahrainis, and others drew closer diplomatically and enhanced their secret security cooperation to ensure Iran's isolation. Successive American presidents have worked hard to achieve closer ties between Israel and Washington's Arab partners, but these relations developed after the JCPOA—not because of the United States, but despite it. Ironically, this left the United States outside the regional strategic consensus that American policymakers had worked so hard to build over the previous almost forty years.

As the nuclear agreement came under attack from nearly all quarters, the Obama administration and its supporters contended that the JCPOA was the best agreement the United States could have obtained. That is likely true, but it was also proved too ambitious given the diplomatic and political opposition to the deal. Although it was different in kind from the transformative efforts of the Clinton and Bush years, President Obama's determination to strike a nuclear deal also sought to remake the region, though in a different way. This was lost on most observers.

Of course, the view within Washington was that whatever shortcoming and opposition there was to the JCPOA, it did not matter. The working assumption in Washington was that America's regional partners and congressional Republicans were going to have to live with the agreement because President Obama's (more than) likely successor, Secretary of State Hillary Clinton, would never walk away from it. Like many of the American foreign-policy community's assumptions about the Middle East, the belief that Clinton would become president proved to be erroneous.

Ending Forever Wars

On June 16, 2015, with Neil Young's "Rockin' in the Free World" blaring in the background, Donald Trump rode the escalator to the lobby level of his flagship building in Manhattan, Trump Tower, to announce that he was seeking the presidency. Onlookers lined the landings near the escalators, some dressed in Trump T-shirts and others holding what looked like homemade signs expressing support for the real-estate developer and reality-television star. A large banner that read "TRUMP—Make America Great Again" hung off to one side. A lectern with a smaller version of the banner framed by eight American flags stood on a raised dais along with Ivanka Trump—who clapped along to the beat, apparently unaware that Young's song was an angry and searing indictment of American society and capitalism. When Trump ascended the stage, she kissed her father and departed to take a place off to the side along with her husband and the future first lady. A large contingent of the press crowded around just below the new candidate, snapping photos on every kind of camera from every imaginable angle. It was what Trump does best: create a spectacle.

Only two minutes into the start of his remarks, which would last the better part of an hour, Trump set the tone for his campaign and subsequent tenure in the Oval Office. He proclaimed that: "When Mexico sends its people, they're not sending their best. They're not sending you. They're not sending you. They're sending people that have lots of problems, and they're bringing those problems with us. They're bringing drugs. They're bringing crime. They're rapists. And some, I assume, are good people."[15] Video clips of those eight sentences have been played over and over again to the extent that they have become an indelible moment in American politics. Lost in the miasma of these racist tropes was the fact that the majority of Trump's address was devoted to foreign policy, with particular attention to the Middle East. In addition to decrying the state of America's relationship with China, comparing America's manufacturing capabilities unfavorably to Japan's, denouncing US trade policy, and highlighting the flight of American jobs to Mexico, Trump assailed Washington over the Islamic State, the civil war in Syria, the conflict in Yemen, the invasion of Iraq, and the American-Saudi codependency.

By the time of Trump's announcement, the United States had been at war in the Middle East for more than a decade. The previous June, the Islamic State had captured territory in Iraq equivalent in area to the size of the state of Maryland, compelling the Obama administration to deploy American combat forces back to the country. Syria's civil war had contributed to instability among its neighbors and in Europe as millions of Syrians sought safety from the Assad regime. Iran continued to sow chaos in the region while the Obama administration negotiated with its leaders over Tehran's nuclear program.

From Trump's perspective, this parlous state of affairs was the fault of America's elites—both Democrats and Republicans—who'd gotten the United States involved in the Middle East but did not know how to withdraw, all the while wasting trillions of dollars that would be better spent at home. Revolt against American elites over the invasion of Iraq and Washington's transformative project in the Middle East more generally would be a theme that Trump would return to at every opportunity on the campaign trail, to devastating effect. For example, at the ninth presidential-primary debate at the Peace Center in Greenville, South Carolina, in February 2016, he attacked Jeb Bush—brother of George W. Bush:

Obviously the war in Iraq was a big fat mistake . . . it took him [Jeb Bush] five days before his people told him what to say and he ultimately said it was a mistake . . . the war in Iraq . . . we spent $2 trillion, thousands of lives . . . we don't even have it, Iran has taken over Iraq with the second largest oil reserves in the world. Obviously, it was a mistake . . . we should never have been in Iraq, we have destabilized the Middle East . . . they lied.[16]

In Greenville, Trump was blasting Bush and his brother, but he was also assailing the foreign-policy community writ large. As a candidate and as president, Trump's boorish and peculiar style often obscured a simple but important question he was asking the experts: "Why do we do what we do?" The answer was essentially a combination of "because that is what we do" and attacks on Trump for his laziness, ignorance, and lack of seriousness.

As president, Trump ignored much of what the State Department, CIA, Pentagon, and a legion of foreign-policy experts advised him, relying instead on his gut. Trump's skepticism of the diplomats, ambassadors, and analysts was reflected in several unorthodox moves and initiatives. These included his willingness to meet with North Korean leader Kim Jong-un, the president's unusually public and critical approach to NATO allies, the imposition of trade tariffs for national-security reasons on close allies such as Canada and European countries, and the decision to negotiate directly with the Taliban without the Afghan government. Each of these policies was met with howls of protest from American elites. When it came to the Middle East, President Trump's instinct was to "end forever wars," a catchphrase taken up by activists ranging from the so-called Progressive Democrats all the way through the Libertarian and nationalist wings of the American Right.

The slogan "ending forever wars" (sometimes referred to as "endless wars") suggests a reordering of priorities, but as a strategy it was ill-defined. The words *endless* and *forever* intimate that there is some knowable time when conflicts become forever and endless.[17] Advocates don't offer a metric, though. The idea also seems to suggest "a military intervention that failed to achieve its goals," but that can happen relatively quickly in a conflict.[18] None of this may matter at a political rally intended to harvest votes from the grievances of Americans, but without a rigorous definition, ending so-called forever wars can lead to policy failures. It did not matter much during the Trump era, however. Despite using the phrase consistently, he did not follow through on the pledge to end forever wars. In fact, during his first three years in office, the president actually deployed more forces to the Middle East than he brought home.[19]

Consistent with his incoherent policymaking in other spheres, he also pursued bellicose policies that foreign-policy experts and Trump's political opponents feared would draw the United States ever deeper into the area. For example, in May 2018, President Trump withdrew the United States from the JCPOA and replaced the agreement with a policy that came to be known as "maximum pressure." Depending on who in the administration was articulating the policy—which featured enhanced sanctions targeting

Iranian oil exports and Tehran's ability to conduct business with multi-national firms, among other measures—the president's goal was either to compel Iran's leader to sign a new deal that would be superior to the JCPOA or to facilitate the collapse of the regime.

Maximum pressure did not produce a new agreement, nor did Iran's people rise up and bring down the Islamic regime. Instead, the policy impelled the Iranians to step up their efforts to disrupt and destabilize the American-led order in the region. In Iraq, Iran's allies often targeted American forces with rocket fire. At times, even the massive US embassy complex in Baghdad's Green Zone came under assault. In the summer of 2019, Iran's air-defense forces shot down an American surveillance drone operating over the Gulf and, in a 1980s redux, the Islamic Revolutionary Guard Corps attacked five oil tankers and a bunkering ship. Then, in September, the Iranians launched a drone and missile attack on Abqaiq, the largest oil-processing facility in the world, and the Khurais oil field—both in Saudi Arabia—temporarily taking about 6 percent of global oil supply offline.

President Trump did not respond militarily to any of Iran's provocations. When the Iranians brought down the American drone, the president dismissed the incident, telling journalists that it must have been an Iranian general acting "stupid." In response to the Abqaiq and Khurais attacks, President Trump broke from forty years of declared policy, committing the United States to ensuring the security of Persian Gulf oil fields. He deflected questions about any potential American response by reminding members of the press that the Iranians had attacked Saudi Arabia, not the United States. This attitude was consistent with both his campaign rhetoric and his long-standing skepticism about the American role in the Gulf. As far back as the 1980s, he had been declaring that the Saudis and others in the Gulf should pay for their protection.[20]

More revealing than the president's reaction to Iranian provocations was that of the American foreign-policy community. With large amounts of Saudi Arabia's oil off the market, American officials, members of Congress, and analysts shrugged. Perhaps there was no sense of crisis because global oil supplies were high, the Saudis were able to make up for some losses by releasing petroleum in storage, and they were able to repair both facilities relatively quickly. At the same time, the broad agreement in Washington that Iran's attacks did not warrant an American military response suggested that Trump was not alone in his desire to do away with the Carter Doctrine and its Reagan Corollary.

Yet less than three months after declining to respond militarily to the Abqaiq and Khurais attacks, the president gave an order that risked pulling the United States into military confrontation in the Middle East. On January 3, 2019, at 12:47 A.M. Baghdad time, an American MQ-9 drone—known as a Reaper—fired missiles at a Toyota sedan and a Hyundai minivan traveling together along the access road that runs to and from Baghdad International Airport. In the vehicles were Abul Mahdi al-Muhandis, the leader of an Iraqi terrorist group called Kataib Hizballah, and Iran's Major General Qassem Soleimani. During the previous week, Muhandis's forces had fired about thirty rockets at an airbase in north central Iraq, killing a contractor and injuring several American and Iraqi soldiers. Then, on New Year's Eve, a mob under the direction of Iranian proxies had assaulted the US embassy in Baghdad, breaching its main gate.

Muhandis was a valuable target. His group had been particularly lethal to American troops in Iraq, and his Iranian patrons could reliably count on him to spill blood and intimidate Iraqi officials to ensure that Tehran got its way in Baghdad. Yet Muhandis's presence in the vehicle may have been a happy coincidence for the Pentagon and CIA because the operation's target was Soleimani. The head of the Islamic Revolutionary Guard Corps Qods Force had taken on an almost-mythic status in the Middle East. Soleimani pulled the political levers in Iraq, rescued Syria's Bashar al-Assad from what seemed like certain defeat, helped ensure Hizballah's vice grip on Lebanon, and took full advantage of Saudi Arabia's ill-conceived intervention in Yemen to pin down Iran's adversary in an unwinnable war. He had rendered four Arab capitals satellites of Tehran and seemed untouchable, slipping from one war zone to another without suffering so much as a scratch. Until, that is, President Trump brought an end to Soleimani's bloody campaign.

There were few outside of Iran who mourned the major general's demise, but it was nonetheless a head-scratching moment in Trump's US Middle East policy. The president had said he wanted to end forever wars, made bringing troops home from the region part of his "Make America Great Again" campaign, and studiously kept his finger off the trigger when Tehran threatened global oil supplies, yet he ordered the assassination of one of the Iranian regime's most important figures. The very fact that Soleimani was revered and feared throughout the region rendered him among the most valuable instruments of Iran's foreign policy.

In Washington, there were concerns that President Trump's heedlessness would plunge the United States into war. It was certainly possible.

The Iranians would have to respond. But the worst fears of columnists, TV talking heads, and foreign-policy analysts were not realized. The Iranians fired a barrage of medium-range missiles on American positions in Iraq, injuring twenty-nine soldiers. Iran's leaders also vowed further revenge at a time and place of their own choosing. Having made their respective points, the Americans and Iranians holstered their weapons and went back to business as usual prior to Soleimani's killing. The entire episode reflected the competing impulses at the core of the Trump administration's approach to the Middle East—impulses that were never reconciled. The president often struck an aggressive tone and goaded the Iranians, but he sought to avoid conflict in the region to the point of discarding the American commitment to protect the flow of oil.

The only other area of the Middle East where President Trump evinced an interest was in peace between Israelis and Palestinians. As he made clear during his run for the presidency, he did not lack the ambition of previous administrations when he vowed to strike the "deal of the century." The president's approach was a departure from the past, but his administration merely replaced the fever dream of a two-state solution with a wholly unworkable solution of its own. After pursuing a policy that sought to convince the Palestinians of the hopelessness of their cause during the first three years of his administration, President Trump and his advisors tabled their idea for a territorial settlement of the conflict called "Peace to Prosperity: A Vision to Improve the Lives of the Palestinian and Israeli People."[21] The plan left the Palestinians with a not-quite-sovereign statelet that closed off the possibility of the return of refugees, territorial contiguity, and a capital in Jerusalem. Mahmoud Abbas, the leader of the Palestinian Authority, rejected it out of hand.

Despite the failure of his deal of the century, President Trump could count the 2020 Abraham Accords as an accomplishment. The agreement, which established peace and the normalization of relations between Israel and the United Arab Emirates, Bahrain, Sudan, and Morocco, was historic. Upon leaving office in January 2021, President Trump could credibly claim that under his watch, Israel took steps toward becoming more integrated into the Middle East. Critics are right that the Abraham Accords did little to address the question of Palestine, but the deal's Arab signatories did not seem to mind. The Emiratis, Bahrainis, Moroccans, and Sudanese clearly believed that waiting for a resolution to the Palestinian problem detracted from national goals like economic development, security, and, in Sudan's case, reintegration into the rest of the world after years of international sanctions. There were two important implications of the Abraham Accords in terms of American interests. First, the American role in clinching the agreement was, in part, the further fulfillment of US efforts to widen the circle of peace in the region. Second, if Israel's incorporation into the Middle East were to proceed, helping to ensure the country's security will become less important to Americans and their leaders.

Incoherence and Confusion

The Obama and Trump years amounted to an incomplete revolution in US Middle East policy. President Obama's instincts were for retrenchment, but he departed from this approach a number of times including when he committed forces to what was essentially a NATO-led effort at regime change in Libya and the renewal of democracy promotion after the Arab uprisings when he affirmed that the fall of regional leaders was an opportunity "to pursue the world as it should be."[22] Then there was the nuclear agreement with Iran. It was a paradox. The JCPOA was to be the instrument through which President Obama intended to extricate the United States from the Middle East, but his way out was through transformation—a shared region— that few Middle Eastern leaders supported. Of course, it was hardly the "stupid [stuff]" akin to President George W. Bush's zeal to vouchsafe freedom to Middle Easterners, but President Obama demonstrated that, despite his stated convictions, the idealist-transformative impulse in American foreign policy ran deep.

As for Trump, one of the underlying rationales for his run for the presidency was to fix the errors of America's political elite, which he and his constituents believed had undermined America's greatness. The so-called endless wars in the Middle East were the most visible manifestation of the perfidy of elites. Yet Trump's record on retrenchment is decidedly mixed. He both surged US forces to the region and withdrew them, at times promising withdrawals that never happened. He also ordered the killing of Iran's Qassem Soleimani that threatened wider conflict, but Trump also repudiated the Carter Doctrine and the Reagan Corollary when he did not—with bipartisan support—respond to Iran's September 2019 attack on Saudi oil facilities. That episode reinforced for Washington's regional partners that the United States, beset with its own problems, was exhausted and unwilling to play the role it had claimed for itself as the provider of regional security. In turn, Saudis, Emiratis, Israelis, Bahrainis, and Egyptians decided to try to resolve regional problems on their own, which did not end well for Syrians, Yemenis, or Libyans. They also banded together to manage the Iran challenge and looked for alternative external powers for help. America's confusion about its role and the incoherence of its half in, half out policies yielded an entirely predictable result: the big hedge.

6

Retrenching and Hedging

Nestled among Washington's ecosystem of ambassadors; ambassadors plen-ipotentiary; first, second, and third secretaries; and counselors of all stripes are the defense attachés. Typically of mid-rank in the diplomatic pecking order, they are part military professional, part diplomat, and part communications specialist whose job is to look after the defense relationships between their home countries and the United States. They are also a great resource for anyone interested in how the people in uniform view the often-complex relations between their ministries, the US Congress, and a given American president.

It was with that unique perspective in mind that, on a cold morning in early 2013, I met a Middle Eastern defense attaché for breakfast at a small café in Georgetown. During a wide-ranging conversation that crisscrossed the region, he relayed to me that, by his estimation, there would come a time—sooner rather than later—when his country would no longer be able to rely on the United States to provide security and stability in the region. He mentioned Rand Paul of Kentucky, a Senate Republican of the libertarian strain, who was consistently an opponent of foreign assistance. It was also in the defense attaché's view that Democrats were eager to wash their hands of the Middle East, pointing to President Obama's withdrawal from Iraq in 2011. He added that it was clear to him that Americans were looking inward with increasing anger.

In the time since we met, American politics has become more polarized. There are many reasons for this, of course, but the Middle East seems to have played an outsize role. In a narrative that has taken hold among parts of the electorate, American elites caused significant damage to the United States in the years after the 9/11 attacks. The wars in Afghanistan and Iraq squandered resources and shattered the families of those killed and wounded. When Barack Obama derided "stupid wars" and Donald Trump declared that the United States could have been rebuilt with the money spent on the Middle East, they were both speaking to disaffected Americans who had grown weary of the international social engineering projects of the political class.

They were tired of their fathers, mothers, brothers, sisters, uncles, and cousins being deployed to the Middle East for their third, fourth, or even fifth tours in Iraq (or Afghanistan). It would have been one thing if there was a return on Washington's investment, but there was none.

Concomitant with the efforts to re-engineer Middle Eastern societies was the transformation of America. In parallel to its military expeditions in the Middle East and Central Asia, the United States embarked on a massive expansion of both the reach and capabilities of its domestic-security agencies, which, with the exigencies of the global war on terror, were left unaccountable. Then, in 2008, years of irresponsible practices resulted in the failure—or near failure—of a number of investment banks, mortgage lenders, and insurance companies. The collapse of the housing market, the near destruction of the iconic American auto industry, the spike in unemployment, and the sharpest economic contraction since the Great Depression produced widespread economic and social dislocation as well as racial animus. The combination of all of these problems seemed to coalesce in Americans' rage at elites and each other culminating in the election of Donald Trump in 2016.

Washington's overly ambitious foray to transform the Middle East had wrought instability in the region and contributed to the palpable anger in American politics that widened existing societal cleavages and opened new ones. This dismal state of affairs contributed to a debate within the foreign-policy community about the proper role for the United States in the region.

Retrenchment, Reduction, and Withdrawal

Donald Trump's answer to the crises that had been buffeting the United States was to "Make America Great Again," which contained unmistakable parallels with, and allusions to, the nativism, racism, and fascism of the America First movement that became prominent in the 1930s and 1940s.[1] Its updated "MAGA" form was based on a specific grievance: elites had made suckers out of ordinary Americans whose well-being they had undercut with an almost treasonous devotion to what he and his supporters derisively called "globalism." For Trump, the post–World War II order in which the United States nurtured global peace and prosperity through free trade and an assortment of international organizations and institutions rendered everyone except Americans wealthier and more secure.

On an emotional level, one could understand the appeal of Trumpism for his voters after almost two decades of foreign conflict and domestic tribulations. Yet MAGA was deeply at odds with itself. One of the ways that Trump claimed he would achieve this vision was by reducing America's presence around the world, especially in the Middle East. The savings associated with this kind of change, he insisted, could be devoted to America's myriad needs. That is an entirely reasonable position, one that President Trump's predecessor also held. At the same time, with no apparent awareness of the contradiction, his administration also wanted the United States to remain the dominant actor in the Middle East, and indeed around the globe.

This is not to suggest that President Trump had an intellectually grounded worldview. By his own admission, he followed his gut. Unknowingly, he was also tapping into ideas with roots across the political spectrum, which had also aimed to bring an end to America's foreign-policy activism. They were the Libertarians, progressive Left, and Realists/Neorealists.[2] The former had long been concerned that an activist foreign policy requires the accumulation of government power, which, in the libertarian worldview, is always a threat to freedom. The Cato Institute was the leading light of libertarian ideas in Washington, but despite occupying choice real estate halfway between the White House and Capitol Hill, the libertarians had a limited influence, at best, on foreign policy. They could claim Senator Paul and his father, Ron, who had represented Texans for almost three decades in the House of Representatives, but few others of note.

Over the years, writers at the *Nation* and *Mother Jones* along with analysts at the Center for International Policy and the Institute for Policy Studies were the standard-bearers of a Leftist foreign policy. These experts, journalists, editors, and pundits, now known as the "Progressives," abhor what they have long considered to be the militarism, imperialism, and neoliberal economics baked into Washington's approach to the world through the post–World War II era. Despite its popularity on college campuses, however, this critique mostly remained on the foreign-policy margins. There were prominent progressive voices in Congress, the best-known among the old guard including Senator Bernie Sanders; Representative Dennis Kucinich, who left Congress in 2013; and Representative Maxine Waters. There was also a younger group of legislators who rose to prominence during the Trump years, such as Alexandria Ocasio-Cortez, Pramila Jayapal, Cori Bush, Rashida Tlaib, Ilhan Omar, Mark Pocan, and Jamie Raskin, among others. Yet collectively, they had less influence on foreign policy than their legions of Twitter (now X) followers would suggest. Other groups that labeled themselves "Progressive," but did have clout among policymakers, such as the Center for American Progress, were rebranded centrist Democrats.

Unlike the Libertarians and Progressives, Realists have been influential in American foreign policy.[3] Figures such as Hans Morgenthau, the theologian Reinhold Niebuhr, George Kennan, and, most of all, Henry Kissinger, helped to shape both the way that foreign-policy practitioners thought about the world and about policy itself. Given their central concern with the distribution of power among states, the Realists' progeny—the Neorealists who argue that the structure of the international system explains the behavior of states—became increasingly vocal in their opposition to American foreign policy throughout the post–Cold War period.[4] They had been skeptical of NATO expansion, arguing that it was unnecessarily provocative toward Russia and likely to be destabilizing in Europe—arguments that came to the fore once again in early 2022 when Russia invaded Ukraine. In the early 2000s, the Neorealists had turned their fire on the invasion of Iraq and the related efforts to transform the Middle East, arguing perceptively that these projects amounted to needless expenditures of resources that sapped the power of the United States to the benefit of other states in the international system—in particular, China. The leading lights of this school of thought were primarily academics who often appeared in the journal *International Security*, but also, at important moments, in the flagship magazine of the foreign-policy establishment of which they were so critical, *Foreign Affairs*.[5] They were by many measures more influential in Washington than either the Libertarians or the Progressives, but for much of the post-9/11 era, their critiques made little headway inside the Beltway's foreign-policy community.

In 2019, the Libertarians, Progressives, and Neorealists came together under the umbrella of a new Washington-based think tank called the Quincy Institute for Responsible Statecraft. Founded with money from the unlikely corporate and Left-Right philanthropic duo of George Soros and Charles Koch, the organization and its scholars advocate for a foreign policy based on limiting the exercise of American power around the world. Despite having a roster of well-known scholars, Quincy was not necessarily a welcome addition in the Washington ideas industry. One magazine article delving into the sources of its funding, ideological inclinations, and suspected Iranian ties of one of its founders called it "Washington's Weirdest Think Tank."[6] In ways it surely is, but some of the disdain for Quincy can be traced to the iconoclastic views of its experts who have challenged prevailing Beltway orthodoxies. The inclusion of new ideas in Washington was a healthy development and should have been welcomed, but few people like to have their long-held beliefs and arguments challenged. There was also an odd in-your-face social-media presence of some of Quincy's less-accomplished employees, who clearly preferred to engage in muckraking rather than engage in sober analysis, adding to the thinly veiled antagonism between the organization and other more well-established think tanks.

Most of the Washington foreign-policy community was decidedly liberal internationalist in orientation, in no small part because they believed that the post–World War II American-led order worked. Millions around the world were safer, freer, and more prosperous under that system than they might have been otherwise. And, for America's elected leaders, foreign-policy officials, analysts, and journalists, an international order predicated on American military, diplomatic, and economic dominance around the globe had become common sense. No one in the mainstream of American foreign-policy thinking ever reexamined the basic assumptions about US primacy in the world.[7] There was no apparent need for this exercise. After all, America had been successful around the world.

Yet the Progressives saw imperialism, the Libertarians' autocracy, and the Neorealists' overextension in the liberal-internationalist approach to the world. And as the initial optimism after the Cold War curdled in the face of repeated foreign-policy failures, ideas associated with these competing strands of thought became integrated into the work of mainstream foreign-policy analysts. The Carnegie Endowment for International Peace's Task Force, "Making U.S. Foreign Policy Work Better for the Middle Class," was emblematic of that change.[8] This group, which was made up of a who's who of George W. Bush, Barack Obama, and future Joe Biden administration officials, started from the perspective that US trade policy, which undermined American manufacturing jobs and wars in faraway lands, had destabilized American society. In this way, the report was an implicit acceptance of one of Trump's primary critiques of America's foreign-policy elites. The authors of the task-force report only mentioned the Middle East once, but because the United States had expended so many resources on the region, it was clear that they were responding to the meager returns on America's investment there over the previous two decades.

The financial, human, and diplomatic costs of the global war on terror, the invasion of Iraq, the Freedom Agenda, and the effort to build a Palestinian state were staggering. Added to this unfortunate situation was the parallel and unsuccessful effort in Central Asia to build a state in Afghanistan. To the Carnegie task force and to many experts on Middle East policy, the idea of continuing in the same policies was unsustainable, compelling officials and analysts to re-examine prevailing assumptions. Foreign-policy analysts picked up and explored ideas like retrenchment, reduction, and even withdrawal as the proper courses for the United States in the Middle East. And while these concepts mean different things, analysts often used them interchangeably to underline the need for fundamental change in the American approach to the region. Of course, there were some who argued that retrenchment, reduction, and withdrawal were the wrong approach to the dilemmas the United States confronted in the Middle East, but the overall weight of the debate favored a diminished American presence in the region.[9]

Implicit in all of the work advocating for a reduced American presence in the region was the recognition that the United States was overextended. Thus there was a need for "recalibration," which would focus policymaking on achieving US interests, thereby making that task easier.[10] Other analysts perceptively argued that it did little good for Americans to be half in, half out of the region, especially since changes in both places—resurgent authoritarianism after the Arab uprisings and a distracted, polarized America—made it an inauspicious moment for Washington in the Middle East. Consequently, the United States should "reduce" its presence there.[11] Others reluctantly concluded that, as the post–Cold War world in which the United States could drive events was coming to an end, there was no longer an interest in the Middle East worth defending. To do so would distract from new geostrategic priorities elsewhere in the world.[12]

One could understand why, after two difficult decades, analysts believed it was necessary to revisit policies that were unsuccessful. At the same time, the proposals for a new direction in America's Middle East policy had a perplexing quality to them. Although they recognized previous failures, few, if any, mainstream analysts were willing to shed the liberal internationalism that had shaped their worldview. So, while they called for more modest approaches to the region, some experts nevertheless laid out a significant agenda for the United States. Despite declaring a need for the United States to undertake some form of withdrawal, some of the very same analysts called on Washington to push for the establishment of a Palestinian state, to resolve the Syrian conflict, stabilize Lebanon, and protect human rights in Egypt. These were all laudable goals, but they were also some of the Middle East's most complex problems. Addressing them would require significant financial, political, diplomatic, and perhaps even military resources, with little guarantee of success. These proposals clearly ran counter to the idea that the United States should reduce its presence and goals in the region.

A substantial part of the problem with the literature on retrenchment, reduction, and withdrawal was not so much that it was wrong, but that some of it lacked historical depth.[13] Without a doubt, Operation Iraqi Freedom and much of the rest of the Bush administration's post-9/11 foreign policy in the Middle East were overly ambitious in their faith that the United States could transform the Middle East, but history did not begin with regime change in Iraq. As previous chapters have highlighted, since the early 1990s, the United States had sought to use its power to transform the region. Obviously, there were differences in emphasis and approach between the Clinton and Bush administrations, but these variations—no matter how significant—should not obscure the underlying and ambitious goals for the Middle East that were at the heart of US policy for the better part of thirty years. This analytic blind spot erroneously demarcates the 1990s and the 2000s into distinct eras. It is more accurate to see them as phases within a broad framework in which Washington embarked on international re-engineering in the Middle East.

An important exception to the commentary about reduction, realignment, and withdrawal was the work of actual advocates of retrenchment—specifically, those who believed that "offshore balancing" was the wisest approach to the Middle East.[14] To their credit, these analysts understood that ensuring the free flow of oil from the region was a core American interest, but they nevertheless believed that the way Washington had gone about it over the previous three decades had wasted American resources. In their diagnosis of the problem, offshore balancers were not wrong, but their approach had a having-one's-cake-and-eating-it-too aspect to it. In their conception of the world, the United States would provide copious amounts of weaponry to its partners to ensure a regional balance. At a moment of "disequilibrium," Washington would intervene in the crisis and re-establish stability. Once that was accomplished, the United States could safely withdraw and resume working to maintain equilibrium through support for its partners.

Offshore balancing seems like an elegant response to America's previous ambition in the Middle East. It solved the problem of securing a critical interest without overinvesting in the region. Given the right tools, regional partners can be the sources of stability and security without risking the lives of US military personnel and freeing up resources to meet geostrategic challenges in other parts of the globe.

Yet, offshore balancing had a number of significant shortcomings. First, it had been tried before and had failed. It was, after all, essentially a restatement of the Nixon Doctrine, which manifested in the Middle East with the Twin Pillar strategy. Yet, as Chapter 2 explains, this approach collapsed under the weight of the Iranian Revolution and the siege of Mecca. Past failure does not preclude future success, however. Operation Desert Shield/Storm is a good example of how offshore balancing should work. In response to a crisis, the United States deployed more than half a million soldiers to Saudi Arabia to push Iraqi forces from Kuwait. Of course, the United States never left after the Iraqis surrendered. Yet offshore balancers would be correct to call that a policy failure rather than a defect in their analytic concept.

More germane to the critique of offshore balancing is the important recognition that, on the eve of Saddam Hussein's invasion of Kuwait, the United States was not exactly offshore even though it was not quite onshore. After the breakdown of the Twin Pillars strategy in 1979, American air and naval assets appeared in the region on a rotating basis to confront Iran and ensure free navigation in the Persian Gulf. It is true that the American Airborne Warning and Control Systems that guided the Saudis in confrontations with Iranian aircraft in the mid-1980s and naval armada that protected American-flagged Kuwaiti tankers had departed the region by the time the Iraqis rolled into Kuwait. Even so, there were about two thousand American service members in the Gulf, the vast majority of whom (1,283) were serving in Saudi Arabia.[15] Whether the United States was onshore or offshore before August 2, 1990, was a matter of perspective.

Another problem stems from different interpretations of balance. In the late 2010s and early 2020s, John Mearsheimer and Stephen Walt, the two most prominent advocates for offshore balancing and restraint, did not perceive a need for the United States to rebalance the region given their assessment of the prevailing power dynamics in the Gulf. Others, notably America's Middle Eastern partners, perceived the regional balance to be dangerously in favor of Iran and wanted the United States to be more engaged in deterring and containing Tehran's malign influence. Who was correct? That depends on whether one sits in Chicago, Cambridge, Riyadh, Jerusalem, Manama, or Abu Dhabi. The problem of perception underscores a final problem with offshore balancing: it assumes a confluence of interests between the balancer and its regional partners. This is not always a good assumption. Since at least the invasion of Iraq, mistrust has marked America's relations with its clients in the Middle East.

Fear and Loathing in the Middle East

Perhaps the best way to explicate this distrust between the United States and its clients in the Middle East is by way of analogy to Russia's invasion of Ukraine in early 2022. There was an interesting parallel between Moscow's advance into its neighbor and Baghdad's takeover of Kuwait in August 1990 that Arab leaders in the Gulf should have appreciated. Like Russian President Vladimir Putin and Ukraine, Saddam Hussein rejected Kuwait's sovereignty, calling it the "nineteenth province of Iraq." And like the Iraqi takeover of its neighbor three decades earlier, American policymakers and their counterparts in Europe concluded that if Russia's invasion of Ukraine was allowed to stand, it would set a terrible precedent emboldening countries to use force to address their grievances, whether real or imagined. President Biden also made the public case that the struggle in Europe was about democracy versus autocracy, which it was, but he also needed a number of nondemocracies, notably Middle Eastern oil producers, to be part of the effort.

These parallels between the summer of 1990 and the winter of early 2022 were lost on the region's decision makers as they—especially the Saudis—leaned toward Moscow. Riyadh steadfastly refused American entreaties to pump more oil, which would have meant breaking with its partner, Russia, in what was called OPEC+ (the thirteen members of the oil cartel, plus ten nonmembers, which set targets for petroleum production and thus have significant influence on price). In the spring of 2022, the Saudi and Emirati oil ministers argued that stability of the oil market was more important than playing politics with OPEC+.[16] This was a noticeable diplomatic swipe at President Biden, who would have benefited two ways from a significant increase in the amount of oil on the global market. First, the inevitable fall in the price of crude would have hurt the Russian war effort. Second, more oil would put downward pressure on the price of gasoline for American consumers. Yet the hard realities of supply and demand severely limited the Biden administration's powers of persuasion. America's Gulf partners and the Russian government had a common interest in high petroleum prices, which would advance their ambitious development goals even as it also helped Moscow's effort to destroy Ukraine. Among the most elaborate of these plans were in Saudi Arabia, which experienced a 9.6 percent GDP growth rate in the first quarter of 2022 on the strength of increased oil prices. In those three months, a barrel of oil averaged about $100, peaking at $125.

During the same period a year earlier, the average price of oil was $60 per barrel, which was good for American consumers and politicians, but made it difficult for oil producers to balance budgets, no less construct lavish new cities in the desert as the Saudis planned.

Riyadh's position on the Ukraine crisis was encapsulated in an interview Prince Turki al-Faisal gave to an English-language Saudi television program called *Frankly Speaking* in early May 2022. The prince—who had been Saudi Arabia's head of intelligence and then served as ambassador in London and Washington—held no official position but, since the end of his long government service, was often used to send unpleasant messages to American officials through a variety of media outlets. During the interview, the Saudi royal protested that, contrary to the commentary of some Western analysts and journalists, Saudi Arabia had not taken Moscow's side, emphasizing the Crown Prince's offer to mediate the conflict. (The friendly interviewer did not point out that proposing to mediate had become standard political and diplomatic cover for those leaders who did not necessarily support Ukraine.) Never missing an opportunity to assail the United States for its support of Israel, Prince Turki highlighted the hypocrisy of Washington's response to Russia's invasion of Ukraine while it consistently had acquiesced to Israeli military operations in Arab countries over the years.

More important, he also made clear that Saudi Arabia had been "let down" by the United States when it came to security, pointing to the Biden administration's decision to remove Yemen's Houthis from the State Department's list of foreign terrorist organizations.[17] The Saudis had intervened in their neighbor's civil war against the Houthis in 2015 expecting a cakewalk, but they found themselves in a quagmire. With Iranian help, the Houthis acquired the technology to fire missiles and drones on Saudi population centers, which they did regularly. Even in light of the Houthi attacks, Biden's team had concluded that lifting the terrorist-group designation would facilitate the flow of badly needed humanitarian aid into Yemen. It did have that effect, but it also emboldened the group. Afterward, more missiles fell on Saudi cities, as well as population centers in the UAE. At around the same time, the Biden team delisted the Houthis and removed Patriot missile batteries from Saudi Arabia as part of an effort to reduce the American military presence in the Middle East.

Feeling burned by the White House for leaving them vulnerable to the Houthis and enjoying the benefits of high oil prices, Saudi leaders were not inclined to join the American effort to punish Russia for its war in Ukraine.

In addition, some Saudis also had bitter memories of the debates around the JCPOA and specifically President Obama's view of what was best for the region.[18] They sought to apply the former president's logic to the war in Europe. On March 1, 2022, the Saudi political scientist and director of the Center for Strategic Studies at the Prince Saud Al Faisal Institute for Diplomatic Studies, Mansour Almarzoqi, tweeted, "Dear Europe: your Russia is our Iran. US once said: 'try to share the neighborhood.' EU once said: 'find a regional solution.'" It was clever trolling that captured the profound ambivalence toward the West and United States among Saudi elites.

This thinly veiled hostility broke into an open war of words seven months later, in October 2022, when OPEC+ agreed on a production cut of two million barrels per day. In Washington, policymakers and analysts accused Saudi Arabia of reneging on an unwritten agreement between the Biden administration and the Royal Court that was struck in the summer of 2022. The Saudis, American officials alleged, had agreed to increase the amount of oil on world markets gradually. Instead, they prevailed on OPEC+ to undertake a sharp cut. In response, mostly Democratic members of Congress, fearful that a sudden jump in gas prices would hurt their party in the 2022 midterm elections, took to Twitter to denounce the Saudi alignment with Russia. They proposed removing American forces and withdrawing remaining Patriot missile batteries from the Kingdom. For good measure, they also called on President Biden to cancel weapons contracts with Saudi Arabia's armed forces. The Saudis and their allies took notice and responded in kind. A prominent Emirati political scientist named Abdulkhaleq Abdalla told the *Financial Times*, "At this moment everybody needs Gulf oil, everybody needs Saudi Arabia and the UAE onboard. Some in Washington definitely don't realise there is a new Gulf and we no longer take orders from Washington."[19]

Some Saudis were more pointed. In response to criticism of Crown Prince Mohammed bin Salman for lining up with Putin and for being neither a reliable nor responsible partner, Ali Shihabi, who for a time ran an organization inside the Beltway that reflected the Royal Court's views, tweeted, "If U want history let's start with the US invasion of Iraq which Biden and Hillary supported and which opened the door to Iran etc. Talk about irresponsibility when not one US official has been held accountable for that."[20] It was unfortunate that these recriminations were being articulated via Twitter, which places a premium on vitriol and smarter-than-thou one-upmanship, but the claims and counterclaims of Americans, Saudis, and Emiratis nevertheless captured the general tenor of relations. In response to what they saw as American fecklessness, officials in Riyadh and Abu Dhabi refused to toe Washington's line on Ukraine and sought to develop their ties with Moscow and Beijing.

It is important to note that the Saudis and Emiratis were not outliers. Other than Qatar, which was quick to denounce the Russian aggression, all of the region's political and military heavyweights—including Israel—sought to maintain their ties with Moscow while simultaneously expressing support for the Ukrainian people and a mediated solution to the conflict.

It is important to note, however, that trust between the United States and its Middle Eastern partners deteriorated well before Russia's incursion into Ukraine. In the early 2000s, the Egyptians believed that Washington sought to replace Egypt's political system with a new one under the Muslim Brotherhood. This was not accurate, but it was the way the Egyptian government had interpreted US policy toward Egypt, which was only reinforced six years later when, during a popular uprising against Mubarak, President Obama made it clear to the Egyptian leader that he must get on with a transition from power.[21] Mubarak's fall was not only a threat to the defenders of the Egyptian regime, but it was also a significant blow to Gulf leaders who regarded Egypt, with its enormous population and large military, as their strategic depth. Within the Middle East, including in Israel, it quickly became a fact that the Obama administration had turned its back on the Egyptian leader who had carried Washington's water during his almost thirty years in power. This account fed the suspicion among the region's leaders that the United States supported the accumulation of Islamist power. Part of what made Mubarak so important to Washington was that, in addition to keeping the Suez Canal open and maintaining peace with Israel, his boot was planted firmly on the throat of Islamists. The latter was especially important to America's partners in the Gulf. When, in 2012, the Obama administration accommodated itself to the election of a Muslim Brotherhood apparatchik to be Egypt's president, those suspicions were seemingly vindicated.

It was not just Egypt, however. The Saudis, Emiratis, Israelis, Bahrainis, and Egyptians (after the Brothers were overthrown in a 2013 coup d'état) chafed at what they regarded as Washington's solicitous approach toward Turkey's Islamist leader, Recep Tayyip Erdoğan. At the beginning of his multidecade rule, Turkey began negotiations to join the European Union, but in time, Erdoğan became both repressive and a leading patron of fellow Islamists around the region. These included Tunisia's Ennahda Party whose leaders avowed themselves to be Muslim Democrats, Egypt's Muslim

Brothers who found sanctuary in Istanbul, and the Palestinian terrorist group Hamas. Erdoğan had also turned a blind eye to extremists using Istanbul as a gateway to wage war against the regime in Syria, and Turkish intelligence was suspected of supporting al-Qaeda–linked groups in the conflict there. From the perspective of other leaders in the region, Erdoğan had much to answer for given his role sowing instability in Syria. The Turkish president was also much like the Arab autocrats that Washington had targeted in its push for democracy, but nevertheless got a pass from US officials. And then there were America's strategic ties with Qatar, whose neighbors accused it of being, among a range of things, a fount of financial support for Islamist movements of all stripes.

Added to this list of complaints and suspicions about American policy was the chaotic withdrawal from Afghanistan in August 2021 that left the Taliban in power in Kabul once again. Middle Eastern officials and diplomats were dumbfounded. Not long after the last C-17 lifted off from Kabul, an Arab minister visiting the United States relayed his shock to a small group of Americans that the Biden administration would hand power back to the Taliban at a time when Islamists across the region—whether it was a palace coup in Tunisia, an election in Morocco, or ongoing repression in Egypt—had suffered major political blows. The minister wondered aloud what message the apparent success of a violent, extremist group would send to the broader universe of Islamists.

For America's regional partners, if there was any indication of American fecklessness in the Middle East, it was the way in which the United States approached Iran. This was clear from the Almarzoqi and Shihabi tweets, which, while being unofficial, fairly reflected more authoritative views. As previous chapters described in some detail, Middle Eastern leaders concluded that the American invasion of Iraq, President Obama's refusal to intervene directly in Syria against the Assad regime, Washington's support for the Arab uprisings, the JCPOA, the ambivalent American approach to Yemen, President Trump's decision not to respond to Iran's aggressions in the Gulf during the summer of 2019, and all the patter in Washington about retrenchment and de-emphasizing the region represented a conscious tilt toward Iran.

There were, of course, groups and individuals in Washington who either explicitly or implicitly favored a shift toward the Iranians, but US policy was far less coherent than the Saudis, Emiratis, Israelis, and Bahrainis perceived. Rather, it was a manifestation of a variety of pathologies that had impinged upon American foreign-policy making. These included hide-bound bureaucracies, incompetent political appointees, far too much crisis management and far too little policy planning, bad assumptions about the way the Middle East works, a large number of issues erroneously identified as American interests, and domestic political polarization. In particular, America's political divisions contributed to wild swings in policy, which alternated between Republican foreign policy and Democratic foreign policy, but only rarely was it US foreign policy. This problem was perfectly encapsulated in the ill-fated JCPOA that President Obama signed in 2015, which most Democrats hailed as a great foreign-policy achievement despite the consternation of Washington's regional partners. In the 2016 presidential campaign, Donald Trump called the nuclear deal "the worst ever" and, little more than a year into his presidency, pulled the United States out of the agreement in favor of a campaign of maximum pressure to the general acclaim of Republicans and much to the relief of the Saudis, Israelis, Emiratis, and Bahrainis. Then, in 2021, President Biden vowed to return to the nuclear agreement, contributing, once again, to the dismay of both his political opponents and important US partners in the Middle East.

America's friends certainly had a point when it came to Iran, but in their eagerness to impugn US Middle East policy more generally, Middle Eastern leaders willfully overlooked a number of salient facts: Mubarak was overthrown because of internal Egyptian political dynamics; Turkey was often a troublesome partner, but it was also a valuable NATO ally; and Qatar's relations with Islamists were necessary for the United States because it provided a way for American officials to communicate with these groups. Presidents representing the two different political parties concluded—with the support of the American people—that Afghanistan was no longer worth the investment. The diverging perspectives of US policymakers and their Middle Eastern counterparts led inevitably to disenchantment on both sides. In the region, however, the increasingly jaundiced view of American commitments to security and stability encouraged Washington's friends to seek support elsewhere.

The Hedge

When Crown Prince Mohammed bin Salman leaned toward Moscow after Vladimir Putin ordered his armies into Ukraine, he was not the first Middle

Eastern leader to seek relations and benefits from several major powers simultaneously. In the 1950s, during the era of Egypt's Free Officers and the
group's leader, Gamal Abdel Nasser, the Egyptians called it "positive neu-
tralism." Foreign-policy experts now refer to this approach as "hedging."
Because their trust in the United States had faltered as Washington's policy
failures piled up and American domestic politics grew increasingly fraught,
Middle Eastern leaders sought relations with other major powers to com-
pensate. They did not seek to replace the United States, and there was no indication that leaders in the region sought to alter their general orientation
toward America. They wanted nothing more than a partnership with the
United States, but the Middle East's crown princes, kings, presidents, and
prime ministers came to question whether Washington wanted to—or even
could—play the role it had previously assigned itself as the anchor of security
and stability in the region. This all happened at the same time an old power
was beginning to re-emerge and a new ambitious country was establishing
itself as a global force.

Russia's 2015 intervention in Syria to save Bashar al-Assad's regime from
defeat contributed to the legend of Vladimir Putin in the region's capitals.
Having rescued his client, the Russian leader established himself as the pow-
erbroker in the Syrian civil war. With Putin in such a powerful position and
with the United States sitting on the sidelines, some of America's friends were
compelled to upgrade their ties with Moscow.[22] Notably, the Israeli prime
minister and the Turkish president remained in regular contact with Putin
and made numerous sojourns to Sochi—Putin's Black Sea getaway—seeking
to ensure their national-security interests in Syria. Both Israel and Turkey
needed Russian clearance to strike at their enemies in Syria—Iran's Islamic
Revolutionary Guard Corps and Kurdish separatists, respectively.

The Turkish government went further than soliciting Putin's support
in Syria, however. In Washington's fight against extremists, Turks were
outraged that those same separatists were American allies in the fight against
the Islamic State. At the same time, Turkish officials were frustrated at the
steadfast US refusal to bring down the Assad regime, whose brutal response to peaceful demonstrations drove almost four million Syrians into
Turkey, creating a variety of social and economic challenges. Added to these
problems was a host of other irritants in the bilateral relationship, including
an erroneous Turkish charge that the United States was harboring the mas-
termind of a failed coup d'état that sought to overthrow Erdoğan. As a result, Ankara developed its ties with Moscow. Not only did trade and tourism

expand, but so did security ties. In 2019, Turkey took delivery of a Russian-manufactured air-defense system that threatened the aircraft of its own allies in NATO.

For their part, King Salman of Saudi Arabia, Egypt's president Abdel Fatah al-Sisi, and Crown Prince of Abu Dhabi Mohammed bin Zayed (who later became president of the UAE) all paid high-profile visits to Moscow. In return, President Putin made splashy visits to Riyadh and Abu Dhabi, where he inked a variety of agreements. Whether any of the parties had any intention of following through with these deals was less important than the optics of it all. President Putin was indicating that Russia was back in the Middle East, and Gulf leaders were signaling their independence from Washington. The Egyptians actually became major customers for Russian weaponry, purchasing more arms from Moscow than they had since the early 1970s.[23] Egypt was also cooperating with the Kremlin-aligned mercenary army, Wagner Group, which fought alongside the Libyan National Army under wannabe strongman General Khalifa Haftar against his foes in the internationally recognized government in Tripoli. It should not have been lost on anyone that Putin's interest in Libya stemmed in large part from the fact that the country boasts the largest reserves of oil in Africa—much of it located in areas under Haftar's control—and the fourth largest deposits of gas on the continent. When President Biden entered the Oval Office, Russia's influence extended into the Gulf and in a crescent-shaped swath of territory extending from Turkey through Syria into Israel and from there to Egypt and Eastern Libya.

Like Putin, Chinese President Xi Jinping also looked competent and ready to lead, but in a different way from his Russian counterpart. The Chinese government maintained its strict neutrality on regional conflicts and was not as big a player in the regional arms market as the United States, European countries, and Russia, though Beijing was not entirely absent from this bazaar. Saudi Arabia is believed to have purchased ballistic missiles from Beijing over the years and, in early 2022, reports surfaced that Riyadh was producing missiles with Beijing's help.[24] The Saudis, Emiratis, Jordanians, and others in the region were also customers for China's low-cost (and low-capability) drones.[25]

In time, the Chinese government may supply more weaponry to the region, but for the most part, Beijing has pursued a different track in the Middle East: investment, trade, and infrastructure development. China has become such an important economic actor in the Middle East that no US partner has been willing to choose between Washington and Beijing. For example, despite a very public American pressure campaign in 2019 to coerce Middle Eastern countries to drop the use of technology that the Chinese telecom firm Huawei developed, the company has a strong presence in Egypt, Saudi Arabia, and the UAE, among other places. The Chinese were also building, buying, or investing in other critical infrastructure around the region, including ports and industrial parks in the UAE, Oman, Israel, and Egypt.[26] Beijing also made it difficult for American firms to compete in the region when Chinese state-owned companies often underbid on large infrastructure projects by as much as 40 percent.[27]

The Egyptian hedge with Beijing (and Russia for that matter) is not strictly about economic development, but it contains an additional, related dimension. Leaders in Cairo chafed at what they perceived to be Washington's interference in their internal affairs concerning Egypt's appalling human rights record.[28] Unlike American officials, neither Beijing nor Moscow was concerned with the issue given their own abysmal treatment of dissidents and, in China's case, the tyranny and cruelty visited upon the Uighurs.[29] Equally important for Egypt's political class was its belief that the Chinese Communist Party had solved the riddle that they had been pondering since China's rise began in the early 2000s. Specifically, how does a country generate spectacular levels of economic growth without relinquishing political control? For the generals in Egypt, what the Chinese government was able to accomplish in both the economic and political spheres represented a far more appealing model of development than the United States, which, while continuing to boast the globe's most dynamic economy, also featured messy, uncertain, and polarized politics.

As America's regional partners developed their political, economic, and security ties with Washington's global competitors, there were consequences. In response to Turkey's purchase of the Russian-manufactured air-defense system, the US Congress forced the Turks out of the development program for the F-35 Joint Strike Fighter, barred Ankara from purchasing these fifth-generation fighter jets, and levied sanctions against Turkish defense entities. The growing links between China and the UAE jeopardized the sale of fifty F-35 fighters to the latter's air force that the Trump administration promised Emirati leaders after they normalized relations with Israel in 2020.[30] As noted, when the Saudis pushed for a cut in oil production in late 2022, helping both themselves and the Russians, Congress and the Biden administration threatened punitive measures in response.

Josh Rogin, a foreign-policy columnist for the *Washington Post*, summed up the prevailing views inside the Beltway in the spring of 2022 when he savaged the Saudis and Emiratis in an article titled "America's Gulf 'Allies' Are Now Putin's Enablers." The penultimate paragraph captures how frustrating and perplexing the changing regional dynamics had become in Washington:

> The new de facto alliance among Putin, MBS [Mohammed bin Salman] and MBZ [Mohammed bin Zayed] is understandable: All three dictators see the spread of freedom, democracy and human rights as existential threats to their holds on power. But the entire rationalization for U.S. partnerships with these Gulf countries is based on their role as important players in maintaining energy stability. If they aren't doing it, what exactly are we getting in return for our investment?[31]

Gulf leaders responded to this type of criticism with self-serving declarations that the crude-oil market in the spring of 2022 was actually in balance, but that the problem for American consumers at the pump was the lack of refining and production capacity. From their perspective, the shift toward alternative energy had undermined investment in these areas, leaving the world without the ability to produce and refine what it needed.[32] These technocratic arguments convinced few in Washington and reinforced a point that Rogin left implicit: Russia and America's Middle East partners were enjoying the benefits of high oil prices. And because the Saudis, in particular, no longer trusted America's commitment to regional security, they saw no reason to help the United States by pumping more oil. The OPEC+ commitment to cut output by two million barrels per day in October only reinforced this dynamic and deepened the growing disaffection between Washington and Riyadh.

Even Israel was not spared. The Israelis had taken steps to distance themselves from China and insulate their infrastructure from Chinese penetration, but Jerusalem's ties with Moscow remained strong.[33] That brought it into the crosshairs of members of Congress, which was atypical. With the exception of a small group of progressives, members of Congress do not usually criticize Israel publicly. Yet Senator Lindsey Graham—a pro-Israel stalwart—and Representative Adam Kinzinger blasted the Israelis in the press for their unwillingness to sell arms to Ukraine. Other pro-Israel figures, such as Senator Ted Cruz and then–House Minority Leader Kevin McCarthy, reportedly assailed the Israelis in private meetings.[34] As noted above, Israel's leaders actually had valid reasons to maintain ties with Russia due to the exigency of keeping the Iranians off-balance in Syria and disrupting Tehran's supply lines to Lebanon's Hizballah. Even so, the traditional deference with which US senators and representatives treated Israelis, especially when it came to the Jewish state's security policy, did not apply after Putin invaded Ukraine.

The opprobrium heaped upon America's regional partners may have caused their ambassadors in Washington moments of discomfort as they interacted with US officials and the media, but nothing changed as a result of scorching editorials and diplomatic dressing-downs. Even after Turkey and the UAE did not get their F-35s and Congress threatened to cut off Saudi Arabia, the Turks, Emiratis, Saudis, Egyptians, and Israelis all still hedged. None of these countries always saw eye to eye with the United States on a variety of issues, but in the roughly three decades after Saddam Hussein's defeat in the first Gulf war and the collapse of the Soviet Union, they almost always fell in line with Washington.

The willingness of America's partners to lean toward Moscow and Beijing reflected a significant change in an evolving regional order in which Middle Easterners believed they had alternatives to a partnership with the United States. There was a feedback-loop quality to this change. As American officials and analysts came to terms with US failures in the region, they turned to scholarly traditions and ideas that were skeptical of the promise of liberal internationalism. Progressive, Libertarian, and Neorealist interpretations of history in turn gave intellectual cover to the policy community's impulse to retrench. There were elements of each of these strands of thought that contained wisdom—notably, the doubt about America's capacity to transform the world—but taken together, they impelled Washington's partners in the region to look elsewhere in the world for support. That may be fine with elements within the American foreign-policy community who no longer wish to be complicit with the transgressions of Washington's Middle Eastern friends. Without dismissing or diminishing the human rights records of US partners, there is a contradiction within the various forms of the withdrawal argument. If the United States is now engaged in a global competition with the likes of Russia and China, it seems prudent to shore up Washington's ties with the Saudis, Emiratis, Egyptians, Bahrainis, and Israelis, rather than signal to them that the region no longer matters.

The debates about America's proper role in the Middle East reflected the uncertainty that came with an international order that was changing but had not yet changed. No one knew what the outcome would be. The Saudis, Egyptians, Emiratis, Israelis, Turks, and others would not have hedged had they gotten what they wanted—unequivocal American support. Yet Washington's partners detected confusion, ambiguity, indecision, and exhaustion in the United States when it came to the Middle East, sowing fears of American retrenchment. Under these circumstances, hedging with Russia and China was rational, but the answer for the United States in the Middle East was not to withdraw. Retrenching was less a strategy than a reaction to two decades of failure. There was a better way.

7

Back to the Future

A few weeks after President Joe Biden took the oath of office in January 2021, he made the short drive from the White House to the Department of State. In the building's ornate Benjamin Franklin Room, the new chief executive declared that "America is back," to the great relief of the gathered foreign service officers and civil servants whose job it is to look after American interests around the world. The Trump years had been particularly tough on US diplomats as the then president made foreign policy both on the fly and by tweet, forcing them to play catch-up.

Biden's visit came on the heels of a flurry of executive orders he signed during his first hours in office. Among those related to foreign policy were directives that made the United States a member of the World Health Organization once again after a two-year absence, recommitted Washington to the Paris Climate Accord after President Trump pulled out of the agreement, and ended the previous administration's ban on travelers from five predominantly Muslim countries entering the United States. Also, in the months that followed, President Biden reassured America's allies in Europe and Asia that the United States remained steadfast in support of their security after his predecessor had equivocated on this issue.

The administration's efforts pleased NATO officials, climate activists, public health officers, and America's friends in Asia. When it came to the Middle East, Biden and his team were more reserved. The president took his time reaching out to regional leaders. And the four goals that Biden's team initially outlined—returning to the Joint Comprehensive Plan of Action (JCPOA), extricating Saudi Arabia from Yemen, holding authoritarian leaders in the region "accountable" for human rights violations, and supporting the two-state solution—were an odd mixture of priorities, reflecting two competing impulses: retrenchment and transformation. The overall drift seemed more the former than the latter, however.

In practice, the administration reduced the US military's presence in the region, withdrawing both equipment and personnel; chose—like its predecessors—to overlook Iranian provocations throughout the region;

broke with three decades of US policy by not appointing a Special Middle East Peace envoy; and continued to work with the region's authoritarian leaders. At the same time, the White House and State Department officials repeatedly declared that the United States was not leaving the Middle East and that it would remain as engaged as ever. In February 2023, Brett McGurk, the White House's coordinator for the Middle East and North Africa, laid out five principles that guided the administration in the region: security partnerships, deterrence, diplomacy, integration, and values.[1] A month later, Assistant Secretary of State for Near Eastern Affairs Barbara Leaf held a briefing for journalists, during which she emphasized, "President Biden's priority of an affirmative framework for America's engagement in the region," which included "support for de-escalating conflicts, support for democratic principles and elections, human rights, and key economic reforms that are central to our engagement in the region."[2]

The competing instincts in US policy reflected the fact that there was little agreement within the American foreign-policy community about how to approach the Middle East and what was important there. It was as if the United States stood at a crossroads but failed to choose a direction. Instead, American officials sought to paper over the contradictions, hoping no one would notice. Setting out that "vision thing," in the words of President George H. W. Bush, is both thankless and difficult. Any broad statement about foreign policy is vulnerable to pundits, journalists, and experts who will invariably declare it unworkable, under-resourced, too ambitious, not ambitious enough, and thus dead on arrival. This is not to suggest that officials have not staked out a vision in the past. There were the Clinton, Bush, and Obama doctrines, which few, if any, can remember. Only the authors of a "Foreign Policy for the Middle Class"—a bipartisan group of former and future policymakers—can recall what it entailed.

The articulation of a vision to guide US–Middle East policy is urgent, however. Washington is emerging from an era in which its approach to the region alternated between crisis management and a grab bag of issues, all of which were identified as priorities. Yet when everything is important, nothing is. In addition, a broad statement about US policy will diminish the mixed signals that Washington has sent to its regional partners and adversaries. For the last half of the 2010s and during the early 2020s, few officials in the Middle East (or Washington, for that matter) understood whether the United States remained committed to playing a role in the region or whether it was leaving.

The watchwords for American policymakers in the Middle East should be: judiciousness, discretion, balance, and efficiency. This prudential conservatism—not to be confused with conservatism in contemporary political parlance, but rather to sustain or conserve—places a premium on seeing the world as it is, safeguarding against transformational impulses, and enabling policies that do as little harm as possible to US interests in the Middle East.

From prudential conservatism flows a mix of old and new interests and goals whose hierarchy is in flux. What has been important to the United States over many years—oil and Israel—may, in time, prove not to be as central to US policy for a variety of political, technological, economic, and cultural reasons. Other issues like counterterrorism and non-proliferation will remain crucial interests for the United States in the Middle East, if only because of the damage extremists and weapons of mass destruction pose to the United States and its citizens.

A foreign policy in the Middle East based on prudential conservatism must also address the climate crisis, though not in some ambitious effort to solve so-called climate conflicts or use climate initiatives to solve conflicts, but in a more modest way, leverage American diplomacy to help this vulnerable region adapt to the worst ravages of this phenomenon. To do otherwise would risk the stability of the Middle East and regions beyond, especially Europe. Finally, Washington is abuzz with discussion and study of great power competition. Without a doubt, the exercise of Russian and Chinese power in the Middle East represents a challenge to the United States and requires an American response. At the same time, if policymakers see the world the way it is, they will recognize that while the policies of Washington's global adversaries add complexity to the American presence in the Middle East, it is not at all clear that in all instances Russia and China are in conflict with the United States in the Middle East. This runs counter to the Beltway zeitgeist, but a Middle East policy based on balance, prudence, and doing the least amount of harm as possible is superior to the new Cold War that, in the early 2020s, Washington policymakers seemed intent on having.

As noted in previous chapters, years of failure had made it understandable for members of the foreign policy community to conclude that the Middle East is not worth the investment. It certainly was not worth the outlays that the United States made in the decades following the successful end of Operation Desert Storm to transform the region. Nonetheless, the Middle

East remains important to the United States in various ways that warrant a different kind of investment.

Success and Failure in the Middle East

Despite the competing tensions inherent to Biden's approach to the Middle East, officials framed American policy as an effort to "get back to basics." It was not entirely clear which basics they proposed to return to, though the administration did repudiate regime change. Even if the president's advisors were vague about the phrase's meaning, it is useful to understand how US–Middle East policy of the past can help inform the present and future American course of action in the region. There was a time when the United States was successful in the region. Washington can be effective once again, but this will require policymakers to choose priorities based on interests that are achievable at an acceptable cost. That is the essence of prudential conservatism. Moreover, the framework implicitly acknowledges the folly of transformation and the risks of overextension. Instead of redeeming the world, Washington would do well to pursue policies intended to prevent "bad things" from happening to American interests. It is an approach that once served the United States well. There is no reason that it cannot do so in the decades to come.

Critics would, no doubt, argue that the world is a different place from where it was during the roughly five decades of US success in the Middle East. That is true, but it would be a mistake to conclude that there are no lessons to be learned from that era. History is not a roadmap to the future, but it can be a guide for policymakers and analysts, especially when it comes to understanding the limits and consequences of using US power. Supporters of a transformative approach could argue that prevention can be costly and employing power to promote positive change can be inexpensive, meaning that transformative policies are not much of a burden. At first blush, this seems like a compelling argument. The costs of the State Department's post-9/11 efforts to promote democratic change in the Middle East were minuscule compared to the resources necessary to ensuring the sea lanes of the Gulf.

Yet the costs of a policy are not only denominated in dollars spent. In its ambitious effort to promote democratic change in the Middle East, the United States marred its relations with important—if problematic—partners such as

Egypt, Saudi Arabia, and the UAE. It also fueled mistrust among people the policy was supposed to help. There were Arab liberals who rejected US help, arguing that the United States was engaged in democracy promotion out of its own self-interest, which was accurate. They were also all too aware of the persistent gap between American values and Washington's actual conduct in the world and did not want to get caught up in the hypocrisy of accepting assistance from the country that also generously supported their oppressors. It was also hard to believe that Arab leaders would reform themselves out of power.

Indeed, part and parcel of developing a policy is calculating what it can reasonably be expected to achieve in the service of a given national interest. Deploying a squadron of naval vessels and an air wing to ensure freedom of navigation through the Strait of Hormuz is no doubt expensive. Yet ensuring the free flow of energy resources from the Gulf is also a goal that policymakers can realistically expect to accomplish. That was not the case with the Freedom Agenda.

Looking back over the arc of US foreign policy in the Middle East since the end of World War II, the oil flowed, Israel remained secure, and American power ensured that neither the Soviet Union nor any other country (or groups of countries) could threaten those interests. This is a record of success. Of course, the fact that the United States was successful in the Middle East is not the same as saying that US policy was cost-free. Washington has been complicit in human rights violations, the denial of Palestinian rights, and has spilled a significant amount of blood. Yet on balance, given the goals of US policy from administration to administration, the United States achieved what it set out to do.

The desire to do better among the American foreign policy community was laudable. Yet when Washington sought to use its power to transform the social, political, and economic orders of societies half a world away, it failed. Iraq was transformed as a result of American efforts, but not in the ways that Washington imagined: the United States brought no democracy to the Middle East, and a Palestinian state is further away from reality than it was when the United States began its intensive efforts to build one three decades earlier. The policymakers, officials, analysts, journalists, and activists who advocated for these efforts believed they were acting with the best intentions. That was not enough, however. In order to have a sound foreign policy, officials need good assumptions about the world and those that formed the basis of America's ambitious transformative project for the Middle East were faulty. Contrary to much thinking within the American foreign policy community in the 1990s and 2000s, reform does not necessarily flow from peace; peace does not necessarily advance from reform; democracy does require democrats, and the United States did not have the power to overcome the political, economic, and social realities of the Middle East to forge positive change there.

It should be clear after the failures of the preceding decades that change in the region is up to Middle Easterners, not Americans. This is not to suggest that US presidents abandon the ideals and positive myths that animate American life in favor of cynicism. There is a place in US foreign policy for the rhetoric of freedom and democracy, but understanding the world the way it is means also recognizing that there is little the United States can do to change the patterns of authoritarian politics in the Middle East. And there is potential considerable harm Washington can do in trying. Americans now have three decades of data to support this claim.

A Better Way Forward

Among critics of American foreign policy, there is a demand that American officials who presided over failures in the Middle East be held "accountable." This seems unlikely to occur. A more productive exercise would involve a concerted effort—free of the partisanship and virtue signaling that had become so common inside the Beltway—to understand both Washington's mistakes in the region and clarify its priorities in the Middle East.

The Prime Directive Continues

By the early 2020s, it was clear that a new international order was emerging, but no one knew exactly what it would look like. Analysts had some idea of the changes that might be wrought by China's global ambitions, Russia's war on Ukraine, the diplomatic assertiveness of the Global South, the emergence of new technologies, and the growing significance of rare earth minerals during what was likely to be an extended interregnum from the post–World War II system to a new one. Yet there were also likely be continuities, among them what has been Washington's prime directive in the Middle East: the free flow of oil from the region.

The idea that oil would remain central to the global economy runs counter to what had become conventional wisdom among environmentalists, policymakers, some Middle East analysts, and commentators who envisioned a world in which demand for oil would decline as a transition to alternative, clean energy got underway. Yet for all the fervent belief in a "net zero" future, no one actually knew when that would happen or if it was achievable given the enormous economic, political, and cultural shifts that it would require. Organizations like OPEC, the influential International Energy Agency (IEA), and the US government's Department of Energy produced study after study, outlook upon outlook, and ran scenarios on top of scenarios that offered widely divergent predictions concerning the future of oil demand. For example, at the height of the global COVID-19 pandemic, when some commentators speculated that the long-term effects of the crisis would hasten a significant overall decline in the demand for oil, the IEA was more skeptical. It estimated, rather, that the rate of demand would slow, but that the overall upward trajectory would continue, albeit on a more gradual slope.[3] Another, more aggressive scenario assumed that significant invest-ment in alternative energy not just in the industrialized West, but also in Africa and India would result in a 75 percent decline in demand for oil. For its part, OPEC predicted steadily increasing demand for its product throughout much of the twenty-first century.

Prediction is perilous, however. Few expected the global scramble for oil and gas supplies in late 2021 and early 2022 stemming from the end of COVID-19 lockdowns in the United States and Russia's invasion of Ukraine. Moreover, even if an energy transition were to gain momentum in the 2030s, as the eighteen US intelligence agencies estimated, it is likely to be "jagged."[4] This means that there will be times during the changeover to clean energy when fossil fuels and the countries that produce them will take on great importance, as Saudi Arabia and other oil and gas producers unexpectedly did after Moscow commenced military operations to overthrow the Ukrainian government.

It would be a positive development if the energy transition was both as-sured and faster, but given the world the way it is, oil will remain central to the health of the global economy, the wealth of the United States, and the well-being of the American consumer. This is a principal reason why Washington cannot wash its hands of the Middle East. The prime directive will remain just that. Still, the resources necessary to prevent disruption of oil flows from the Middle East are different from those that were required for the ill-fated effort to transform the Middle East.

In response to the question: "What does it take to ensure freedom of navigation in the Gulf, including the Strait of Hormuz?" both military professionals and civilian analysts agree that a squadron of four to seven naval vessels along with a wing of fighter aircraft plus the periodic rotation of an aircraft carrier into the region are sufficient.[5] This still requires thousands of American personnel in the region, but hardly the tens of thousands that had been stationed there over three decades in support of an overly ambitious effort to transform the region. Leveraging artificial intelligence in support of this mission, which the US Navy and its regional partners are already doing, will complement and enhance the efficacy of this more modest force.[6] Indeed, until the imagined post-oil future materializes, Washington has little choice but to continue its role as regional sentry and with it the moral costs of maintaining close ties with its non-democratic partners of the Middle East. While those drawbacks remain, rightsizing America's military presence has the combined benefit of conserving resources, providing policymakers greater flexibility to deploy military assets elsewhere in the world, and, importantly, providing a brake on the transformative tendencies in American foreign policy. It is harder to pursue "wars of choice" if American forces are not poised to undertake regime change.

Unbreakable, but Changing Bonds

On the morning of October 7, 2023, close to 2,000 terrorists from Hamas, other Islamist factions, and local militias breached Israel's sophisticated security perimeter around the Gaza Strip. They attacked twenty-two different locations including military bases, towns, and collective farms near the border as well as a music festival. At the same time, Hamas let loose a barrage of thousands of rockets on Israeli cities. The toll was staggering for Israelis—1,200–1,400 killed, more than 3,000 wounded, and more than 200 taken hostage. In addition, Hamas dealt a heavy blow to the Israel Defense Forces' reputation, which, in turn, potentially compromised its ability to deter Israel's other adversaries.

It took military units and police forces close to three days to regain control of Israeli territory. What they found when clearing the areas that had borne the brunt of the Hamas attack was wanton and grisly murder, including that of women, children, and the elderly. There were reports of rape and beheadings that prompted American officials to characterize the attacks as

"ISIS-level savagery."[7] The National Security Council's coordinator for strategic communications, Admiral John Kirby, broke down in tears during a live television interview in response to the photos of the victims.

President Biden, an old-time centrist Democrat who has referred to himself as a Zionist, was immediate and resolute in his support for the Jewish State. In a series of statements, he expressed a heartfelt understanding of historical Jewish trauma and promised that Israel would get whatever it needed in the coming conflict. At the end of remarks he gave from the White House's State Dining Room on the afternoon of October 10, the president declared:

And let there be no doubt: The United States has Israel's back.

We will make sure the Jewish and democratic State of Israel can defend itself today, tomorrow, as we always have. It's as simple as that.

These atrocities have been sickening.

We're with Israel. Let's make no mistake.[8]

Toward those ends, Biden ordered two aircraft carrier battle groups to the Middle East—one to the Eastern Mediterranean and the other to the Persian Gulf. He also deployed US Air Force assets closer to the Middle East and put as many as 2,000 Marines on standby for deployment to the region. While there was probably significant coordination between the Israeli Ministry of Defense and the Pentagon, the US military was moving into the Middle East not to fight alongside Israel but rather to deter Iran and its proxy Hezbollah from any effort to start a regional war. This was a significant concern. During the second week of the conflict, Iran-aligned militias in Iraq and Syria launched drone attacks on American forces in both countries, eliciting airstrikes from the United States. The Houthis in Yemen launched salvos of Iranian-supplied long-range rockets at Israel via the Red Sea, but the US Navy shot them down. Despite the demonstration of American firepower, there remained significant concern that a second front along Israel's frontier with Lebanon would erupt given Hizballah's self-conception as the "resistance" (to Israel) *par excellence* and its suspected arsenal of more than 100,000 rockets.

The American action to support Israel was perfectly consistent with US policy in the region dating back to the October 1973 War. Initially, it was also noncontroversial with the American public. In the early stages of the Gaza conflict, Americans responded to "Israel's 9/11" as one might expect with symbolic outpourings of support. Buildings in New York City—which has the second-largest Jewish population in the world outside of Israel—were lit up in the blue and white of the Israeli flag, as was the enormous Ferris wheel at National Harbor just outside of Washington. Jews and non-Jews posted "I Stand with Israel" messages on their social media accounts, and the news media focused on the Israelis that were murdered or missing. In one viral video, a multicultural group of construction workers confronted a man in one of New York City's outer boroughs who was tearing down leaflets of Israeli hostages. They told him that he could scream "Death to Israel" all he wanted because he was in America, but they would not permit him to erase from public consciousness Hamas's captives.

The leaflet vandalism was bewildering in its indifference to human suffering and unfortunately cast a pall on Americans of Arab, but particularly Palestinian, descent. Many Palestinian-Americans were wracked with sorrow and fear over Israel's pummeling of the Gaza Strip. Events in the Middle East also heightened their considerable anxiety over hate crimes in America. The Arab American and Muslim American community had experienced the bigoted fallout after the September 11 attacks and were braced for a repeat of those terrible days, weeks, and months—a concern that was vindicated after the stabbing murder of a six-year-old Palestinian American boy in Chicago four days after the war in Gaza began and the shooting of three Palestinian college students in Vermont some weeks later. Arab Americans were not supportive of President Biden's full-throated support for Israel, but many were resigned to it.

As the conflict unfolded, it became clear that there were redoubts on the American Left where pro-Palestinian—and in some cases pro-Hamas—sentiment ran strong. This was most evident on university campuses, where students turned out to demonstrate solidarity with the Palestinian cause along with apparently large numbers of faculty members within the social sciences and humanities who supported a boycott of Israel. The Democratic Socialists of America organized street demonstrations in major American cities during which demonstrators clearly aligned themselves with Hamas. In Congress, a resolution in support of Israel won the unanimous support in the Senate and all but ten members of the House of Representatives. Of those voting no, only one was Republican, Thomas Massie of Kentucky, while the rest were Progressives with a history of pro-Palestinian activism. The question was whether the demonstrations championing Palestinian rights while assailing Israel for war crimes were a continuing exception to the rule of ironclad support for the Jewish state or a harbinger of change.

Although the crisis that began on October 7 seemed to vindicate the idea of unbreakable bonds between the United States and Israel, even at a moment of maximum presidential and congressional backing for the Jewish State, the pro-Israel coalition seemed to be under stress. As the Israeli air force undertook withering airstrikes on the Gaza Strip ahead of its promised ground invasion, a CNN poll revealed that only 27 percent of Americans aged 18–34 believe that Israel's response to Hamas's attack was "fully justified."[9] A Harvard CAPS–Harris Poll conducted twelve days after the war began was revealing: 51 percent of American 18- to 24-year-olds and 48 percent of people between 25 and 34 years old believed that Hamas's attacks on Israeli civilians was "justified by the grievances of Palestinians."[10] A little less than half of the 18- to 24-year-olds surveyed sided with Hamas, as did almost 30 percent of people in the next higher age range.[11] A combined half of Americans between 18 and 34 years of age did believe that Israeli civilians, including women and children, were murdered, raped, and otherwise abused.[12] Perhaps these results reflected the mis- and disinformation campaigns that a very online generation were subjected to as they sought news about the Israel-Hamas war. This sentiment could not be dismissed, however. Months before the conflict in the spring of 2023, a Gallup poll revealed that for the first time ever, more Democrats expressed sympathy for the Palestinian cause than they did for Israel.[13] Some politicians understood that there was a softening of support for Israel and acted accordingly. Separate from the House Progressives, during their presidential campaigns, Mayor Pete Buttigieg, who became Secretary of Transportation in the Biden administration, and Senator Elizabeth Warren (D-MA) supported conditioning aid to Israel over its policies in the West Bank and Gaza Strip.

Looking beyond the war in Gaza, however, neither admonishing Israel for its treatment of Palestinians and its occupation/annexation nor open-ended military assistance is the best way for the United States to continue to help ensure Israeli security. Even with shifts in public opinion among Democrats and young people, a punitive approach to cutting or conditioning aid is not politically realistic. At the same time, the Israelis no longer need the roughly $5 billion annual allotment of American largesse. This is the logical outcome of America's successful effort to help prevent challenges to Israeli security over the last five decades. With American assistance, Israel has built a sophisticated and capable military force atop an advanced economy with a well-developed defense-industrial base. The problem on October 7 was not a lack of Israel's capabilities, as the subsequent war demonstrated, but rather Israeli complacency and lack of imagination.

Hamas, Islamic Jihad, and Iran's primary proxy, Hizballah, are dangerous, but it seems quite unlikely that, despite the death and destruction of October 7, these groups can push the "Jews into the sea," as Gamal Abdel Nasser once infamously threatened. Like Nasser, Iranian leaders were often full of bluster about what they alleged to be Israel's imminent demise. Still, because Iran has latent and potential capabilities, including in the area of nuclear weapons, it remains a significant challenge to both Israel and the regional order. For that reason, the United States should continue to help Israel, but after the war in the Gaza Strip comes to an end, it should do so in a different way. A more realistic approach, based on the world as it is, would be for Washington and Jerusalem to enter into an agreement that would gradually end the aid relationship over a period of ten years and replace it with a series of military, diplomatic, and commercial agreements that will help ensure Israel can defend itself.[14]

It might seem odd or unnecessary to undertake a change in the assistance program, especially since Israel continues to enjoy broad bipartisan support on Capitol Hill. Yet this support is precisely what makes it a propitious moment to alter the way Washington helps prevent threats to Israel's security. In the prevailing American political context, phasing out aid will not be punitive, especially if the assistance is replaced with a series of treaties and agreements that forge strong bilateral ties well into the future. Changing the US-Israel aid relationship while there remains strong support for Israel in Congress and among the public will pave the way for more normal diplomatic, economic, and military relations between the two countries and diminish some of the moral costs the United States pays for its relations with Israel.

Fighting Terrorists

In addition to oil and Israel, countering terrorists should remain a core US concern in the Middle East for several reasons. First, it is paramount for America's leaders to protect the United States. Second, 9/11 produced lasting trauma and continues to be politically salient for Americans and their elected leaders.[15] Third, after the attacks on New York and the Pentagon, the prevailing narrative indicated that Islamist extremism emanating from the Middle East was and continues to be an existential threat to the United States. These ideas contributed to the rapid augmentation of an already large national security bureaucracy, including the creation of the Department of Homeland Security, the Office of the Director of National Intelligence, and the National Counterterrorism Center as well as the securitization of domestic policing.

The all-encompassing way that Washington pursued its "Global War on Terror" in the decades following 9/11 was intertwined with its broad effort to transform the Middle East. Not only was American foreign policy militarized and US domestic politics securitized, but the war in Iraq, the Freedom Agenda, and building a Palestinian state were justified in one way or another by appealing to the need to fight extremism.

When President Obama entered the White House, he dropped the transformative justifications and moral zeal of his predecessor in favor of cold calculation. No post-9/11 president, especially one whose opponents assailed him for not donning an American flag lapel pin, could be seen letting up on the jihadist threat. Consequently, Obama maintained a "kill list" of the world's most-wanted terrorists and used drone warfare liberally, especially in Yemen and Pakistan. It was in those two countries that Obama had his two greatest counterterrorism successes. On May 2, 2011, the president ordered US special-forces operators to raid a villa in the northern Pakistan city of Abbottabad. There, soldiers found and killed the world's most-wanted man, Osama bin Laden. Later the same year, Anwar al-Awlaki, a US citizen of Yemeni heritage whom American officials described as an inspirational leader of al-Qaeda of the Arabian Peninsula, was obliterated (along with his son) when an American drone fired two hellfire missiles at him and his companions.

This muscular approach to counterterrorism continued under President Trump. Despite vowing to bring troops home from the Middle East, the president and his advisors emphasized military action exclusively in the fight against terrorists. In April 2017, he authorized the Pentagon to drop the GBU-43/b Massive Ordinance Blast—called the "Mother of All Bombs"—on a suspected Islamic State hideout in Afghanistan and gave the military greater leeway to fight terrorists.

For his part, President Biden sought to expand and advance ideas for counterterrorism based on the experience of the United States during the previous decades. In September 2021, Homeland Security Advisor Elizabeth Sherwood-Randall stated that:

> Countering terrorism will require a new approach that prioritizes agility and greater investment in a broad set of tools, including diplomacy, development, and prevention efforts both abroad and at home that can shape environments in which terrorists thrive and recruit.[16]

The references to development and shaping environments abroad were echoes of the immediate post-9/11 years when counterterrorism was also social engineering. At the same time, the Biden administration made it clear that the parallel militarization of US policy from that era, including the Obama administration's drone-centric strategy, had been a mistake.[17] In his *National Security Strategy*, which was released in late 2022, Biden shifted the axis of US counterterrorism policy, moving from "'U.S.-led, partner-enabled' to one that is 'partner-led, U.S.-enabled.'"[18] Within this new context, Washington would work with friendly governments to improve law enforcement, intelligence, information sharing, and judicial systems. And yet, there was no perceptible change in US conduct. The pace of American counterterror operations may have slowed after US forces tracked down the leader of the Islamic State, Abu Bakr al-Baghdadi, in 2019, but in May 2022, for example, President Biden deployed five hundred soldiers to Somalia to help the government in Mogadishu destroy an extremist group called al-Shabab. A few months later, a CIA drone killed Ayman al-Zawahiri, who had led al-Qaeda since bin Laden's death in 2011, as he relaxed on a balcony in Kabul, the Afghan capital. In early April 2023, US Central Command announced that it had killed a senior ISIS leader, Khaled Ayyad Ahmad al-Jabouri, in a drone strike, and two weeks later US forces killed one of his colleagues in a helicopter raid.

It is hard to criticize successful military operations that have slayed some of the world's most dangerous terrorists. Yet the military-centric approach to terrorism contains risks. As successive national-security strategies have made clear, there will always be a place for force in counterterrorism, but the other components of the policy like law enforcement, federal prosecution, and information-sharing have often been secondary to military might. Instead, the United States has deployed what amounts to a global expeditionary force that has routinely violated the sovereignty of other countries to execute America's most wanted. From the perspective of many Middle

Easterners, the way in which the United States sought to prevent terrorist attacks amounted to a "war on Islam," leaving the country open to charges of neo-colonialism, and resulted in the deaths of a fair amount of innocent people, especially in Yemen, Syria, and Pakistan. No doubt it has had its successes, but US counterterrorism policy had strategic, diplomatic, moral, and political costs including at home, where Americans were required to surrender rights in the name of security as surveillance increased, due process was weakened, and airports became Constitution-free zones.

Some elected leaders and analysts believe that a new approach to counterterrorism must include an American withdrawal from the Middle East. This prescription is based on the idea that if the United States is not in the region, there would be less motive to threaten Americans.[19] This downplays the complex reasons behind violent extremism and why the United States is a target of terrorists. There is a wiser policy than either the overly militarized approach of the first two decades of the twenty-first century or withdrawal. The stunning irony is that presidents Obama, Trump, and Biden have all advocated for it. The official policy statements from all three administrations recognize that the United States can neither bomb its way out of the terrorism threat nor transform the region in ways that will mitigate it. Consider, for example, President Obama's official statement on the issue:

> U.S. CT [counterterrorism] efforts require a multidepartmental and multinational effort that goes beyond traditional intelligence, military, and law enforcement functions. We are engaged in a broad, sustained, and integrated campaign that harnesses every tool of American power—military, civilian, and the power of our values—together with the concerted efforts of allies, partners, and multilateral institutions. These efforts must also be complemented by broader capabilities, such as diplomacy, development, strategic communications, and the power of the private sector.[20]

President Trump's policy did not differ substantially from Obama's:

> We must confront terrorists with the combined power of America's strengths—our strong military, our law enforcement and intelligence communities, our civilian government institutions, our vibrant private sector, our civil society, our international partnerships, and the firm resolve of the American people.[21]

And President Biden's formal strategy for countering terrorism resembles those of his predecessors.[22] The more balanced approach set out in official US government documents has better chances of success because its underlying logic recognizes the limits of American power while also seeking to mitigate the damage that can result from exercising that power. Instead of following their own guidelines, however, American presidents have emphasized violence at the expense of other aspects of their own broad strategies. That may insulate presidents from political sniping, but it is not likely to make the United States or Americans safer.

Proliferation

Non-proliferation will also remain an important US goal in the Middle East, but how best to achieve it is subject of a polarizing and fraught debate. President Bush ordered the invasion of Iraq in part, he claimed, because he did not want the smoking gun (of Saddam Hussein's weapons program) to be "a mushroom cloud."[23] It turned out badly for Americans and Iraqis and would likely be unsuccessful if the United States pursued a similar strategy in Iran. It was fortunate that, even among Iran hawks, an American invasion to topple the Iranian regime was not considered an option. Yet what about "maximum pressure," a limited military strike, or diplomacy, which, when it comes to Iran, would mean a return to the JCPOA, as ways to prevent Iranian proliferation? Since almost the moment the JCPOA was signed in 2015, a debate has raged within the policy community about the wisdom of diplomacy versus coercion. When President Trump withdrew the United States from the nuclear agreement in 2018, that debate intensified with partisans on one side arguing that team Trump was warmongering while the president's supporters made the case that strong-arming the Iranians with what they dubbed "maximum pressure" was the best way to replace a flawed agreement with a better one.

At times, it was hard to tell precisely what the Trump administration wanted in Iran. Some advisors seemed to have sought regime change, while others did not. This may have been part of a deliberate strategy to keep the Iranians off-balance, or perhaps it was an example of the kind of incoherence that was emblematic of Trump's presidency. Regardless, the entire JCPOA episode offered two insights about the efficacy of coercion as a means of prevention, especially when it comes to a state like Iran that is in an advanced stage of nuclear development. First, American officials clearly believed that limited military operations would not do sufficient damage to Iran's nuclear program and would likely draw the United States into a potentially costly, open-ended conflict. Second, both Obama and Trump employed maximum pressure—though Obama never called it that—to compel the Iranians to pursue policies favorable to the United States. In Obama's case, it worked. By ramping up the pressure on Iran in 2010 (in parallel with the UN) and in 2012 with an array of sanctions, the White House brought Iranian leaders to the negotiating table, which resulted in the JCPOA. After Trump broke out of the agreement, he tried the same tactic to force the Iranians into new talks. The Iranians balked, however, and despite the efforts of the Biden administration to return to the agreement, leaders in Tehran remained unwilling to commit to the JCPOA once again.

Biden's renewed efforts for an agreement, Trump's attempt to coerce the Iranians into negotiations for a new nuclear deal (if that was, in fact, what he was doing), and the original JCPOA all failed for a variety of reasons: the ambitious nature of the deal, domestic US politics, mistrust among the parties, and Iranian intransigence. It is true that the JCPOA sought to prevent Iran from acquiring nuclear weapons technology, but it was also a means to change the Middle East. The internal logic of the agreement with its sunsetting clauses after which the Iranians could pursue further nuclear work indicated a belief that the JCPOA would produce change both within Iran and among its adversaries. The deal was not just about arms control, but rather a means by which Iran would be integrated into a "shared region," in the words of President Obama.[24] This would, of course, facilitate American retrenchment and a turn toward the challenges and opportunities in Asia. The president and his team were correct that the United States had overinvested in the Middle East, but they vastly overestimated the transformative nature of the agreement. Not only was the JCPOA vulnerable to America's poisonous politics, but the Saudis, Emiratis, Bahrainis, and especially the Israelis, all opposed it because they believed that Tehran would give up neither its four-decades-long quest drive to become nuclear capable nor its regional hegemonic ambitions. Indeed, no one in the Middle East actually seemed to want to share the region.

There were—and there remain—better policies aimed at Iran and other potential proliferators in the Middle East. It would place a premium on deterrence and containment at the expense of complex accords and the good faith of governments whose trustworthiness is suspect. It is also superior to the use of military force as a means of disarmament. The premise of the policy is a recognition of reality: Iran is or is likely to become a nuclear-capable state. The combination of deterrence and containment is a realistic way the United States can prevent Iran from brandishing its nuclear weapons and thwart its destabilizing activities in the region. Without getting into the arcana of the theoretical literature that developed during the Cold War, it is possible to discourage the Iranian regime from using its presumed nuclear weapons through the threat of dire consequences should Tehran unsheathe its arsenal. In other words, deterrence. At the same time, even a more modest American military presence can also limit—or contain—Tehran's destabilizing activities throughout the region. Deterrence and containment are policies that tend to make American policymakers uncomfortable because they involve an ongoing military commitment, the policy can limit the United States' own freedom of action, and, at least in the Iran case, the approach is an implicit recognition that US non-proliferation policy has failed.

Like the mission to ensure freedom of navigation, the United States would not need tens of thousands of service members spread across bases throughout the region. Washington could accomplish its goals with a smaller number of naval ships, aircraft, and ground personnel than it had for most of the first two decades of the twenty-first century.[25] It is important to note that despite a reduced force in the region, deterrence and containment entails the willingness of American policymakers to send these forces into action if necessary to demonstrate to the Iranians what is acceptable conduct, thereby establishing (or re-establishing) the rules of the game between Washington and Tehran.

Of course, deterrence and containment are not risk-free. Misread signals could lead to escalation, but the approach reduces the likelihood of this outcome because it does not preclude dialogue between the two countries. And, in an odd way, deterring and containing Iran might actually improve bilateral communication between the two countries because US-Iran relations would operate within an implicit, but well-understood, framework for conduct.[26]

The policy is hardly as romantic as secret back channels established in neutral capitals or high-stakes, marathon negotiations in Viennese ballrooms. Deterrence and containment are also not as bold or daring as forcing out a regime whose leaders are responsible for so much blood, including that of Americans. But it is a superior way to prevent Iran from employing its nuclear capabilities and hindering Tehran's regional malevolence while "simultaneously reduc[ing] the risk of war, protect[ing] Americans, and render[ing] the U.S. presence in the region less expensive."[27]

Iran is not the only proliferation risk in the Middle East, just the most urgent one. What if one of or a combination of US partners in the region sought to become nuclear capable? Analysts have warned that if Iran developed a nuclear weapon, it is likely that Saudi Arabia would follow suit and that other regional powers such as Egypt and Turkey might also be compelled to become nuclear powers. These risks are real but are often overstated.[28] Would-be nuclear powers face significant financial outlays, bureaucratic politics, scientific and technological challenges, reputational costs, and security threats that can compromise an effort to develop nuclear weapons capabilities.[29] If proliferation were not so hard, the Iranians would not have needed five decades to work at it, and Egypt would have long ago developed nuclear weapons to match Israel's arsenal. In the decades since President John F. Kennedy made the non-proliferation of nuclear weapons a primary feature of his foreign policy, the number of countries in the nuclear club has remained relatively small, and even shrinking after ex-Soviet states relinquished their warheads to Russia for destruction. In addition, international agreements such as the 1968 Treaty on the Non-Proliferation of Nuclear Weapons (NPT) and the Missile Technology Control Regime (MTCR), which was founded in the late 1980s to control the export of material and technology for missiles, have helped make the development and deployment of nuclear weapons more difficult.

Of course, it is hard to predict what Saudis and others might do in a dynamic security environment. Yet as Iran continues its determined effort to become nuclear weapons–capable, the Saudis have incentives to acquire a weapon even if the resumption of diplomatic relations that was consummated in the spring of 2023 diminishes the rivalry between Riyadh and Tehran. The Saudis would confront the range of impediments referenced above. And the United States should work to strengthen the NPT and the MTCR along with pursuing diplomacy to persuade the Saudis and others not to proliferate. Washington has wisely offered to help Riyadh with a civilian nuclear program on the condition that they not enrich or reprocess nuclear material for a weapon. The United States has also demanded that, in return for its help, the Saudis sign the International Atomic Energy Agency's "Additional Protocol." The AP, as it is known, "significantly increases the IAEA's ability to verify the peaceful use of all nuclear material in States with comprehensive safeguard agreements."[30] Saudi leaders have rejected these conditions, indicating that they want the option to proliferate.

If a US partner like Saudi Arabia is determined to access nuclear technology despite diplomatic, economic, and other efforts to forestall this development, the United States should provide it with expertise to develop nuclear safeguards, transparency, redundancy, and the means to communicate with their regional adversaries. This runs counter to conventional thinking about proliferation, but under those circumstances it is the best way to prevent the worst potential consequences of proliferation. The case of Pakistan is instructive in this regard. Throughout the 1970s and 1980s, the United States did much to forestall Islamabad's acquisition of nuclear weapons. Henry Kissinger promised Islamabad military assistance if it did not proliferate, the Carter administration initially threatened to cut aid for development and then suspended it, and under President George H. W. Bush, the United States applied congressionally mandated military sanctions on Pakistan, prohibiting the transfer of F-16s to the country. Despite these efforts, the United States still failed.[31] In May 1998, the Pakistanis conducted their first nuclear-weapons test. Recognizing reality, beginning in the early 2000s, Washington provided training, financial assistance, and technology aimed at securing Islamabad's arsenal.[32]

It is important to underscore that Washington should not pursue a policy aimed at fostering proliferation in the region based on the theory that a greater number of nuclear-capable countries will produce a more stable region.[33] Rather, based on trends in the Middle East, as Iran makes gains toward developing a nuclear weapons capability, the best way to prevent the most destabilizing aspects of proliferation is for Washington to help its partners manage the hazards of being a nuclear-capable state. Like the deterrence and containment, assisting would-be proliferators is not risk-free, but it will help avoid the worst potential outcomes associated with uncontrolled proliferation.

Earth, Wind, and Fire

In 2022, Shush, a city of about fifty thousand in the Khuzestan region of Iran, recorded the hottest temperature on Earth for that year—128.5 degrees Fahrenheit. That same year, Iraq's Milh Lake (also known as Lake Razzaza) experienced a significant decline in water levels. The famous marshlands in southern Iraq, which were first destroyed under Saddam Hussein and were then restored through conservation efforts, were once again endangered due to excessive heat and insufficient rainfall. In the northern part of the country, the reservoir of the Mosul Dam became so depleted that it revealed an ancient city called Kemune. The six countries of the Gulf Cooperation Council—Saudi Arabia, the UAE, Qatar, Bahrain, Kuwait, and Oman—are warming at twice the rate of the global average, with temperatures expected to increase by five to seven degrees Fahrenheit by the end of the twenty-first century. On the region's present trajectory, Gulf countries will not be able to sustain human life for one-third of the year because of extreme heat. There is near universal consensus among scientists that on every metric—water scarcity, high heat, food insecurity, desertification, and climate migration—the Middle East will bear the brunt of the dramatic transformation of Earth's climate.

Of course, the United States cannot prevent the climate crisis. The best approach to mitigating its effects is to invest in clean energy and its related infrastructure at home. At first glance, it is not all evident that Washington should prioritize climate change–related policies in the Middle East, but it should. Climate change often coincides with migration and as the region suffers the effects of a warming planet, people will be on the move seeking safety. This has profound implications not only for the countries in the Middle East, but also beyond the region, especially in Europe whose stability and prosperity are critical to the United States. At a more basic level, if the United States can play an important role helping to prevent the catastrophic effects of extreme heat and drought, it would demonstrate an important shift away from the destructive American policies of recent decades and toward regional stability. There is also the potential benefit of establishing American leadership on a critical issue at a time when Washington's regional partners have hedged with other great powers.

But, before addressing how the United States can help prevent some of the worst effects of the climate crisis in the Middle East, it is important to clarify what Washington should not do. As the foreign-policy community has become more attuned to climate change in the Middle East, it has tended to focus on how its effects are linked to conflict.[34] The heuristic example for this claim is Syria, but this is a misreading of what happened in that country and risks the development of bad policies.

In February 2012, a small think tank in Washington called the Center for Climate and Security published a report titled "Syria: Climate Change, Drought and Social Unrest," which argued that there were causal connections between environmental crises and the origins of the Syrian conflict.[35] The paper made a significant impact in Washington, where a diverse group of journalists and policymakers took up its themes, but it suffered from a combination of misinterpreted scientific data, exaggeration of the intersection of climate and political grievances, and erroneous assertions about Syrian politics.[36] It could well be that climate change made the conflict likely, but this hypothesis is without scientific support. This uncertainty is consistent with the US government's assessment that "complex dimensions of human and state decision making and the challenge of connecting climate, weather, and sociopolitical models" render it difficult to say for certain that climate change is a driver of conflict.[37]

Rather than linking climate to conflict, Washington should help the region adapt to climate change through technical efforts aimed at shared resources, especially water. It is not an easily resolved problem, of course. As long as the conflicts that beset the region persist, the kind of cooperation necessary for Middle Eastern societies to adapt to the climate crisis will be difficult.[38] Across the arc of North Africa, throughout the Levant, and into the Gulf region, borders, sovereignty, and political legitimacy are contested. These include tensions between Morocco and Algeria, Libya and Egypt, Israelis and Palestinians, Iraq and Turkey, Syria and Turkey, Syria and Jordan, Yemen and Saudi Arabia, the UAE and Oman, as well as Iran and Iraq.

The conflict between Israelis and Palestinians over land, sovereignty, and legitimacy extends to natural resources and demonstrates the challenges of climate adaptation. As water in the region becomes scarcer due to changing rainfall patterns and declining aquifers, water resources have become defined in zero-sum terms.[39] The Palestinian Authority (PA) accuses Israel of drawing far more water than what should rightfully be the Israeli share, worsening water scarcity for the Palestinian population. The Israelis deny this, but because relations between Israel and the PA are so fraught, Palestinian water scarcity remains unresolved. It is not just the Israelis and Palestinians, of course. Water resources are important aspects of tension between or within any number of countries in the region including Turkey and Syria, Iraq and Turkey, Egypt and Ethiopia, and Yemen.

The aim of US policy should not be to resolve conflicts in order to address the climate crisis, but rather to help countries manage their shared natural resources, which can go a long way toward preventing the deleterious consequences of climate change. This is a significant challenge, but it is hardly impossible. The 2022 maritime boundary agreement between Lebanon and Israel is not climate-friendly, as it allows both countries to exploit natural gas deposits, but it does provide a template for forging mutually beneficial agreements between implacable enemies. According to American diplomats, they were able to insulate a technical agreement from the politics of the conflict between Israel and Lebanon by pushing Israeli and Lebanese officials to focus not on how a potential agreement benefited their adversary, but rather on what they wanted out of the maritime boundary deal. This reframing allowed the parties to concentrate on each country's individual gains, which facilitated an agreement. By all measures, they were hard and difficult negotiations, but the creative way in which Americans subtly shifted their discussions with each country to de-emphasize the zero-sum nature of the Israel-Lebanon relationship in favor of a dialogue that stressed the country-specific benefits of a maritime border agreement is potentially replicable in pursuit of climate adaptation across conflict zones.[40]

It is unlikely that technical agreements can overcome political obstacles in every case. The Egyptian-Ethiopian stalemate over the Grand Ethiopian Renaissance Dam (GERD), which threatens to reduce the flow of the Nile, demonstrates how technical solutions remain vulnerable to nationalism. Still, Washington should not accept this as a foregone conclusion. Yes, politics is powerful, but so is the need for leaders—even authoritarian ones—to ensure that there is water and food for their populations. Although not analogous to the state of war that exists between Israelis and Lebanese, Washington can help foster adaptation in ways that diminish the threat GERD poses to Egypt's well-being despite tense relations between Cairo and Addis Ababa. With the example of the Israel-Lebanon deal and how American officials were able to protect negotiations from politics, the United States can help Middle Easterners share critical resources, especially water, and address other environmental problems. In ways, these issues are much easier to address than political reform, fixing borders, and disputed sovereignty, and their impact may be even greater given the stakes involved with the climate crisis—higher temperatures, intensifying water scarcity, challenges to food security, and both internal and external migration, especially in poorer Middle Eastern countries.

Although leaders in the region have sought to diversify their relations, the United States remains appealing to them because it is the global leader in technology. Whatever doubts and differences Arab leaders and their people harbor about the United States, they have long wanted to benefit from America's know-how. As a result, US advice, expertise, and resources for climate adaptation would, without a doubt, be welcomed in the region. Washington has the capability to help Middle Easterners prevent some of the worst consequences of their warming neighborhood without getting bogged down in regional politics. Indeed, it would be best to approach climate change in the Middle East with modesty. That means understanding what is realistically possible—fostering adaptation—through deft diplomacy, technological sophistication, and sufficient financial resources in order to head off some of the worst effects of the climate crisis in the region.

Between China and Russia

Many in the foreign-policy community have embraced the idea that great-power competition has become the defining feature of American foreign policy. The point of departure for this new (but old) paradigm was the Pentagon's 2018 *National Defense Strategy* and its *Nuclear Posture Review* of the same year. Both documents declared that "inter-state strategic competition" would define the Department of Defense's mission in the coming years instead of countering terrorism.[41] The officials responsible for drafting each of these reports recognized that the unipolar moment of the post–Cold War era had passed, and that the United States was entering an age in which Russia and China would challenge American primacy around the globe. Of the two countries, it was the latter, in particular, that garnered the most attention from political leaders, officials, experts, and journalists (at least until Russia's invasion of Ukraine in early 2022). That is because of China's startling economic growth over the previous three decades, Beijing's commitment to building a large and technologically advanced military, the Chinese leadership's stated intention to extend Beijing's political influence around the globe, and the Chinese Communist Party's ideological challenge to Western liberalism.[42]

The Chinese government's success in achieving these goals has been uneven, especially as it confronted the prospect of slower economic growth due to the global COVID-19 pandemic and Beijing's "zero-COVID" policies. China's aging workforce and the CCP's effort to assert more control over the economy at the expense of the private sector may also hamper future growth and development. Yet despite these potential challenges, China has amassed the kind of global prestige that places the country in the category of peer competitor—or near-peer competitor—of the United States.

Both China and Russia are globally ambitious powers, which means they are also competitors and potential adversaries of the United States in the Middle East. It is important to note that great-power competition is not as acute in the Middle East as it is in either Asia or Europe. This issue is often overlooked in Washington's overall approach to Beijing and Moscow, which tends to veer toward maximalism. China and Russia face a range of challenges that could hinder their ability to challenge the United States over time. In the present, however, Chinese and Russian leaders have sought to use their power and influence to undermine US policy, raising questions about their long-term objectives in the Middle East. As a result, American policymakers have concluded that confronting China and Russia in the region is a core interest of the United States.

China's Middle East

In the early 2020s, there were a number of perspectives within the American foreign-policy community on China's role in the Middle East. The one that gained the most currency posited that Beijing's growing prominence in the region was a sign that the Chinese government sought to supplant Washington as the dominant power in the Middle East.[43] According to this view, China's multidimensional threat to the United States stemmed from its potential to project power into the region. Analysts and US officials warned that the development of ports and other Chinese infrastructure around the Middle East would eventually become militarized. This, in turn, would pose a challenge to America's freedom of action in the region and Washington's ability to ensure the shipping lanes. China's growing assertiveness in the Middle East would also make it more difficult for the United States to apply diplomatic and financial pressure on Iran. The Chinese government's decision in 2020 to make a multibillion-dollar investment in Iran that relieved American economic pressure on Iran seemed to bolster this argument. Another data point was the deal the Chinese brokered in March 2023 between Saudi Arabia and Iran aimed at restoring diplomatic relations between the two Gulf adversaries. Many in Washington feared that the agreement was part of a Chinese effort to weaken the American led political order that had helped the United States achieve its goals in the region.

Parallel to these concerns, the Saudis raised the possibility of denominating energy transactions in the Chinese currency instead of the US dollar, giving Beijing the kind of market influence that would allow it to set prices in global energy markets. This would add to China's growing prestige in the Middle

East and beyond. Taken together, Beijing's economic and diplomatic influence along with its military potential combined with the willingness of US partners in the region to lean into their relations with the Chinese government would—according to a growing consensus among analysts, journalists, officials, and elected leaders in Washington—place China at an advantage in its global competition with the United States.

A smaller group of observers tended to view Beijing's presence in the Middle East as less directly threatening to Washington. They questioned why China would seek the burden of being the provider of regional stability and security in the Middle East. After all, the region and the Chinese government already enjoy the security that the US Fifth Fleet and the thousands of American service members provide. This allows Beijing to pursue its largely mercantilist objectives without the burden and expense of assuming regional predominance.[44] These analysts further suggested that the image of China aggressively pursuing projects in the region aimed in large part toward superseding the United States was also inaccurate. In East Asia, China sought predominance and worked hard to push out the United States, but a number of China analysts contended that the "Middle East was not that high on Beijing's agenda."[45]

Instead of domination, these experts contended that China pursued a policy of strict neutrality in the region. No doubt there were times that this undercut the United States, such as the timely $25 billion investment in Iran in 2020 that helped to stabilize the regime in Tehran. This complicated American efforts to coerce Iran to halt its nuclear activities, but—in keeping with Beijing's primary goal of ensuring the health of the Chinese economy—it was primarily interested in shoring up a major oil exporter to China. This interest in the free flow of energy parallels that of the United States and undermines the notion that Beijing is Washington's adversary in all instances. Despite sharing this interest, unlike Washington, the Chinese are intent on keeping their distance from the politics and rivalries of the Middle East. This was a lesson Chinese leaders learned from, in particular, the US invasion of Iraq, which they regarded as an historic strategic blunder.[46]

Still, the maximalist approach carried the day in part because China is a rising power with an ambitious leadership and in part due to the way the issue was framed inside the Beltway. There was only political upside for members of Congress and presidential contenders to be tough on China. The problem for the United States was clear to anyone who had been paying close attention to developments in the Middle East. The previous chapter explained how

America's partners in the region are also friends with China—the largest investor in oil fields, gas facilities, industrial parks, and ports stretching from North Africa to the Persian Gulf. Because Middle Eastern countries benefit from their bilateral relations with both Washington and Beijing, Egyptians, Saudis, Emiratis, and others want to be able to develop their ties with both great powers.

Few in Washington want to wrestle with these complications. Instead policymakers were intent on making competition with China a priority in the Middle East. Under these circumstances, they needed to do a better job convincing leaders in the region that their futures lie with Washington, not Beijing. During the Obama years, the Chinese challenge was primarily an issue for the United States and Asia, which was, in part, the rationale for the so-called pivot to Asia. But by the time President Trump took office, China was widely—and correctly—regarded as an emerging global power, and while the president deserved credit for elevating the issue, he did little more than browbeat US partners in the Middle East over their use of Chinese telecom technology. For its part, the Biden administration, which was tough on China through a variety of diplomatic, financial, and military measures, especially in Europe and East Asia, had difficulty responding to Beijing's challenge in the Middle East. Early in his administration, the president sought to counter China's Belt and Road Initiative with something his administration called Build Back Better World. The initiative sought to "collectively catalyze hundreds of billions of dollars of infrastructure investment for low- and middle-income countries" in cooperation with the Group of Seven.[47] Build Back Better World died in Congress and was too small to challenge China's considerable investments around the globe, including the Middle East. In addition, despite concern in Washington about widespread adoption of China's 5G technology among US partners in the region, the best President Biden could muster during his summer 2022 visit to Saudi Arabia was an offer of a joint US-Saudi committee on 5G/6G development.

The kinds of initiatives the Biden administration pursued in the Middle East were too little in the face of the Chinese government's massive investments (and potential arms supplies) in the region.[48] To its credit, the White House responded to the China challenge in the area where the United States excels—security. It returned Patriot missile batteries to Saudi Arabia in March 2022 after withdrawing them the previous year. A few months later, after meeting with members of the Gulf Cooperation Council plus Egypt, Jordan, and Iraq, the Department of Defense embarked upon the development of a regional integrated air-defense system. Then, in 2023, the US military announced that it would conduct counter-drone warfare exercises in Saudi Arabia. Overall, between the summer of 2022 and the spring of 2023, the United States conducted more than a dozen military exercises in the Middle East with both regional partners and European allies. These were signals to Arab leaders that Washington took threats to their security seriously, which, in turn, was aimed at forestalling the Chinese government's effort to capitalize further on its already significant economic influence in the realm of arms sales and security cooperation.

Although the United States remained the primary provider of security in the region, a significant part of China's allure (as noted in the previous chapter) was its willingness to share technology and invest in infrastructure, areas where the United States is at a disadvantage. There is little the United States can do about the latter, however. Unlike Beijing, Washington does not command a vast state-owned enterprise sector that can be leveraged to advance its foreign-policy agenda. As the ill-fated Build Back Better World demonstrated, the vicissitudes of domestic politics can undermine even creative foreign-policy ideas. Yet the risk of China's work in this domain may not be as great as some suspected. It should not matter to the United States that Chinese firms are building Neom, a futuristic city planned for Saudi Arabia's Red Sea coast. The use of commercial ports as Chinese naval bases remains theoretical, and given the continuing commitment of the United States to freedom of navigation in the Gulf, this seems less of a problem than what some of the alarming analysis and commentary have suggested.[49]

In contrast, Washington can and should address the issue of technology, but the United States needs to be smarter about it than it has been. It was good news that the Biden administration announced plans in late 2022 to invest $1.5 billion into the development of a "standards-based alternative for modern cellular networks."[50] Only a handful of companies, including Huawei and another Chinese company called ZTE, dominate the manufacture of equipment for these networks. In order to resolve the commercial and national security risks associated with a concentrated market of Chinese, South Korean, and European firms, Washington is looking toward alternatives, notably Open Radio Access Network (ORAN).[51] This is promising, but as alternatives like ORAN become more available, American policymakers need to be more discerning about their concerns regarding Chinese technology in the region. Ripping out and replacing all Huawei technology is possible but expensive and perhaps unnecessary. That is to say, not all networks are the same. A smart technology policy in the Middle East would focus attention on government networks, cellular networks, the switches that go into them, and other areas like undersea cables, which are all potentially vulnerable and areas where the United States should encourage its partners to use technology such as ORAN.[52] There is no reason to believe that Middle Eastern leaders, who have always wanted to work with Washington, would balk at the opportunity to use Western technology, which is often superior to what the Chinese or others can offer.

Washington will also need to rethink how it manages sensitive topics such as human rights. The American tone about political reform has changed since the halcyon days of the Freedom Agenda, but President Biden's commitment to infuse his foreign policy with values created tension with Washington's regional partners. America's elected leaders will rightly never give up on their rhetorical commitment to values, but policymakers must also understand that it is precisely because Beijing does not "politicize human rights"—in the words of a Saudi interlocutor—that China is appealing to some of America's partners in the region.[53]

It was on this issue that, in 2021 and 2022, the Biden administration set itself up for a deepening rift with Saudi Arabia, a problematic but nevertheless important regional partner, compromising Washington's ability to counter China's influence with the Saudi leadership. President Biden may have been sincere in his desire to incorporate values into his foreign policy, but he did not recognize the limits of American power in trying to hold Saudi Crown Prince Mohammed bin Salman accountable.[54] What became known as the "Khashoggi ban"—named for the Saudi journalist and *Washington Post* columnist who was murdered by Saudi agents in 2018—that barred individuals who threatened journalists and oppositionists from entering the United States and the release of the intelligence community's report about the killing were smart ways of getting the American point across on human rights. Yet the Biden administration went further, freezing out the Crown Prince, initially placing a hold on weapons sales to the kingdom, and withdrawing Patriot missile batteries from Saudi Arabia at a time when the Houthis in Yemen were firing missiles at Saudi cities.[55] These policies opened Washington to accusations of interfering in the internal affairs of Saudi Arabia and of purposefully compromising its security, sowing mistrust, and providing an opening through which America's competitors could capitalize. Since that time, Saudi Arabia has drawn closer to Beijing, directing more of its oil shipments to Asia, where China is the largest consumer of Saudi crude, purchasing more Chinese weaponry, and convening a summit with Chinese leader Xi Jinping in late 2022.

Some analysts and officials argue that the United States must stand for something in the ideological battle between the CCP and that of Western liberalism in the competition for regional influence.[56] They make a strong point about defending democracy, but the best way to outmaneuver the Chinese in the Middle East is to recognize the significant constraints of a values-forward foreign policy and the damage that such an approach does to the effort to compete with China in the region. A policy that endeavors not to give America's Middle Eastern partners a reason to align more closely with Beijing may not be consistent with American values. Yet if the goal of US foreign policy is to prevent the further development of China's influence in the Middle East, then it is more likely to be effective than reprimanding leaders about their relations with China, non-starters like Build Back Better World, and mixed signals about the importance of the region that have been a hallmark of the American approach to the Middle East across administrations.

From Damascus with Love

Perhaps of greater concern to the United States in the early and mid-2020s than China was Russia. This seems curious given the fact that thirty years after the end of the Cold War, the US economy dwarfs that of Russia, which is largely dependent on oil and gas exports. Throughout much of this period, the post-Soviet military was not capable of projecting power beyond Russia and what is commonly referred to as its "near abroad," the Caucasus and Central Asia. At the same time, the United States remained the overwhelmingly dominant military power in the Middle East. But that changed in the 2010s when Russia first brokered an agreement that was intended to dispose of Syria's stock of chemical weapons, forestalling a possible American military strike, and then, two years later, when Russian president Vladimir Putin ordered his military to intervene directly in Syria's civil war to save the Assad regime. Since then, Moscow has regained, and even extended, the influence it lost in the Middle East when the Soviet Union withered and died.

By January 2021, Moscow had become an important player in the region from Damascus north to Ankara, south to Jerusalem and Cairo, and then west into Libya. Whatever Beijing's designs on the region were, Moscow was clearly making a bid to rival Washington in the Middle East. The exercise of Russian power and the Saudi, Emirati, Egyptian, Turkish, and Israeli receptivity to it complicated a range of American policies including fighting ISIS in Syria, stabilizing energy prices, or helping Ukraine.

By important measures of state power, Putin's growing influence in the Middle East was curious. Unlike Beijing, Moscow is neither a source of foreign direct investment nor a provider of contracting services in the region.[57] Also, although its weapons systems were attractive to some Middle Eastern states—such as Egypt, Algeria, and Syria—after the Russian military's debacle in Ukraine, the superiority of Western, especially American, arms was clear.

Rather, Moscow's prestige in the Middle East is based on two factors: its ability to troll the United States and its oil reserves. The combination of US hegemony in the region and the failures of Washington's ambitious effort to transform Middle Eastern societies brought into sharp relief the contradictions between American principles and practice, defective assumptions that served as the foundations for regional policies, and basic incompetence. This left Washington open to Moscow's well-honed whataboutism and lies on terrorism, human rights, democracy, and a variety of other issues. It is a practice that Russian foreign minister Sergey Lavrov has perfected.

Lavrov's discursive tactics of Russian officials was a weapon of the weak, however. There was little need for Washington to engage in verbal sparring with Moscow. Rather, American policymakers should stop giving the Russians grist for their diplomacy for the Twitter (now X) age. That means an approach to the region that strives to do no harm, is geared toward prevention, and recognizes the limits of American power in the region.

Russia's role in the region is not just a function of its "troll power." Moscow's influence in the Middle East is also directly linked to its status as the world's third-largest producer of oil.[58] This has created a common interest among the Russians and the region's energy producers on oil production and price. That was not always the case, as countries within OPEC+ often disagree over these issues as they jockey for market share. It was clear from the state of the global market after Russia's invasion of Ukraine in early 2022, however, that there were powerful incentives for Moscow and its fellow oil producers in OPEC+ to keep oil prices high. There was little that Washington could do to alter the production decision of OPEC+ other than pursue more-rational energy policies including conservation, exploitation of domestic sources of energy, and investment in alternative energy. Yet, as noted above, Middle Eastern oil will remain important well through the mid-twenty-first century.

As a result, regardless of the quality of Russia's relations with its partners in OPEC+, the United States should continue its efforts to prevent disruptions of oil flow from the region—a responsibility that Russia does not have the capacity to take on—while reining in Washington's proclivities for projects of international social engineering.

The preventive policy solution in a dynamic strategic environment where the United States, China, and Russia are vying for power and influence is straightforward: American officials must avoid the false promises of transformation and retrenchment, each of which provides an open invitation for Moscow and Beijing to deepen their influence in the Middle East. It is important to remember that most of the leaders in the region remain predisposed toward the United States for political, diplomatic, and cultural reasons. They also like the security that Washington provides. To the extent that Washington wants to prevent them from falling into the orbit of the Russians and the Chinese, American policymakers need to offer them a reason not to lean into their ties with Moscow and Beijing.

Sine Waves

If there is a metaphor for American foreign policy in the Middle East since the early 1990s, it is the sine wave. The upward trajectory or slope of the waveform represents the transformative goals that followed victory over Saddam Hussein's Iraq in February 1991 and the Soviet Union's collapse at the end of that year, reaching its peak with the invasion of Iraq and the Freedom Agenda after the 9/11 attacks. The amplitude diminished both because of circumstance—Operation Iraqi Freedom failed to achieve its goals—and because leaders in the region proved resistant to America's efforts to build a Palestinian state and forge democratic change.

After this intense period of transformative activity in the Middle East, Americans elected a president who regarded those projects to be folly. Yet, the slope increased again after Washington briefly returned to policies designed to democratize the region after four Arab leaders were toppled in a year of popular uprisings. The upward trajectory continued as the United States sealed a nuclear deal with Iran that was intended both to facilitate transformation of the region, especially the Persian Gulf, and America's retrenchment from the Middle East. The next downward undulation came with the election of another president who also questioned the wisdom of investing vast amounts of time, energy, and, importantly, resources in the Middle East. It was then poised to rise once again with a new president who promised a foreign policy based on American values and committed himself to resurrecting the JCPOA. At the same time, his advisors underscored the White House's intention to de-emphasize the Middle East even as the United States has sought to reassure its partners that it remains committed to their security and the region's stability.

Despite the efforts of presidents Obama, Trump, and Biden, the corrective revolution in US–Middle East policy remained incomplete. This was, in part, a result of circumstance and their own ambitious policies despite themselves. At a level of greater abstraction, however, over the course of the first two decades or so of the twenty-first century, the combination of American failure, interest creep, old habits that never die, and a bruising domestic political environment has left the United States without a strategy in the region. Instead, the United States was stuck in an in-between place in the Middle East that invited competitors like China and Russia to capitalize on America's past failures and its present indecisiveness. The necessary change in US–Middle East policy was not as challenging as it seemed, however. This concept had implicitly been part of the American playbook in the past. Beginning in the mid-1990s, American officials lost sight of the fact that when they pursued policies of prevention rather than transformation, they were more likely to be successful protecting US interests and, in the process, they may even help redeem the world.

Notes

Chapter 1

1. Hamid, "World Must Aid Syria's Rebels"; Cook, "It's Time to Think Seriously about Intervening in Syria"; Weiss, "Break the Stalemate! A Blueprint For a Military Intervention in Syria"; Weiss, "Threat of Force Would Work."
2. Mandelbaum, *Mission Failure*, 3.
3. Walt, "The World Wants You to Think Like a Realist."
4. Waltz, *Theory of International Politics*.
5. Cook, *False Dawn*.
6. Indyk, *Innocent Abroad*, 50.
7. Gordon and Nephew, "Two Years On, the Iran Deal Is Working"; Samuels, "The Aspiring Novelist Who Became Obama's Foreign-Policy Guru."
8. Walt, *The Hell of Good Intentions: America's Foreign Policy Elite and the Decline of U.S. Primacy.*
9. Wertheim, "The Only Way to End 'Endless War.' "
10. See, e.g., Takeyh, *The Last Shah: America, Iran, and the Fall of the Pahlavi Dynasty*; Wilford, *America's Great Game: The CIA's Secret Arabists and the Shaping of the Modern Middle East*; Ricks, *Fiasco: The American Military Adventure in Iraq*; Quandt, *Peace Process: American Diplomacy and the Arab-Israel Conflict since 1967*; Cooper, *The Oil Kings: How the U.S., Iran, and Saudi Arabia Changed the Balance of Power in the Middle East*; and Haass, *War of Necessity, War of Choice: A Memoir of Two Iraq Wars*, although an exhaustive list would include many others.

Chapter 2

1. Bowman, "Anti-War Demonstration Draws 75,000 to Washington Protests Take Place across the Nation."
2. Chrisafis et al., "Millions Worldwide Rally for Peace."
3. "Cities Jammed in Worldwide Protest of War in Iraq."
4. Yergin, *The Prize: The Epic Quest for Oil, Money, and Power*, 4.
5. Bronson, *Thicker than Oil: Quest for Oil, Money, and Power*, 15.
6. Ibid.
7. Ibid.
8. "Anglo-French Oil Agreement Is Out."

9. Krasner, "Defending the National Interest: Raw Materials Investments and U.S. Foreign Policy," 111.

10. Office of the Historian, "The 1928 Red Line Agreement."

11. Ibid.

12. Hull, "109: The Near East Looms Big."

13. Ibid.

14. Vitalis, "America's Kingdom," 129.

15. Bronson, *Thicker than Oil*, 20.

16. Painter, "Oil and the American Century."

17. Takeyh, *The Last Shah*, 8–13.

18. The shah, as Mohamed Reza Pahlavi became known, is widely regarded to have been an American client in the Middle East. Yet, his foreign policy was far more nuanced than this one-dimensional view suggests. He was not only a partner of the United States, but also cultivated ties with the Soviet Union and enjoyed good relations with neighboring Arab states as well as Israel. For a full exposition of the Shah's foreign policies, see Takeyh, *The Last Shah*.

19. The royalty agreement between Great Britain and Iran stood in contrast to the 1950 agreement between the then-American-owned Aramco and Saudi Arabia, which split the profits equally between the two parties. For a full discussion of the arrangement, see Galpern, *Money, Oil, and Empire in the Middle East: Sterling and Postwar Imperialism, 1944–1971.*

20. Krasner, "Defending the National Interest," 119.

21. Takeyh, *The Last Shah*, Chapter 4.

22. Krasner, "Defending the National Interest."

23. Ibid.

24. DeForth, "U.S. Naval Presence in the Persian Gulf."

25. Galpern, *Money, Oil, and Empire in the Middle East.*

26. Ibid.

27. Kupchan, *The Persian Gulf and the West*, 35–6.

28. Bronson, *Thicker than Oil*, 106.

29. Cook, *The Struggle for Egypt*, 135.

30. Adjusted for inflation, the price increase of a barrel of oil was equivalent to $49.77 and the price of a gallon of gas went from $1.76 to $2.71 in 2022 dollars.

31. Painter, "Oil and the American Century."

32. Rutledge, *Addicted to Oil: America's Relentless Drive for Energy Security.*

33. Ibid.

34. Bronson, *Thicker than Oil.*

35. Ibid.

36. "Questions from Louis Harris & Associates Poll: January 1974 (Roper #31107689) | Roper IPoll—Roper Center for Public Opinion Research."

37. "Louis Harris Associates Poll: January 1975."

38. ORC International, "Opinion Research Corporation Poll."

39. "Questions from Louis Harris & Associates Poll: August 1975 (Roper #31107868) | Roper IPoll—Roper Center for Public Opinion Research."

40. Carter, "State of the Union Address 1980."
41. Hoagland, "A Carter Doctrine for Mideast Oil?"
42. McGovern, "How to Avert a New 'Cold War' "; Gelb, "Beyond the Carter Doctrine"; Newsom, "America Engulfed."
43. Brands et al., "RIP the Carter Doctrine, 1980–2019"; Lawson, "The Reagan Administration in the Middle East."
44. Assistant Secretary of State for Near Eastern Affairs Richard Murphy told members of the Congress at the time that "ready access to Gulf oil is critical to the economic well-being of the West."
45. In their article, "The Case for Offshore Balancing: A Superior Grand Strategy," John J. Mearsheimer and Stephen M. Walt suggest that the Rapid Deployment Force was an instrument of offshore balancing. It was, but only by default. American officials at the time sought basing for the force in the region, but due to political sensitivities no countries volunteered to host it. In time this would change dramatically and, by 2021, American forces totaling about forty-four thousand spread across bases, ports, and airfields in Bahrain, Saudi Arabia, the United Arab Emirates, Qatar, Oman, Kuwait, and Iraq.
46. "President George H. W. Bush: Address before a Joint Session of Congress, September 11, 1990." Bush quoted from the joint press conference with Soviet president Mikhail Gorbachev in his address to a joint session of Congress two days later.
47. Haass, *War of Necessity, War of Choice*, 132.
48. Ibid.
49. Indyk, "The Clinton Administration's Approach to the Middle East."
50. Ibid.
51. Yergin, *The Prize*, Chapter 33.
52. Brenner, "Why Is the United States at War with Iraq?"
53. Sharp, "Egypt: Background and U.S. Relations."
54. "2020 Country Reports on Human Rights Practices."
55. Garfinkle and Pipes, *Friendly Tyrants: An American Dilemma*, x; Kirkpatrick, "Dictatorships and Double Standards."
56. Cook, *The Struggle for Egypt*, 230–44; Cook, *Ruling but Not Governing: The Military and Political Development in Egypt, Algeria, and Turkey*, 87.
57. Jones, "What Iran Air Flight 655 Says about America's Role in the Middle East."
58. Ibid.

Chapter 3

1. Sachar, *A History of Israel: From the Rise of Zionism to Our Time*, 15.
2. UN Resolution 181 envisioned a Jewish state and an Arab state. Neither community in Palestine was supportive of the borders of the proposed states. In their effort to amass as many Jews in the Jewish state as possible and include as many Arabs as possible in the Arab state, the UN Special Commission on Palestine (UNSCOP) created a map with territorial discontinuities. Nevertheless, the Jewish community accepted

the partition while the Arab Higher Committee—representing the Palestinians—rejected it. There are two reasons offered for this rejection. First, Palestinian academics and supporters of the Palestinian cause make the case that the proposed partition gave anywhere from 53 to 55 percent of the land to the Jewish state, despite the fact that there were fewer Jews in Palestine than Arabs. Second, other scholars and supporters of Israel argue that the Arab Higher Committee rejected partition because the Palestinian leadership rejected the idea of a Jewish state in Palestine to begin with, on principle. Instead, the committee believed, on this view, that the appropriate course of action for the UN was to support the independence of an Arab state in the area where UNSCOP was proposing two states. For illustrative examples of these widely differing perspective, see Khalidi, *The Hundred Years' War on Palestine*; Erakat, *Justice for Some: Law and the Question of Palestine*; Kramer, "Why the 1947 UN Partition Resolution Must Be Celebrated"; Sachar, *A History of Israel*.

3. Israeli Ministry of Foreign Affairs, "The Declaration of the Establishment of the State of Israel."

4. Sachar, *A History of Israel*; Morris, "The Birth of the Palestinian Refugee Problem Revisited"; Khalidi, *Palestinian Identity*.

5. Lustick, *Arabs in the Jewish State*, 123–9; Manna, "Palestinians under Military Rule in Israel."

6. McCullough, *Truman*, 595–7.

7. Mead, *The Arc of a Covenant: The United States, Israel, and the Fate of the Jewish People*, Chapter 4; McCullough, *Truman*, 597.

8. McCullough, *Truman*, 596. President Truman ended up losing New York State in the 1948 election.

9. Mead, *The Arc of a Covenant: The United States, Israel, and the Fate of the Jewish People*, 196.

10. Stillman, *The Jews of Arab Lands in Modern Times*.

11. "Tripartite Declaration Regarding the Armistice Borders: Statement by the Governments of the United States, the United Kingdom, and France."

12. Cook, *The Struggle for Egypt*, 69; Barak, "Between Reality and Secrecy."

13. Bass, *Support Any Friend*, 151.

14. Ibid., 53–5.

15. "Press Release from Office of Senator JFK to Secretary of State, Dulles, March 5, 1956."

16. "Remarks by Senator John F. Kennedy at Yankee Stadium, New York, New York, on April 29, 1956."

17. "Speech by Senator John F. Kennedy, Zionists of America Convention, Statler Hilton Hotel, New York, NY | The American Presidency Project."

18. "Message from Vice President Richard Nixon to the Annual Convention of the Zionist Organization of America, New York, NY | The American Presidency Project."

19. Mead, *The Arc of a Covenant*, 310–11.

20. It turns out that Kennedy was only half right. The Israelis proliferated despite his efforts, but no other country in the region followed suit.

21. Bar-Siman-Tov, "The United States and Israel since 1948."

22. Bass, *Support Any Friend*.

23. Oren, *Six Days of War: June 1967 and the Making of the Modern Middle East*, 26.
24. Ibid.; Parker, *The Politics of Miscalculation in the Middle East*; Quandt, *Peace Process*; Quandt, "Lyndon Johnson and the June 1967 War: What Color Was the Light?"
25. Quandt, *Peace Process*, Chapter 2; Quandt, "Lyndon Johnson and the June 1967 War: What Color Was the Light?"
26. Cook, *The Struggle for Egypt*, Chapter 3.
27. This was the case even after it came to light that Israeli forces had attacked an American naval vessel, the USS *Liberty*, operating off the Egyptian coast. The official story from which the American and Israeli governments have never deviated is that the attack was an accident: Israeli aircrews and torpedo boats mistook the US naval intelligence-gathering ship for an Egyptian vessel. The *Liberty*'s survivors and other observers do not accept that explanation and accuse the Israelis of deliberately targeting the ship and the Johnson administration of looking the other way, despite 34 killed and 171 wounded American servicemen. Critics of the official story indicate that Israel attacked the *Liberty* because it was providing valuable information about Israel's operations to Washington that the Israelis feared the Johnson administration could use as part of any effort to impose a ceasefire.
28. "UN Security Council Resolution 242."
29. President Johnson likened Israel to the frontier much as he imagined his home state of Texas.
30. "Public Papers of the Presidents of the United States."
31. Cook, *The Struggle for Egypt*, 134.
32. Sharp, "U.S. Foreign Aid to Israel." In 1982, Secretary of State Alexander Haig was the first American official to use the term "qualitative military edge" in relation to Israel, but maintaining Israeli military superiority had become American policy for much of the preceding decade.
33. Ibid.
34. Ibid.
35. "About the BSF."
36. Ibid.
37. "Israeli Cyber Security Industry Continued to Grow in 2021." Israeli firms have not always been good stewards of the technology they have developed. There is, for example, the notorious case of the NSO Group. The firm's spyware, Pegasus, was ostensibly developed to help governments apprehend criminals and thwart terrorist attacks. Yet the NSO Group is believed to have sold its technology to Saudi Arabia, the United Arab Emirates, India, Azerbaijan, Hungary, Rwanda, Germany, Mexico, Bahrain, Morocco, and Togo—countries that have, according to a consortium of university-based tech researchers and journalists, used the spyware to surveil, intimidate, and apprehend their political opponents, journalists, human-rights activists, and the lawyers for these advocates. There is also no ignoring the geostrategic implications of the NSO Group's reported clientele. It is clear that the Pegasus spyware is part and parcel of Israeli statecraft, intended as a way of enhancing or developing relations with countries that perceive common threats from Islamism and Iran like Saudi Arabia, Bahrain, and the UAE. Others such as Azerbaijan, India, and Hungary

provide Israel with various kinds of diplomatic, political, and military support. When Israel's Ministry of Defense approved the sale of Pegasus to these countries, it was not simply a commercial matter.

38. Senor and Singer, *Start-Up Nation*, 181–2.

39. Saba, "UAE Seeks $1 Trillion in Economic Activity with Israel by 2031."

40. Sharp, "Egypt: Background and U.S. Relations."

41. Kampeas, "20 Years Ago, the UN Durban Conference Aimed to Combat Racism. It Devolved into a 'Festival of Hate' against Jews"; Adamson, "U.S. and Israel Officially Withdraw from UNESCO."

42. For example, at this writing only two members of the US Congress support Boycott, Divestment, and Sanctions: Representative Rashida Tlaib (D-MI) and Representative Ilhan Omar (D-MN). A third member, Representative Cori Bush (D-MO), stated in a 2020 campaign flyer that is now only retrievable via Facebook that she "has always been sympathetic to the BDS movement," but since coming to Congress has not indicated her support for the effort. To access the flyer, see: https://www.facebook.com/1000253160054572/photos/pb.100053136128819.-2207520000../3287822621297603/?type=3. In addition, major companies with operations and investments in Israel include Alibaba, Amazon, Apple, Applied Materials, Baidu, Berkshire Hathaway, booking.com, Bosch Group, Citi, Dell, eBay, Facebook, Flex, Ford, GM, Google, HP, Intel, Mastercard, Microsoft, Oracle, Perrigo, and Phillips. In addition to this list, more than two hundred multinational firms have R&D hubs in Israel.

43. Zaken, "Israelis Begin Doing Deals in Saudi Arabia."

44. Zaken, "Qatar, Israel Reach Agreement on Diamond Trade."

45. Public-opinion polling in the Middle East used to be more difficult than it is now, though it continues to be challenging. Given the nature of politics in these countries, pollsters report that there are issues that remain off-limits and questions that local partners are understandably reluctant to ask. The last decade of polling in the Middle East provides critical insight into the way that Arabs view Israel and the conflict between the Palestinians and Israelis. Various polls demonstrate that Palestine remains important to vast majorities of Arabs across the region. They also show that overwhelming majorities oppose the idea of normalization with Israel. And most do not believe that Israel is interested in peace. This is hardly surprising, given the history of the conflict between Palestinians and Israelis. Yet, within the data, there is a recognition of the reality that Israel is a permanent part of the Middle East. Polling conducted by Zogby Research Services between 2011 and 2019 reinforces the importance of Palestine for Arabs, but also indicates that resolving the Palestinian-Israeli conflict is not always a priority for Arabs. In 2011, for example, Zogby found that among eleven priorities, the issue came in ninth in Tunisia; eighth in Egypt; tenth in Lebanon; eleventh in Iraq; and second in Jordan, Saudi Arabia, and the United Arab Emirates. Of course, 2011 was a year of significant political tumult in Egypt and Tunisia, which may be the reason why resolving the conflict may have ranked so low. In subsequent polling (2015), two-thirds of respondents expressed support for the 2002 Arab Peace Initiative. In 2016, a plurality of Egyptians and majority of Saudis believed that the occupation of Palestinian lands was the greatest obstacle to peace and stability. This

is significant given the size and influence of these countries. At the same time, however, Lebanese and Iraqis ranked Israel's occupation as seventh and, in Jordan and the UAE, the issue ranked eighth in importance. By 2019, Zogby found a significant change in attitudes. Majorities in Egypt, Jordan, Palestine, Saudi Arabia, and the UAE believed there was a likelihood of normalization, and majorities in Egypt, Jordan, Saudi Arabia, and the UAE supported it. The poll also found that, as a priority for the region, Palestine was ninth out of nine options for Emiratis, Saudis, and Lebanese; eighth for Iraqis; seventh for Tunisians; and fourth for Egyptians. Yet, just a year later, polling from Arab Barometer and Arab Opinion Index shows that support for normalization was in the single digits in most countries. The latter's 2019 poll also shows that just 2.3 percent of Arabs polled reject Israel, meaning they do not recognize its existence, and 7 percent reject Israel on religious grounds. This is not to suggest that pious people are impervious to changing their minds, but, because religion is linked to identity and because these respondents frame the conflict in religious terms, a shift seems less likely.

46. "Americans Still Favor Israel While Warming to Palestinians"; Saad, "Americans' Views toward Israel Remain Firmly Positive"; "The American Public and Israel | Roper Center for Public Opinion Research"; Rosentiel, "The U.S. Public's Pro-Israel History."
47. Imseis, "Negotiating the Illegal: On the United Nations and the Illegal Occupation of Palestine, 1967–2020"; Imseis, "Critical Reflections on the International Humanitarian Law Aspects of the ICJ Wall Advisory Opinion"; Lapidoth, "The Expulsion of Civilians from Areas Which Came under Israeli Control in 1967: Some Legal Issues."
48. "ארכיון Settlement Watch."
49. Miller, "Israel's Lawyer."
50. Abrams, *Tested by Zion*, 287–92.
51. "The Covenant of the Islamic Resistance Movement."
52. "Hamas in 2017."
53. Ibid.
54. Ibid.
55. "Gaza Strip"; "West Bank."
56. "West Bank." According to the CIA, these data are for both the West Bank and the Gaza Strip.
57. Khalidi, *Palestinian Identity*.
58. Lawrence, *Messages to the World*, xii.
59. World Islamic Front Statement Urging Jihad against Jews and Crusaders.
60. Robinson, *Global Jihad: A Brief History*, 23.
61. Lustick, "We Need to Talk about Israel," October 23, 2020.
62. Ibid.
63. Mearsheimer and Walt, *The Israel Lobby*.
64. Ibid.
65. One of the best-known cases of the alleged power of the pro-Israel lobby dates back four decades and involved a twelve-term Republican congressman from Springfield,

Illinois, named Paul Findley. In the 1970s, he advocated for a dialogue with the Palestine Liberation Organization and had nice words for the organization's leader, Yasir Arafat—Israel's archenemy and a terrorist. Pro-Israel groups opposed Findley with great passion. Findley lost his 1982 re-election bid and parlayed his post-congressional career into anti-Israel advocacy, which included authoring a book about the influence of pro-Israel groups titled *Those Who Dare to Speak Out*. It was, however, mostly a self-serving myth. In the 1980 election, Findley prevailed (by twelve percentage points) over a candidate who also had the backing of pro-Israel groups. During his losing campaign two years later, Findley had to contend with 20 percent unemployment in his district, unfavorable redistricting, lackluster fundraising, and a formidable political opponent, as well as the opposition of pro-Israel groups. Contrary to legend, there were multiple factors that contributed to Findley's loss.

66. The controversy involved whether the funds Israel raised on international credit markets with American guarantees could be used to settle immigrants from the Soviet Union in Jewish communities in the West Bank and Gaza Strip, which the administration opposed. When the president sought a four-month delay to consider the Israeli request, he was met with fierce resistance and political pressure. At one contentious moment he stated, "We're up against very strong, and effective, sometimes groups that go up to the Hill. I heard today that there were something like a thousand lobbyists up on the Hill working the other side of the question. We've got one lonely guy down here." The clear implication was that the president of the United States—"the lonely guy"—was no match for the power of Israel's supporters. It turned out that pro-Israel groups actually lost that battle with President Bush.

67. In September 2021, despite objections from House progressives over Israel's request for supplemental security assistance to help restock its Iron Dome system after a conflict with Hamas, the House voted in favor of the funding 420 votes to 9. In 2019, House Resolution 246 "Opposing efforts to delegitimize the State of Israel and the global boycott, divestment, and sanctions movement targeting Israel" passed the House of Representatives with 398 votes.

68. Flynn, "Edwards, Ivey Face Off Tuesday after Tense Home Stretch in Md. Primaries."

69. Ibid.

70. "The Post Endorses Glenn Ivey for Maryland's 4th District Democratic Primary."

71. The reverse case of Donna Edwards's loss was Pennsylvania Democrat Summer Lee, who prevailed in a general election race against a candidate who enjoyed AIPAC's support.

Chapter 4

1. Haass, *War of Necessity, War of Choice*.

2. Bush and Scowcroft, *A World Transformed*, 374.

3. "President George H. W. Bush: Address before a Joint Session of Congress, September 11, 1990."

4. Turner, "To a New World Order"; Buruma, "Bush's 'New World Order': It Is Right to Be Encouraging Democracy"; Muravchik, "Opinion: At Last, Pax Americana"; *New York Times*, "The New World Order So Far."

5. Bush and Scowcroft, *A World Transformed*, xiii, 115, 151, 205.
6. Talbott, "Why NATO Should Grow."
7. Daalder, "NATO in the 21st Century: What Purpose? What Missions?"
8. Crossette, "Democracy's Desert; A Rising Tide of Freedom Bypasses the Arab World."
9. Indyk, *Innocent Abroad*, 16.
10. Ibid., 17–18.
11. Lake, "From Containment to Enlargement."
12. Indyk, *Innocent Abroad*, 58.
13. Ibid., 392.
14. "Saddam Must Go."
15. Ibid.
16. Abrams et al., "Letter to President Clinton on Iraq."
17. Makiya, *Republic of Fear*.
18. Leigh, "New Bank Scandal Evidence against Family of Leader in Waiting."
19. The Iraq Liberation Act passed in the House of Representatives with 360 yeas, 38 nays, and 26 not voting on October 5, 1998. It was passed by unanimous consent in the Senate on October 7, 1998.
20. Gilman, "H.R. 4655—105th Congress (1997–1998)."
21. "President Declares 'Freedom at War with Fear.' "
22. Bin Laden, "Declaration of Jihad against the Americans Occupying the Land of the Two Holiest Sites"; Robinson, *Global Jihad*, 26.
23. Interview with a former US government official, February 18, 2022 (Washington, DC).
24. Kaye et al., "More Freedom, Less Terror? Liberalization and Political Violence in the Arab World."
25. "President Bush Discusses Freedom in Iraq and Middle East."
26. "President Bush Presses for Peace in the Middle East."
27. Rice, "Remarks at the American University in Cairo."
28. Boot, "The Case for American Empire."
29. Boot, "What the Neocons Got Wrong."
30. "President Bush Outlines Iraqi Threat."
31. "Erased in a Moment: Suicide Bombing Attacks against Israeli Civilians."
32. Rice, *Democracy: Stories from the Long Road to Freedom*, 276–7.
33. Kristol and Kaplan, *The War over Iraq: Saddam's Tyranny and America's Mission*; Sullivan, "Yes, a War Would Be Moral"; Zakaria, "It's Time to Talk to the World"; Friedman, "Iraq, Upside Down"; Adelman, "Cakewalk in Iraq"; Indyk, O'Hanlon, and Gordon, "Getting Serious about Iraq"; Kagan and Kristol, "What to Do about Iraq?"; Perle, "The U.S. Must Strike at Saddam Hussein"; Ajami, "The Reckoning"; Ajami, "Hosing Down the Gulf's Arsonist"; *Wall Street Journal*, "How to Liberate Iraq."
34. Kaiser and Ottaway, "Saudi Leader's Anger Revealed Shaky Ties."
35. Gerstenzang, "Saudi Prince Warns Bush to Rein In Israel."
36. Interview with a former US government official, February 18, 2022 (Washington, DC).
37. Democratic peace theory remains contested among scholars.
38. Belasco, "The Cost of Iraq, Afghanistan, and Other Global War on Terror Operations since 9/11"; "Costs of the 20-Year War on Terror."
39. "American War and Military Operations Casualties: Lists and Statistics."
40. "Presidential Approval Ratings—George W. Bush."

Chapter 5

1. "Remarks by the President at Cairo University."
2. Mazarr, *Leap of Faith: Hubris, Negligence, and America's Greatest Foreign Policy Tragedy*, 7.
3. Cook, *False Dawn*, Chapter 1.
4. "Remarks by the President on the Middle East and North Africa."
5. Obama, *A Promised Land*, 655–68.
6. "Remarks by the President in Address to the Nation on Libya."
7. Power, *The Education of an Idealist*, 304–5.
8. Cook, *False Dawn*, Chapter 5.
9. Mazarr, *Leap of Faith*. Interview with a former US government official, February 18, 2022 (Washington, DC).
10. Lee and Solomon, "Obama Wrote Secret Letter to Iran's Khamenei about Fighting Islamic State"; MacAskill, "Obama Sent Letter to Khamenei before the Election, Report Says."
11. "Message, President Bill Clinton to President Mohammad Khatami."
12. Goldberg, "The Obama Doctrine."
13. Samuels, "The Aspiring Novelist Who Became Obama's Foreign-Policy Guru."
14. Gordon and Nephew, "Two Years On, the Iran Deal Is Working."
15. *Time*, "Donald Trump's Presidential Announcement Speech."
16. "CBS Republican Presidential Candidates Debate."
17. Cook, "End the 'Forever War' Cliché."
18. Ibid.
19. The president twice vowed to withdraw America's contingent of special-forces operators from Syria in December 2018 and again in October 2019. In the first instance, which resulted in the resignation of the secretary of defense, the bureaucracy slow-walked the president's orders and the forces remained. In the second episode, 40 percent of the soldiers were ordered out of Syria and the rest redeployed.
20. Daalder and Lindsay, *The Empty Throne: America's Abdication of Global Leadership*, 29.
21. "Peace to Prosperity: A Vision to Improve the Lives of the Palestinian and Israeli People."
22. "Remarks by the President on the Middle East and North Africa."

Chapter 6

1. Churchwell, *Behold, America: A History of America First and the American Dream*.
2. Deudney and Ikenberry, "Misplaced Restraint."
3. Ibid.
4. Waltz, *Man, the State, and War: A Theoretical Analysis*.
5. Porter, "Why America's Grand Strategy Has Not Changed"; Desch, "America's Liberal Illiberalism"; Bueno de Mesquita and Downs, "Intervention and Democracy."

6. Rosen, "Washington's Weirdest Think Tank."

7. Porter, "Why America's Grand Strategy Has Not Changed."

8. Salman and Engel, "Making U.S. Foreign Policy Work Better for the Middle Class."

9. Katulis and Juul, "Strategic Reengagement in the Middle East: Toward a More Balanced and Long-Term Approach for U.S. Policy"; Cook, "No Exit: Why the Middle East Still Matters to America"; Brands, "Why America Can't Quit the Middle East."

10. Jentleson, "Strategic Recalibration."

11. Karlin and Wittes, "America's Middle East Purgatory."

12. Indyk, "The Middle East Isn't Worth It Anymore."

13. Gause, "The Price of Order: Settling for Less in the Middle East"; Bandow, "A Blueprint for Getting Out of the Middle East"; Indyk, "The Middle East Isn't Worth It Anymore"; Karlin and Wittes, "How to Do More with Less in the Middle East"; Pillar et al., "A New U.S. Paradigm for the Middle East"; Miller and Sokolsky, "5 Reasons Why Trump Is Right about Getting America Out of Syria"; Gause, "Should We Stay or Should We Go? The United States and the Middle East"; Jentleson, "Right-Sizing Foreign Policy"; Miller and Sokolsky, "U.S. Democracy Promotion"; Lynch, "Obama and the Middle East: Rightsizing the U.S. Role"; Logan, "Why the Middle East Still Doesn't Matter"; Jones, "Don't Stop at Iraq."

14. Mearsheimer and Walt, "The Case for Offshore Balancing"; Ashford, "Unbalanced: Rethinking America's Commitment to the Middle East."

15. "Worldwide Manpower Distribution by Geographical Area."

16. El Dahan, Alkousaa, and Saba, "UAE, Saudi Say OPEC+ Should Not Play Politics."

17. "Foreign Terrorist Organizations."

18. Goldberg, "The Obama Doctrine."

19. Brower et al., "The New Oil War: OPEC Moves against the US."

20. Shihabi, "Ali Shihabi علي الشهابي on Twitter."

21. Cook, *The Struggle for Egypt*.

22. Washington was not willing to become a party to the Syrian conflict except to fight the Islamic State. For a time, the United States embarked on a halfhearted effort to train and equip Syrian opposition fighters, but the effort ended in failure, in large part because President Obama was ambivalent about it.

23. Wezeman, Kuimova, and Wezeman, "Trends in International Arms Transfers, 2021."

24. Masterson, "Saudi Arabia Said to Produce Ballistic Missiles"; Meick, "China's Reported Ballistic Missile Sale to Saudi Arabia: Background and Potential Implications."

25. Rumley, "China's Security Presence in the Middle East: Redlines and Guidelines for the United States."

26. Ibid.

27. Private conversation with an American business executive, February 12, 2022 (Chicago).

28. Alterman, "The Other Side of the World: China, the United States, and the Struggle for Middle East Security."

29. Ibid.

30. Strobel and Youssef, "F-35 Sale to U.A.E. Imperiled over U.S. Concerns about Ties to China—WSJ."

31. Rogin, "America's Gulf 'Allies' Are Now Putin's Enablers."
32. Di Paola and Bartenstein, "Saudi Oil Chief Says All Energy Sectors Running Out of Capacity."
33. Schanzer et al., "Aligning U.S.-Israeli Cooperation on Technology Issues and China."
34. Magid, "Lindsey Graham Criticizes Israel for Refusing to Sell Weapons to Ukraine"; Samuels, "Israel's Ukraine Position Will Hurt U.S. Ties, Warns Republican Congressman."

Chapter 7

1. "Brett McGurk Sets Out the 'Biden Doctrine' for the Middle East."
2. "Digital Briefing with Barbara Leaf, Assistant Secretary of State for Near Eastern Affairs."
3. "IEA World Energy Outlook."
4. Bordoff and O'Sullivan, "Green Upheaval"; Office of the Director of National Intelligence, "Climate Change and International Responses Increasing Challenges to US National Security through 2040."
5. Interview with American military officials, Washington, DC, February 27, 2023; Pollack, "RIP the Carter Doctrine, 1980–2019."
6. "IMSC Task Force Completes Maritime Exercise with Unmanned Systems, A.I."; Maxwell, "Artificial Intelligence Is the Future of Warfare (Just Not in the Way You Think)."
7. Jeff Seldin, "US Calls Hamas Attack 'ISIS-Level Savagery,'" https://www.voanews.com/a/us-calls-hamas-attack-isis-level-savagery-/7303672.html.
8. "Remarks by President Biden on the Terrorist Attacks in Israel," October 10, 2023, https://www.whitehouse.gov/briefing-room/speeches-remarks/2023/10/10/remarks-by-president-biden-on-the-terrorist-attacks-in-israel-2/.
9. Jennifer Agiesta, "CNN Poll: Americans Are Deeply Sympathetic toward Israelis and See Their Military Response to Hamas Attacks as Justified," https://www.cnn.com/2023/10/15/politics/cnn-poll-israel-hamas-war-americans/index.html.
10. "Harvard Caps Harris Poll," October 19, 2023, https://harvardharrispoll.com/wp-content/uploads/2023/10/HHP_Oct23_KeyResults.pdf.
11. Ibid.
12. Ibid.
13. Saad, "Democrats' Sympathies in Middle East Shift to Palestinians."
14. Bellin and Kurtzer, "3 Bilateral Agreements That Would Improve Israel's Relationship with America"; Cook, "How to End the Special Relationship with Israel."
15. Nadeem, "Two Decades Later, the Enduring Legacy of 9/11."
16. "Remarks as Prepared for Delivery by Assistant to the President for Homeland Security, Dr. Liz Sherwood-Randall on the Future of the U.S. Counterterrorism Mission."
17. Ibid.
18. "National Security Strategy," 2022.

19. Murphy, "America's Middle East Policy Is Outdated and Dangerous"; Thrall and Goepner, "Step Back: Lessons from U.S. Foreign Policy from the Failed War on Terror."

20. National Strategy for Counterterrorism, June 2011.

21. National Strategy for Counterterrorism of the United States of America, June 2018.

22. "National Security Strategy"; "Remarks as Prepared for Delivery by Assistant to the President for Homeland Security, Dr. Liz Sherwood-Randall on the Future of the U.S. Counterterrorism Mission."

23. "Bush: Don't Wait for Mushroom Cloud."

24. Goldberg, "The Obama Doctrine."

25. Interview with American military officials, Washington, DC, February 27, 2023.

26. Cook, "The Only Sensible Iran Strategy Is Containment."

27. Ibid.

28. Mueller, *Atomic Obsession.*

29. Stein, "Kilowatts or Kilotons"; Hymans, *The Psychology of Nuclear Proliferation: Identity, Emotions, and Foreign Policy*; Tannenwald, "Stigmatizing the Bomb: Origins of Nuclear Taboo"; Lavoy, "Nuclear Myths and the Causes of Nuclear Proliferation."

30. "Additional Protocol," 2016.

31. Markey, *No Exit from Pakistan: America's Tortured Relationship with Islamabad*, 90; also see Kux, *The United States and Pakistan, 1947–2000: Disenchanted Allies.*

32. Markey, *No Exit from Pakistan*, 17; Kux, *The United States and Pakistan 1947–2000.*

33. Waltz, "The Spread of Nuclear Weapons: More May Be Better."

34. Fanning and Mekelberg, "The Coming Climate Migration Crisis in the Middle East and North Africa"; Taylor, "Climate Change 'Will Create World's Biggest Refugee Crisis'"; Brown and Crawford, "Rising Temperatures, Rising Tensions: Climate Change and the Risk of Violent Conflict in the Middle East."

35. Femia and Werrell, "Syria: Climate Change, Drought and Social Unrest."

36. Selby et al., "Climate Change and the Syrian Civil War Revisited."

37. Office of the Director of National Intelligence, "Climate Change and International Responses Increasing Challenges to US National Security through 2040."

38. Waterbury, "The Political Economy of Climate Change in the Arab Region."

39. Stang, "Climate Challenges in the Middle East: Rethinking Environmental Cooperation"; Fanning and Mekelberg, "The Coming Climate Migration Crisis in the Middle East and North Africa"; Brown and Crawford, "Rising Temperatures, Rising Tensions."

40. Not for attribution presentation by a US official, November 28, 2022 (Washington, DC).

41. "Nuclear Posture Review," 2018; "Summary of the National Defense Strategy of the United States of America: Sharpening the American Military's Competitive Edge."

42. Rudd, "The World According to Xi Jinping."

43. Doran, "Biden Is Delivering the Middle East to China"; Herzinger and Lefkowitz, "China's Growing Naval Influence in the Middle East"; Rumley, "China's Security Presence in the Middle East: Redlines and Guidelines for the United States"; Doran and Rough, "China's Emerging Middle Eastern Kingdom."

44. Cook and Green, "China Isn't Trying to Dominate the Middle East"; Cook, "Major Power Rivalry in the Middle East"; Alterman, "The Other Side of the World: China, the United States, and the Struggle for Middle East Security."

45. Interviews with former US government officials, March 7, 2023 (Washington, DC).

46. Ibid.

47. "Fact Sheet: President Biden and G7 Leaders Launch Build Back Better World (B3W) Partnership."

48. Essaid, "UAE's IDEX Weapons Fair Brings in Russia, China, and Billion-Dollar Deals—Al-Monitor."

49. Herzinger and Lefkowitz, "China's Growing Naval Influence in the Middle East."

50. Fried, "U.S. to Spend $1.5 Billion to Jumpstart Alternatives to Huawei."

51. Ibid.; "Open RAN Policy Question FAQs."

52. Interviews with former US government officials, March 7, 2023 (Washington, DC).

53. Alterman, "The Other Side of the World."

54. Haass, "The Dangerous Decade: A Foreign Policy for a World in Crisis."

55. Cook, "Biden Was Always Going to Need Saudi Arabia."

56. "National Security Strategy"; Scheinmann, "The U.S. Should Want a Cold War with China"; Brands and Cooper, "U.S.-Chinese Rivalry Is a Battle over Values"; McFaul, "China Is Winning the Ideological Battle with the U.S."

57. Young, "How Russia's Invasion of Ukraine Will Impact Energy Markets."

58. Katulis, "Ukraine Is the World's First Major 'Troll Power' War."

Works Cited

"About the BSF." BSF. Accessed January 7, 2022. https://www.bsf.org.il/about/.

Abrams, Elliott. 2013. *Tested by Zion: The Bush Administration and the Israeli-Palestinian Conflict.* Cambridge: Cambridge University Press.

Abrams, Elliott, Richard Armitage, William J. Bennett, Jeffrey Bergner, John Bolton, Paula Dobriansky, Francis Fukuyama, et al. 1998. "Letter to President Clinton on Iraq." January 26. https://webarchive.loc.gov/all/20030527201806/http://www.newamerican century.org/iraqclintonletter.htm.

Adamson, Thomas. 2019. "U.S. and Israel Officially Withdraw from UNESCO." *PBS Newshour* and *Associated Press*, January 1. https://www.pbs.org/newshour/politics/u-s-and-israel-officially-withdraw-from-unesco.

"Additional Protocol." n.d. Accessed March 10, 2023. https://www.iaea.org/topics/additio nal-protocol.

Adelman, Ken. 2002. "Cakewalk in Iraq." *Washington Post*, February 13. https://www. washingtonpost.com/archive/opinions/2002/02/13/cakewalk-in-iraq/cf09301c-c6c4-4f2e-8268-7c93017f5e93/.

Agiesta, Jennifer. 2023. "CNN Poll: Americans Are Deeply Sympathetic toward Israelis and See Their Military Response to Hamas Attacks as Justified." *CNN.com*, October 15. https://www.cnn.com/2023/10/15/politics/cnn-poll-israel-hamas-war-americans/ index.html.

Ajami, Fouad. 1994. "Hosing Down the Gulf's Arsonist." *U.S. News and World Report*, October 24.

Ajami, Fouad. 1998. "The Reckoning." *The New Republic*, February 23.

Alterman, Jon B. 2017. "The Other Side of the World: China, the United States, and the Struggle for Middle East Security." Washington, DC: Center for Strategic and International Studies.

"The American Public and Israel: Roper Center for Public Opinion Research." March 16, 2015. https://ropercenter.cornell.edu/blog/american-public-and-israel.

"American War and Military Operations Casualties: Lists and Statistics." 2020. RL32492. Washington, DC: Congressional Research Service. https://sgp.fas.org/crs/natsec/RL32 492.pdf.

"Americans Still Favor Israel While Warming to Palestinians." 2021. *Gallup.com*. March 19. https://news.gallup.com/poll/340331/americans-favor-israel-warming-palestini ans.aspx.

"Anglo-French Oil Agreement Is Out." 1920. *New York Times*, July 23.

"A/RES/181(II) of 29 November 1947." 1947. Accessed May 20, 2021. https://docume nts-dds-ny.un.org/doc/RESOLUTION/GEN/NR0/038/88/PDF/NR003888.pdf?Open Element.

Ashford, Emma. 2018. "Unbalanced: Rethinking America's Commitment to the Middle East." *Strategic Studies Quarterly* 12 (1): 127–48. http://www.jstor.org/stable/26333880.

Bandow, Doug. 2021. "A Blueprint for Getting Out of the Middle East." *The American Conservative*, July 8. https://www.theamericanconservative.com/a-blueprint-for-getting-out-of-the-middle-east/.

Barak, Eitan. 2007. "Between Reality and Secrecy: Israel's Freedom of Navigation through the Straits of Tiran, 1956–1967." *Middle East Journal* 61 (4): 657–79. https://www.jstor.org/stable/4330453.

Bar-Siman-Tov, Yaacov. 1998. "The United States and Israel since 1948: A 'Special Relationship'?" *Diplomatic History* 22 (2): 231–62. http://www.jstor.org/stable/24913659.

Bass, Warren. 2004. *Support Any Friend: Kennedy's Middle East and the Making of the U.S.-Israel Alliance.* New York: Oxford University Press.

Belasco, Amy. 2014. "The Cost of Iraq, Afghanistan, and Other Global War on Terror Operations since 9/11." RL33110. Washington, DC: Congressional Research Service. https://sgp.fas.org/crs/natsec/RL33110.pdf.

Bellin, Yossi, and Daniel Kurtzer. 2020. "3 Bilateral Agreements That Would Improve Israel's Relationship with America." *The National Interest*, June 19. https://nationalinterest.org/feature/3-bilateral-agreements-would-improve-israels-relationship-america-163067.

Boot, Max. 2023. "What the Neocons Got Wrong." *Foreign Affairs*, March 10. https://www.foreignaffairs.com/iraq/what-neocons-got-wrong.

Boot, Max. 2001. "The Case for American Empire." *Weekly Standard*, October 15. https://www.washingtonexaminer.com/weekly-standard/the-case-for-american-empire.

Bordoff, Jason, and Meghan L. O'Sullivan. 2022. "Green Upheaval." *Foreign Affairs*, January 24. https://www.foreignaffairs.com/articles/world/2021-11-30/geopolitics-energy-green-upheaval.

Bowman, Tom. 1991. "Anti-War Demonstration Draws 75,000 to Washington: Protests Take Place across the Nation." *Baltimoresun.com*, January 27. https://www.baltimoresun.com/news/bs-xpm-1991-01-27-1991027045-story.html.

Brands, Hal. 2019. "Why America Can't Quit the Middle East." *The Caravan*, March 21. https://www.hoover.org/research/why-america-cant-quit-middle-east.

Brands, Hal, Steven A. Cook, and Kenneth M. Pollack. 2019. "RIP the Carter Doctrine, 1980–2019." *Foreign Policy*, December 15. https://foreignpolicy.com/2019/12/15/carter-doctrine-rip-donald-trump-mideast-oil-big-think/.

Brands, Hal, and Zack Cooper. 2021. "U.S.-Chinese Rivalry Is a Battle over Values." *Foreign Affairs*, March 16. https://www.foreignaffairs.com/articles/united-states/2021-03-16/us-china-rivalry-battle-over-values.

Brenner, Robert. 1991. "Why Is the United States at War with Iraq?" *New Left Review* I/185 (February): 122–37.

"Brett McGurk Sets Out the 'Biden Doctrine' for the Middle East." 2023. Atlantic Council, February 16. https://www.atlanticcouncil.org/commentary/transcript/brett-mcgurk-sets-out-the-biden-doctrine-for-the-middle-east/.

Bronson, Rachel. 2008. *Thicker than Oil: America's Uneasy Partnership with Saudi Arabia.* New York: Oxford University Press.

Brower, Derek, David Sheppard, Andrew England, and Felicia Schwartz. 2022. "The New Oil War: OPEC Moves against the US." *Financial Times*, October 7.

Brown, Oli, and Alec Crawford. 2009. "Rising Temperatures, Rising Tensions: Climate Change and the Risk of Violent Conflict in the Middle East." June 1. Winnipeg,

Manitoba: International Institute for Sustainable Development. https://www.iisd.org/ system/files/publications/rising_temps_middle_east.pdf.

Bueno de Mesquita, Bruce, and George W. Downs. 2006. "Intervention and Democracy." *International Organization* 60 (3): 627–49. https://www.jstor.org/stable/3877822.

Buruma, Ian. 1991. "Bush's 'New World Order': It Is Right to Be Encouraging Democracy." *St. Petersburg Times*, May 14. https://www.tampabay.com/archive/1991/05/14/bush-s-new-world-order-it-is-right-to-be-encouraging-democracy/.

"Bush: Don't Wait for Mushroom Cloud." 2002. *CNN.com*, October 8. https://edition.cnn. com/2002/ALLPOLITICS/10/07/bush.transcript/.

Bush, George H. W., and Brent Scowcroft. 1999. *A World Transformed*. New York: Penguin Random House.

Carter, Jimmy. "State of the Union Address 1980." https://www.jimmycarterlibrary.gov/ assets/documents/speeches/su80jec.phtml.

"CBS Republican Presidential Candidates Debate." 2016. C-SPAN. February 13. https:// www.c-span.org/video/?404611-1/cbs-republican-presidential-candidates-debate.

Chrisafis, Angelique, David Fickling, Jon Henley, John Hooper, Giles Tremlet, Sophie Arie, and Chris McGreal. 2003. "Millions Worldwide Rally for Peace." *The Guardian*, February 16. http://www.theguardian.com/world/2003/feb/17/politics.uk.

Churchwell, Sarah. 2018. *Behold, America: The Entangled History of "America First" and "the American Dream."* New York: Basic Books.

"Cities Jammed in Worldwide Protest of War in Iraq." 2003. *CNN.com*, February 16. https://www.cnn.com/2003/US/02/15/sprj.irq.protests.main/.

Cook, Steven A. 2007. *Ruling but Not Governing: The Military and Political Development in Egypt, Algeria, and Turkey*. Baltimore: Johns Hopkins University Press.

Cook, Steven A. 2011. *The Struggle for Egypt: From Nasser to Tahrir Square*. New York: Oxford University Press.

Cook, Steven A. 2012. "It's Time to Think Seriously about Intervening in Syria." *The Atlantic*, January 17. https://www.theatlantic.com/international/archive/2012/01/its-time-to-think-seriously-about-intervening-in-syria/251468/.

Cook, Steven A. 2017. *False Dawn: Protest, Democracy, and Violence in the New Middle East*. New York: Oxford University Press.

Cook, Steven A. 2020. "How to End the Special Relationship with Israel." *Foreign Policy*, May 20. https://foreignpolicy.com/2020/05/20/israel-palestine-annexation-west-bank-ending-special-relationship.

Cook, Steven A. 2020. "No Exit: Why the Middle East Still Matters to America." *Foreign Affairs*, November/December. https://www.foreignaffairs.com/articles/united-states/ 2020-10-13/no-exit.

Cook, Steven A. 2020. "The Only Sensible Iran Strategy Is Containment." *Foreign Policy*, January 29. https://foreignpolicy.com/2020/01/29/iran-strategy-containment-suleim ani-trump-nuclear-deal/.

Cook, Steven A. 2021. "End the 'Forever War' Cliché." *Foreign Policy*, April 22. https:// foreignpolicy.com/2021/04/22/end-the-forever-war-cliche/.

Cook, Steven A. 2021. "Major Power Rivalry in the Middle East." Discussion Paper on Managing Global Disorder 2. New York: Council on Foreign Relations. https://cdn.cfr. org/sites/default/files/report_pdf/dp-cook-no.-2.pdf.

Cook, Steven A. 2022. "Biden Was Always Going to Need Saudi Arabia." *Foreign Policy*, June 8. https://foreignpolicy.com/2022/06/08/biden-saudi-arabia-mohammed-bin-sal man-mbs-pariah-oil/.

Cook, Steven A., and James Green. 2021. "China Isn't Trying to Dominate the Middle East." *Foreign Affairs*, August 21. https://www.foreignaffairs.com/articles/united-sta tes/2021-08-09/china-isnt-trying-dominate-middle-east.

Cooper, Andrew Scott. 2012. *The Oil Kings*. New York: Simon & Schuster.

"Costs of the 20-Year War on Terror: $8 Trillion and 900,000 Deaths." 2021. Costs of War Project. September 1. https://www.brown.edu/news/2021-09-01/costsofwar.

"The Covenant of the Islamic Resistance Movement." 1988. Avalon Project, Yale Law School. https://avalon.law.yale.edu/20th_century/hamas.asp.

Crossette, Barbara. 1998. "Democracy's Desert: A Rising Tide of Freedom Bypasses the Arab World." *New York Times*, April 26, sec. Week in Review. https://www.nytimes. com/1998/04/26/weekinreview/the-world-democracy-s-desert-a-rising-tide-of-free dom-bypasses-the-arab-world.html.

Daalder, Ivo H. 1999. "NATO in the 21st Century: What Purpose? What Missions?" Washington, DC: Brookings Institution. https://www.brookings.edu/articles/nato-in-the-21st-century-what-purpose-what-missions/.

Daalder, Ivo H., and James M. Lindsay. 2018. *The Empty Throne: America's Abdication of Global Leadership*. New York: Public Affairs.

DeForth, Peter W. 1975. "U.S. Naval Presence in the Persian Gulf: The Mideast Force since World War II." *Naval War College Review* 28 (1): 28–38. https://www.jstor.org/stable/ 44641608.

Desch, Michael C. 2007/2008. "America's Liberal Illiberalism: The Ideological Origins of Overreaction in U.S. Foreign Policy." *International Security* 32 (3): 7–43.

Deudney, Daniel, and John Ikenberry. 2021. "Misplaced Restraint: The Quincy Coalition versus Liberal Internationalism." *Survival* 63 (4): 7–32. https://www.tandfonline.com/ doi/epub/10.1080/00396338.2021.1956187.

"Digital Briefing with Barbara Leaf, Assistant Secretary of State for Near Eastern Affairs." 2023. U.S. Department of State, March 30. https://www.state.gov/online-briefing-with-barbara-a-leaf-assistant-secretary-of-state-for-near-eastern-affairs/.

Di Paola, Anthony, and Ben Bartenstein. 2022. "Saudi Oil Chief Says All Energy Sectors Running Out of Capacity." *Bloomberg.com*, May 10. https://www.bloomberg.com/ news/articles/2022-05-10/saudi-oil-chief-says-all-energy-sectors-running-out-of-capacity.

Doran, Michael. 2023. "Biden Is Delivering the Middle East to China." *Tablet Magazine*, March 16. https://www.tabletmag.com/sections/israel-middle-east/articles/ biden-china-saudi-iran-talks.

Doran, Michael, and Peter Rough. 2020. "China's Emerging Middle Eastern Kingdom." *Tablet Magazine*, August 3. https://www.tabletmag.com/sections/israel-middle-east/ articles/china-middle-eastern-kingdom.

El Dahan, Maha, Riham Alkousaa, and Yousef Saba. 2022. "UAE, Saudi Say OPEC+ Should Not Play Politics." *Reuters*, March 29, sec. Business. https://www.reuters.com/ business/world-economy-will-be-hit-if-oil-supplies-are-threatened-saudi-energy-minister-2022-03-29/.

Erakat, Noura. 2019. *Justice for Some: Law and the Question of Palestine*. Stanford, CA: Stanford University Press.

"Erased in a Moment: Suicide Bombing Attacks against Israeli Civilians." 2002. New York: Human Rights Watch. https://www.hrw.org/reports/2002/isrl-pa/ index.htm.

Essaid, Salim A. 2023. "UAE's IDEX Weapons Fair Brings in Russia, China, and Billion-Dollar Deals." *Al-Monitor*, February 24. https://www.al-monitor.com/originals/2023/02/uaes-idex-weapons-fair-brings-russia-china-and-billion-dollar-deals.

"Fact Sheet: President Biden and G7 Leaders Launch Build Back Better World (B3W) Partnership." 2021. June 12. https://www.whitehouse.gov/briefing-room/statements-releases/2021/06/12/fact-sheet-president-biden-and-g7-leaders-launch-build-back-better-world-b3w-partnership/.

Fanning, Kate, and Yossi Mekelberg. 2021. "The Coming Climate Migration Crisis in the Middle East and North Africa." New Lines Institute, December 8. https://newlinesinstitute.org/climate-migration/the-coming-climate-migration-crisis-in-the-middle-east-and-north-africa/.

Femia, Francesco, and Caitlin Werrell. 2012. "Syria: Climate Change, Drought and Social Unrest." Center for Climate & Security, February 29. https://climateandsecurity.org/2012/02/syria-climate-change-drought-and-social-unrest/.

Flynn, Meagan. 2022. "Edwards, Ivey Face Off Tuesday after Tense Home Stretch in Md. Primaries." *Washington Post*, July 16. https://www.washingtonpost.com/dc-md-va/2022/07/16/maryland-congress-primary-democrats-republicans/.

"Foreign Terrorist Organizations." 2022. Accessed May 5. https://www.state.gov/foreign-terrorist-organizations/.

Fried, Ina. 2022. "U.S. to Spend $1.5 Billion to Jumpstart Alternatives to Huawei." *Axios*, December 7. https://www.axios.com/2022/12/07/huawei-alternatives-5g-cellural-equipment-oran.

Friedman, Thomas L. 2002. "Iraq, Upside Down." *New York Times*, September 18, sec. Opinion. https://www.nytimes.com/2002/09/18/opinion/iraq-upside-down.html.

Galpern, Steven G. 2009. *Money, Oil, and Empire in the Middle East: Sterling and Postwar Imperialism, 1944–1971.* Cambridge: Cambridge University Press.

Garfinkle, Adam, and Daniel Pipes. 1991. *Friendly Tyrants: An American Dilemma.* London: Palgrave Macmillan UK.

Gause, F. Gregory, III. 2019. "Should We Stay or Should We Go? The United States and the Middle East." *Survival* 61 (5): 7–24.

Gause, F. Gregory, III. 2022. "The Price of Order: Settling for Less in the Middle East." *Foreign Affairs*, March/April. https://www.foreignaffairs.com/middle-east/price-order.

"Gaza Strip." 2022. In *The World Factbook*. Central Intelligence Agency. https://www.cia.gov/the-world-factbook/countries/gaza-strip/#people-and-society.

Gelb, Leslie H. 1980. "Beyond the Carter Doctrine." *New York Times*, February 10. https://timesmachine.nytimes.com/timesmachine/1980/02/10/112139632.html.

Gerstenzang, James. 2002. "Saudi Prince Warns Bush to Rein In Israel." *Los Angeles Times*, April 26. https://www.latimes.com/archives/la-xpm-2002-apr-26-mn-40074-story.html.

Gilman, Benjamin A. 1998. "H.R. 4655—105th Congress (1997–1998): Iraq Liberation Act of 1998." Legislation, October 31. https://www.congress.gov/bill/105th-congress/house-bill/4655.

Goldberg, Jeffrey. 2016. "The Obama Doctrine." *The Atlantic*, March 10. https://www.theatlantic.com/magazine/archive/2016/04/the-obama-doctrine/471525/.

Gordon, Philip M., and Richard Nephew. 2017. "Two Years On, the Iran Deal Is Working." *The Atlantic*, July 14. https://www.theatlantic.com/international/archive/2017/07/iran-nuclear-deal-two-years/533556/.

Haass, Richard. 2009. *War of Necessity, War of Choice: A Memoir of Two Iraqs*. New York: Simon & Schuster.

Haass, Richard. 2022. "The Dangerous Decade: A Foreign Policy for a World in Crisis." *Foreign Affairs* 101 (5).

"Hamas in 2017: The Document in Full." 2017. *Middle East Eye*, May 2. http://www.middleeasteye.net/news/hamas-2017-document-full.

Hamid, Shadi. 2012. "World Must Aid Syria's Rebels." *CNN.com*, February 6. https://www.cnn.com/2012/02/06/opinion/hamid-syria/index.html.

"Harvard CAPS–Harris Poll, October 19, 2023." https://harvardharrispoll.com/wp-content/uploads/2023/10/HHP_Oct23_KeyResults.pdf.

Herzinger, Blake, and Ben Lefkowitz. 2023. "China's Growing Naval Influence in the Middle East." Washington Institute for Near East Policy. February 17. https://www.washingtoninstitute.org/policy-analysis/chinas-growing-naval-influence-middle-east.

Hoagland, Jim. 1979. "A Carter Doctrine for Mideast Oil?" *Washington Post*, June 3. https://www.washingtonpost.com/archive/opinions/1979/06/03/a-carter-doctrine-for-mideast-oil/af3fb2c8-5f5e-4ed4-b1df-de980fd60e18/.

Hull, Cordell. 1948. "109: The Near East Looms Big." In *Memoirs of Cordell Hull*. New York: Macmillan.

Hymans, Jacques. 2006. *The Psychology of Nuclear Proliferation: Identity, Emotions, and Foreign Policy*. Cambridge: Cambridge University Press.

"IEA World Energy Outlook: Global Oil Demand Set to Plateau, Not Decline by 2040 | IEA World Energy Outlook." 2020. October 13. https://www.spglobal.com/commodityinsights/en/market-insights/latest-news/metals/101320-global-oil-demand-set-to-plateau-not-decline-by-2040-iea.

"IMSC Task Force Completes Maritime Exercise with Unmanned Systems, A.I." 2023. U.S. Central Command. January 9. https://www.centcom.mil/MEDIA/NEWS-ARTICLES/News-Article-View/Article/3262687/imsc-task-force-completes-maritime-exercise-with-unmanned-systems-ai.

Imseis, Ardi. 2005. "Critical Reflections on the International Humanitarian Law Aspects of the ICJ Wall Advisory Opinion." *American Journal of International Law* 99 (1): 102–18. https://doi.org/10.2307/3246093.

Imseis, Ardi. 2020. "Negotiating the Illegal: On the United Nations and the Illegal Occupation of Palestine, 1967–2020." *European Journal of International Law* 31 (3): 1055–85.

Indyk, Martin. 1993. "The Clinton Administration's Approach to the Middle East." Presented at the Soref Symposium, May 18. https://www.washingtoninstitute.org/policy-analysis/clinton-administrations-approach-middle-east.

Indyk, Martin. 2014. *Innocent Abroad*. New York: Simon & Schuster.

Indyk, Martin. 2020. "The Middle East Isn't Worth It Anymore." *Wall Street Journal*, January 17. https://www.wsj.com/articles/the-middle-east-isnt-worth-it-anymore-11579277317.

Indyk, Martin, Michael O'Hanlon, and Philip M. Gordon. 2002. "Getting Serious about Iraq." Brookings Institution. September 1. https://www.brookings.edu/articles/getting-serious-about-iraq/.

"Israeli Cyber Security Industry Continued to Grow in 2021: Record of $8.8 Billion Raised." 2022. Gov.il. January 20. https://www.gov.il/en/departments/news/2021cyber_industry.

Israeli Ministry of Foreign Affairs. 1948. "The Declaration of the Establishment of the State of Israel." https://www.gov.il/en/departments/general/declaration-of-establ ishment-state-of-israel#:~:text=On%20May%2014%2C%201948%2C%20on,of%20 the%20State%20of%20Israel.

Jentleson, Bruce. 2019. "Right-Sizing Foreign Policy." *Democracy Journal* 54 (Fall). https:// democracyjournal.org/magazine/54/right-sizing-foreign-policy/.

Jentleson, Bruce. 2018. "Strategic Recalibration." The Century Foundation, January 24. https://tcf.org/content/report/strategic-recalibration/.

Jones, Toby C. 2011. "Don't Stop at Iraq: Why the U.S. Should Withdraw from the Entire Persian Gulf." *The Atlantic*, December 22. https://www.theatlantic.com/international/ archive/2011/12/dont-stop-at-iraq-why-the-us-should-withdraw-from-the-entire-persian-gulf/250389/.

Jones, Toby C. 2013. "What Iran Air Flight 655 Says about America's Role in the Middle East." *Washington Post*, October 17. https://www.washingtonpost.com/news/worldvi ews/wp/2013/10/17/what-iran-air-flight-655-says-about-americas-role-in-the-mid dle-east/.

Kagan, Robert, and William Kristol. 2002. "What to Do about Iraq?" Carnegie Endowment for International Peace. January 21. https://carnegieendowment.org/ 2002/01/21/what-to-do-about-iraq-pub-940.

Kaiser, Robert G., and David B. Ottaway. 2002. "Saudi Leader's Anger Revealed Shaky Ties." *Washington Post*, February 10. https://www.washingtonpost.com/archive/polit ics/2002/02/10/saudi-leaders-anger-revealed-shaky-ties/a570bab2-c7c4-4111-b9bc-c03a3cab5ce2/.

Kampeas, Ron. 2021. "20 Years Ago, the UN Durban Conference Aimed to Combat Racism. It Devolved into a 'Festival of Hate' against Jews." *Jewish Telegraphic Agency*, September 9. https://www.jta.org/2021/09/09/politics/20-years-ago-the-un-dur ban-conference-aimed-to-combat-racism-it-devolved-into-a-festival-of-hate-agai nst-jews.

Karlin, Mara, and Tamara Cofman Wittes. 2019. "America's Middle East Purgatory." *Foreign Affairs*, January/February. https://www.foreignaffairs.com/articles/middle-east/2018-12-11/americas-middle-east-purgatory.

Karlin, Mara, and Tamara Coffman Wittes. 2020. "How to Do More with Less in the Middle East: American Policy in the Wake of the Pandemic." *Foreign Affairs*, September 15. https://www.foreignaffairs.com/articles/middle-east/2020-09-15/how-do-more-less-middle-east.

Katulis, Brian. 2021. "Ukraine Is the World's First Major 'Troll Power' War." *The Liberal Patriot*, December 9. https://www.liberalpatriot.com/p/ukraine-is-the-wor lds-first-major.

Katulis, Brian, and Peter Juul. 2021. "Strategic Reengagement in the Middle East: Toward a More Balanced and Long-Term Approach for U.S. Policy." Center for American Progress. December 16. https://www.americanprogress.org/article/strategic-reeng agement-in-the-middle-east/#:~:text=Toward%20a%20More%20Balanced%20 and,away%20from%20direct%20military%20action.

Kaye, Dalia Dassa, Frederic Wehrey, Audra K. Grant, and Dale Stahl. 2008. "More Freedom, Less Terror? Liberalization and Political Violence in the Arab World." Santa Monica, CA: RAND Corporation. https://www.rand.org/content/dam/rand/pubs/ monographs/2008/RAND_MG772.pdf.

Khalidi, Rashid. 2009. *Palestinian Identity: The Construction of Modern National Consciousness*. New York: Columbia University Press.

Khalidi, Rashid. 2020. *The Hundred Years' War on Palestine*. New York: Macmillan.

Kirkpatrick, Jeane J. 1979. "Dictatorships and Double Standards." *Commentary*, November. https://www.commentary.org/articles/jeane-kirkpatrick/dictatorships-double-standards/.

Kramer, Martin. 2017. "Why the 1947 UN Partition Resolution Must Be Celebrated." *Mosaic*, November 27. https://mosaicmagazine.com/response/israel-zionism/2017/11/why-the-1947-un-partition-resolution-must-be-celebrated/.

Krasner, Stephen D. 1978. *Defending the National Interest: Raw Materials Investments and U.S. Foreign Policy*. Princeton, NJ: Princeton University Press.

Kristol, William, and Lawrence Kaplan. 2003. *The War over Iraq: Saddam's Tyranny and America's Mission*. San Francisco: Encounter Books.

Kupchan, Charles. 1987. *The Persian Gulf and the West: The Dilemmas of Security*. Boston: Allen & Unwin.

Kux, Dennis. 2001. *The United States and Pakistan 1947–2000: Disenchanted Allies*. Washington, DC: Woodrow Wilson Center Press/Johns Hopkins University Press.

Laden, Osama bin. n.d. "Declaration of Jihad against the Americans Occupying the Land of the Two Holiest Sites." Accessed April 17, 2022. https://ctc.westpoint.edu/harmony-program/declaration-of-jihad-against-the-americans-occupying-the-land-of-the-two-holiest-sites-original-language-2/.

Lake, Anthony. 1993. "Remarks of Anthony Lake: 'From Containment to Enlargement.'" https://www.mtholyoke.edu/acad/intrel/lakedoc.html.

Lapidoth, Ruth. 1990. "The Expulsion of Civilians from Areas Which Came under Israeli Control in 1967: Some Legal Issues." *European Journal of International Law* 2 (1): 97–109. http://www.ejil.org/article.php?article=2027&issue=101.

Lavoy, Peter R. 1993. "Nuclear Myths and the Causes of Nuclear Proliferation." *Security Studies* 2 (3/4): 192–212.

Lawrence, Bruce, ed. 2005. *Messages to the World: The Statements of Osama Bin Laden*. Translated by James Howarth. London: Verso Books.

Lawson, Fred. 1984. "The Reagan Administration in the Middle East." *MERIP*, December. https://merip.org/1984/12/the-reagan-administration-in-the-middle-east/.

Lee, Carole E., and Jay Solomon. 2014. "Obama Wrote Secret Letter to Iran's Khamenei about Fighting Islamic State." *Wall Street Journal*, November 7, sec. World. https://online.wsj.com/articles/obama-wrote-secret-letter-to-irans-khamenei-about-fighting-islamic-state-1415295291.

Leigh, David. 2003. "New Bank Scandal Evidence against Family of Leader in Waiting." *The Guardian*, April 17, sec. World news. https://www.theguardian.com/world/2003/apr/17/iraq.davidleigh.

Logan, Justin. 2014. "Why the Middle East Still Doesn't Matter." *Politico Magazine*, October 9. https://www.politico.com/magazine/story/2014/10/why-the-middle-east-still-doesnt-matter-111747.

"Louis Harris Associates Poll: January 1975." Roper Center for Public Opinion Research. https://ropercenter.cornell.edu/ipoll/study/31107837.

Lustick, Ian. 1980. *Arabs in the Jewish State: Israel's Control of a National Minority*. Austin: University of Texas Press.

Lustick, Ian S. 2020. "We Need to Talk about Israel." *Foreign Affairs*, October 23. https://www.foreignaffairs.com/articles/middle-east/2019-04-16/commitment-issues.

Lynch, Marc. 2015. "Obama and the Middle East: Rightsizing the U.S. Role." *Foreign Affairs*, September/October. https://www.foreignaffairs.com/articles/middle-east/obama-and-middle-east.

MacAskill, Ewen. 2009. "Obama Sent Letter to Khamenei before the Election, Report Says." *The Guardian*, June 24, sec. US news. https://www.theguardian.com/world/2009/jun/24/khamenei-obama-letter.

Magid, Jacob. 2022. "Lindsey Graham Criticizes Israel for Refusing to Sell Weapons to Ukraine." *Times of Israel*, March 1. https://www.timesofisrael.com/liveblog_entry/lindsey-graham-criticizes-israel-for-refusing-to-sell-weapons-to-ukraine/.

Makiya, Kanan. 1998. *Republic of Fear: The Politics of Modern Iraq*. Berkeley: University of California Press.

Mandelbaum, Michael. 2016. *Mission Failure: America and the World in the Post–Cold War Era*. New York: Oxford University Press.

Manna, Adel. "Palestinians under Military Rule in Israel." n.d. *Interactive Encyclopedia of the Palestinian Question*. https://www.palquest.org/en/highlight/14340/palestinians-under-military-rule-israel.

Markey, Daniel S. 2013. *No Exit from Pakistan: America's Tortured Relationship with Islamabad*. New York: Cambridge University Press.

Masterson, Julie. 2022. "Saudi Arabia Said to Produce Ballistic Missiles." *Arms Control Today*, January/February. https://www.armscontrol.org/act/2022-01/news/saudi-arabia-said-produce-ballistic-missiles.

Mazarr, Michael J. 2019. *Leap of Faith: Hubris, Negligence, and America's Greatest Foreign Policy Tragedy*. New York: Public Affairs.

McCullough, David. 1992. *Truman*. New York: Simon & Schuster.

McFaul, Michael. 2019. "China Is Winning the Ideological Battle with the U.S." *Washington Post*, July 23. https://www.washingtonpost.com/opinions/2019/07/23/china-is-winning-ideological-battle-with-us/.

McGovern, George. 1980. "How to Avert a New 'Cold War.'" *The Atlantic*, June. https://www.theatlantic.com/magazine/archive/1980/06/how-avert-new-cold-war/309181/.

Mead, Walter Russell. 2022. *The Arc of a Covenant: The United States, Israel, and the Fate of the Jewish People*. New York: Alfred A. Knopf.

Mearsheimer, John J., and Stephen M. Walt. 2016. "The Case for Offshore Balancing." *Foreign Affairs*, July/August. https://www.foreignaffairs.com/articles/united-states/2016-06-13/case-offshore-balancing.

Meick, Ethan. 2014. "China's Reported Ballistic Missile Sale to Saudi Arabia: Background and Potential Implications." Washington, DC: U.S.-China Economic and Security Review Commission. https://www.uscc.gov/sites/default/files/Research/Staff%20Report_China%27s%20Reported%20Ballistic%20Missile%20Sale%20to%20Saudi%20Arabia_0.pdf.

"Message from Vice President Richard Nixon to the Annual Convention of the Zionist Organization of America, New York, NY." 1960. The American Presidency Project. August 27. https://www.presidency.ucsb.edu/documents/message-from-vice-president-richard-nixon-the-annual-convention-the-zionist-organization.

"Message, President Bill Clinton to President Mohammad Khatami." 1999. June 1. https://nsarchive.gwu.edu/document/19812-national-security-archive-doc-08-message.

Miller, Aaron David. 2005. "Israel's Lawyer." *Washington Post*, May 23. https://www.washingtonpost.com/archive/opinions/2005/05/23/israels-lawyer/7ab0416c-9761-4d4a-80a9-82b7e15e5d22/.

Miller, Aaron David, and Richard Sokolsky. 2016. "U.S. Democracy Promotion: Aim Lower." *The American Interest*, June 2. https://carnegieendowment.org/2016/06/02/u.s.-democracy-promotion-aim-lower-pub-63718.

Miller, Aaron David, and Richard Sokolsky. 2019. "5 Reasons Why Trump Is Right about Getting America Out of Syria." *Los Angeles Times*, January 3. https://www.latimes.com/opinion/op-ed/la-oe-miller-sokolosky-syria-20190103-story.html.

Morris, Benny. 2003. *The Birth of the Palestinian Refugee Problem Revisited*. Cambridge: Cambridge University Press.

Mueller, John. 2012. *Atomic Obsession: Nuclear Alarmism from Hiroshima to Al-Qaeda*. New York: Oxford University Press.

Muravchik, Joshua. 1991. "At Last, Pax Americana." *New York Times*, January 24, sec. Opinion. https://www.nytimes.com/1991/01/24/opinion/at-last-pax-americana.html.

Murphy, Chris. 2021. "America's Middle East Policy Is Outdated and Dangerous." *Foreign Affairs*, February 19. https://www.foreignaffairs.com/articles/united-states/2021-02-19/americas-middle-east-policy-outdated-and-dangerous.

Nadeem, Reem. 2021. "Two Decades Later, the Enduring Legacy of 9/11." Pew Research Center, September 2. https://www.pewresearch.org/politics/2021/09/02/two-decades-later-the-enduring-legacy-of-9-11/.

"National Security Strategy." 2022. Accessed November 1, 2022. https://www.whitehouse.gov/wp-content/uploads/2022/10/Biden-Harris-Administrations-National-Security-Strategy-10.2022.pdf.

"National Strategy for Counterterrorism." 2011. Accessed March 3, 2022. https://obamawhitehouse.archives.gov/sites/default/files/counterterrorism_strategy.pdf.

"National Strategy for Counterterrorism of the United States of America." 2018. Accessed March 3, 2022. https://www.dni.gov/files/NCTC/documents/news_documents/NSCT.pdf.

Newsom, David D. 1981. "America Engulfed." *Foreign Policy*, no. 43: 17–32.

New York Times. 1991. "The New World Order So Far." January 20, sec. Opinion. https://www.nytimes.com/1991/01/20/opinion/the-new-world-order-so-far.html.

"Nuclear Posture Review." 2018. Department of Defense. Accessed November 14, 2022. https://media.defense.gov/2018/Feb/02/2001872886/-1/-1/1/2018-NUCLEAR-POSTURE-REVIEW-FINAL-REPORT.PDF.

Obama, Barack. 2020. *A Promised Land*. New York: Crown.

Office of the Director of National Intelligence. 2021. "Climate Change and International Responses Increasing Challenges to US National Security through 2040." National Intelligence Estimate NIC-NIE-2021-10030-A. Washington, DC: National Intelligence Council. Accessed March 2, 2022. https://www.dni.gov/files/ODNI/documents/assessments/NIE_Climate_Change_and_National_Security.pdf.

Office of the Historian. "The 1928 Red Line Agreement." Accessed May 6, 2021. https://history.state.gov/milestones/1921-1936/red-line.

"Open RAN Policy Question FAQs." Accessed March 15, 2023. https://www.openranpolicy.org/faqs/.

ORC International. "Opinion Research Corporation Poll: January 1975." https://doi.org/10.25940/ROPER-31107920.

Oren, Michael B. 2002. *Six Days of War: June 1967 and the Making of the Modern Middle East*. New York: Oxford University Press.

Painter, David. 2012. "Oil and the American Century." *Journal of American History* 99 (1): 24–39.

Parker, Richard B. 1993. *The Politics of Miscalculation in the Middle East*. Indiana Masterpiece Editions Series. Bloomington: Indiana University Press.

"Peace to Prosperity: A Vision to Improve the Lives of the Palestinian and Israeli People." 2020. https://trumpwhitehouse.archives.gov/wp-content/uploads/2020/01/Peace-to-Prosperity-0120.pdf.

Perle, Richard. 2001. "The U.S. Must Strike at Saddam Hussein." *New York Times*, December 28, sec. Opinion. https://www.nytimes.com/2001/12/28/opinion/the-us-must-strike-at-saddam-hussein.html.

Pillar, Paul R., Andrew Bacevich, Annelle Sheline, and Trita Parsi. "A New U.S. Paradigm for the Middle East: Ending America's Misguided Policy of Domination." 2020. Quincy Institute for Responsible Statecraft. July 17. https://quincyinst.org/2020/07/17/ending-americas-misguided-policy-of-middle-east-domination/.

Porter, Patrick. 2018. "Why America's Grand Strategy Has Not Changed: Power, Habit, and the U.S. Foreign Policy Establishment." *International Security* 42 (4): 9–46.

Power, Samantha. 2019. *The Education of an Idealist*. New York: HarperCollins.

"President Bush Discusses Freedom in Iraq and Middle East." 2003. November 6. https://georgewbush-whitehouse.archives.gov/news/releases/2003/11/20031106-2.html.

"President Bush Outlines Iraqi Threat." 2002. October 7. https://georgewbush-whiteho use.archives.gov/news/releases/2002/10/20021007-8.html.

"President Bush Presses for Peace in the Middle East." 2003. May 9. https://georgewbush-whitehouse.archives.gov/news/releases/2003/05/20030509-11.html.

"President Declares 'Freedom at War with Fear.'" 2001. September 20. https://georgewb ush-whitehouse.archives.gov/news/releases/2001/09/20010920-8.html.

"President George H. W. Bush: Address before a Joint Session of Congress, September 11, 1990." https://millercenter.org/the-presidency/presidential-speeches/september-11-1990-address-joint-session-congress.

"Presidential Approval Ratings—George W. Bush." 2008. *Gallup.com*. https://news.gallup.com/poll/116500/Presidential-Approval-Ratings-George-Bush.aspx.

"Press Release from Office of Senator JFK to Secretary of State, Dulles, March 5, 1956." JFK Presidential Library.

"Public Papers of the Presidents of the United States: Richard M. Nixon (1970)—Content Details-PPP-1970-Book1." Accessed June 18, 2021. https://www.govinfo.gov/app/deta ils/https%3A%2F%2Fwww.govinfo.gov%2Fapp%2Fdetails%2FPPP-1970-book1.

Quandt, William B. 1992. "Lyndon Johnson and the June 1967 War: What Color Was the Light?" *Middle East Journal* 46 (Spring): 198–228.

Quandt, William B. 2005. *Peace Process: American Diplomacy and the Arab-Israel Conflict since 1967*. Washington, DC: Brookings Institution Press and University of California Press.

"Questions from Louis Harris & Associates Poll: January 1974 (Roper #31107689): Roper IPoll—Roper Center for Public Opinion Research." Accessed May 13, 2022. https://ropercenter.cornell.edu/ipoll/study/31107689/questions#62e603a3-c9a4-4f7d-b2f1-7d64dbdb7bc4.

"Questions from Louis Harris & Associates Poll: August 1975 (Roper #31107868): Roper IPoll—Roper Center for Public Opinion Research." Accessed May 13, 2022. https://ropercenter.cornell.edu/ipoll/study/31107868/questions#a1a79115-fb2a-421c-9307-e553a507a1c6.

"Remarks as Prepared for Delivery by Assistant to the President for Homeland Security, Dr. Elizabeth Sherwood-Randall on the Future of the U.S. Counterterrorism

Mission: Aligning Strategy, Policy, and Resources." 2021. September 9. https://www.
    whitehouse.gov/briefing-room/speeches-remarks/2021/09/09/remarks-by-assistant-
    to-the-president-for-homeland-security-dr-liz-sherwood-randall-on-the-future-of-
    the-u-s-counterterrorism-mission-aligning-strategy-policy-and-resources/.
"Remarks by President Biden on the Terrorist Attacks in Israel, October 10, 2023." 2023.
    https://www.whitehouse.gov/briefing-room/speeches-remarks/2023/10/10/remarks-
    by-president-biden-on-the-terrorist-attacks-in-israel-2/.
"Remarks by Senator John F. Kennedy at Yankee Stadium, New York, New York, on April
    29, 1956." 1956. *JFK Library.* https://www.jfklibrary.org/archives/other-resources/
    john-f-kennedy-speeches/yankee-stadium-19560429.
"Remarks by the President at Cairo University." 2009. June 4. https://obamawhitehouse.
    archives.gov/the-press-office/remarks-president-Cairo-university-6-04-09.
"Remarks by the President in Address to the Nation on Libya." 2011. March 28. https://
    obamawhitehouse.archives.gov/the-press-office/2011/03/28/remarks-President-addr
    ess-nation-libya.
"Remarks by the President on the Middle East and North Africa." 2011. May 19. https://
    obamawhitehouse.archives.gov/the-press-office/2011/05/19/remarks-president-mid
    dle-east-and-north-africa.
Rice, Condoleezza. 2005. "Remarks at the American University in Cairo." June 20. https://
    2001-2009.state.gov/secretary/rm/2005/48328.htm.
Rice, Condoleezza. 2017. *Democracy: Stories from the Long Road to Freedom.*
    New York: Twelve Books.
Ricks, Thomas. 2006. *Fiasco: The American Military Adventure in Iraq.* New York: Penguin.
Robinson, Glenn E. 2020. *Global Jihad: A Brief History.* Stanford, CA: Stanford
    University Press.
Rogin, Josh. 2022. "America's Gulf 'Allies' Are Now Putin's Enablers." *Washington Post,*
    May 5. https://www.washingtonpost.com/opinions/2022/05/05/saudi-arabia-uae-help
    ing-putin-hurting-us-biden-allies-gulf-russia/.
Rosen, Armin. 2021. "Washington's Weirdest Think Tank." *Tablet Magazine,* April 28.
    https://www.tabletmag.com/sections/news/articles/quincy-trita-parsi-soros-koch
    -armin-rosen.
Rosentiel, Tom. 2006. "The U.S. Public's Pro-Israel History." Pew Research Center. July 19.
    https://www.pewresearch.org/2006/07/19/the-us-publics-proisrael-history/.
Rudd, Kevin. 2022. "The World According to Xi Jinping." *Foreign Affairs,* December.
Rumley, Grant. 2022. "China's Security Presence in the Middle East: Redlines and
    Guidelines for the United States." Policy Notes 123. October 18. Washington,
    DC: Washington Institute for Near East Policy. https://www.washingtoninstitute.org/
    policy-analysis/chinas-security-presence-middle-east-redlines-and-guidelines-uni
    ted-states.
Rutledge, Ian. 2006. *Addicted to Oil: America's Relentless Drive for Energy Security.*
    London: I. B. Tauris.
Saad, Lydia. 2016. "Americans' Views toward Israel Remain Firmly Positive." *Gallup.com,*
    February 29. https://news.gallup.com/poll/189626/americans-views-toward-israel-
    remain-firmly-positive.aspx.
Saad, Lydia. 2023. "Democrats' Sympathies in Middle East Shift to Palestinians." *Gallup.
    com,* March 16. https://news.gallup.com/poll/472070/democrats-sympathies-middle-
    east-shift-palestinians.aspx.

Saba, Yousef. 2021. "UAE Seeks $1 Trillion in Economic Activity with Israel by 2031." *Reuters*, September 14, sec. Middle East. https://www.reuters.com/world/middle-east/uae-aims-1-trillion-activity-with-israel-by-2031-2021-09-14/.

Sachar, Howard. 2007. *A History of Israel: From the Rise of Zionism to Our Time.* 3rd ed. New York: Alfred A. Knopf.

"Saddam Must Go." 1997. *Washington Examiner*, November 17. https://www.washing tonexaminer.com/weekly-standard/saddam-must-go.

Salman, Ahmed, and Rozlyn Engel. 2020. "Making U.S. Foreign Policy Work Better for the Middle Class." Washington, DC: Carnegie Endowment for International Peace. https://carnegieendowment.org/files/USFP_FinalReport_final1.pdf.

Samuels, Ben. 2022. "Israel's Ukraine Position Will Hurt U.S. Ties, Warns Republican Congressman." *Haaretz*, March 21. https://www.haaretz.com/israel-news/.premium-failure-to-assist-ukraine-militarily-will-affect-u-s-aid-to-israel-republican-says-1.10688375.

Samuels, David. 2016. "The Aspiring Novelist Who Became Obama's Foreign-Policy Guru." *New York Times*, May 5, sec. Magazine. https://www.nytimes.com/2016/05/08/magazine/the-aspiring-novelist-who-became-obamas-foreign-policy-guru.html.

Schanzer, Jonathan, Shira Efron, Martijn Rasser, and Alice Hickson. 2022. "Aligning U.S.-Israeli Cooperation on Technology Issues and China." Center for a New American Security. March 9. https://www.cnas.org/publications/reports/aligning-u-s-israeli-cooperation-on-technology-issues-and-china.

Scheinmann, Gabriel. 2022. "The U.S. Should Want a Cold War with China." *Wall Street Journal*, February 10. https://www.wsj.com/articles/the-us-should-want-a-cold-war-with-china-xi-jinping-taiwan-geopolitics-military-confrontation-competition-biden-democracy-11644510051.

Selby, Jan, Omar S. Dahi, Christiane Fröhlich, and Mike Hulme. 2017. "Climate Change and the Syrian Civil War Revisited." *Political Geography* 60 (September): 232–44. doi:10.1016/j.polgeo.2017.05.007.

Seldin, Jeff. 2023. "US Calls Hamas Attack 'ISIS-Level Savagery.'" *Voice of America*, October 9. https://www.voanews.com/a/us-calls-hamas-attack-isis-level-savagery-/7303672.html.

Senor, Dan, and Saul Singer. 2011. *Start-Up Nation: The Story of Israel's Economic Miracle.* New York: Grand Central Publishing.

"Settlement Watch." 2022. *Peace Now.* Accessed May 13. https://peacenow.org.il/en/categ ory/settlement-watch.

Sharp, Jeremy M. 2021. "Egypt: Background and U.S. Relations." RL33003. Washington, DC: Congressional Research Service. https://sgp.fas.org/crs/mideast/RL33003.pdf.

Sharp, Jeremy M. 2022. "U.S. Foreign Aid to Israel." RL33222. Washington, DC: Congressional Research Service. https://crsreports.congress.gov/product/pdf/RL/RL33222/44.

Shihabi, Ali. 2022. "Ali Shihabi علي الشهابي on Twitter:" *Twitter.* Accessed October 10. https://twitter.com/alishihabi/status/1578783193221959681.

"Speech by Senator John F. Kennedy, Zionists of America Convention, Statler Hilton Hotel, New York, NY: The American Presidency Project." 1960. August 26. https://www.presidency.ucsb.edu/documents/speech-senator-john-f-kennedy-zionists-amer ica-convention-statler-hilton-hotel-new-york-ny.

Stang, Gerald. 2016. "Climate Challenges in the Middle East: Rethinking Environmental Cooperation." Washington, DC: Middle East Institute.

Stein, Aaron Michael. 2015. "Kilowatts or Kilotons." PhD thesis, King's College London.

Stillman, Norman. 2021. *The Jews of Arab Lands in Modern Times*. Lincoln, NE: Jewish Publication Society.

Strobel, Warren, and Nancy Youssef. 2021. "F-35 Sale to U.A.E. Imperiled Over U.S. Concerns about Ties to China—WSJ." *Wall Street Journal*, May 25. https://www.wsj.com/articles/f-35-sale-to-u-a-e-imperiled-over-u-s-concerns-about-ties-to-china-11621949050.

Sullivan, Andrew. 2003. "Yes, a War Would Be Moral." *Time*, March 3. http://content.time.com/time/subscriber/article/0,33009,1004321-1,00.html.

"Summary of the National Defense Strategy of the United States of America: Sharpening the American Military's Competitive Edge." 2018. Department of Defense. https://dod.defense.gov/Portals/1/Documents/pubs/2018-National-Defense-Strategy-Summary.pdf.

Takeyh, Ray. 2021. *The Last Shah: America Iran, and the Fall of the Pahlavi Dynasty*. New Haven, CT: Yale University Press.

Talbott, Strobe. 1995. "Why NATO Should Grow." *The New York Review of Books*, August 10. https://www.nybooks.com/articles/1995/08/10/why-nato-should-grow/.

Tannenwald, Nina. 2005. "Stigmatizing the Bomb: Origins of Nuclear Taboo." *International Security* 29 (4): 5–49.

Taylor, Matthew. 2017. "Climate Change 'Will Create World's Biggest Refugee Crisis.'" *The Guardian*, November 2, sec. Environment. https://www.theguardian.com/environment/2017/nov/02/climate-change-will-create-worlds-biggest-refugee-crisis.

Thrall, A. Trevor, and Erik Goepner. 2017. "Step Back: Lessons from U.S. Foreign Policy from the Failed War on Terror." Policy Analysis, no. 814. June 26. Cato Institute. https://www.cato.org/sites/cato.org/files/pubs/pdf/pa-814.pdf.

"Tripartite Declaration Regarding the Armistice Borders: Statement by the Governments of the United States, the United Kingdom, and France." 1950. Avalon Project, Yale Law School. https://avalon.law.yale.edu/20th_century/mid001.asp.

Trump, Donald J. 2015. "Presidential Announcement Speech." *Time*. June 16. https://time.com/3923128/donald-trump-announcement-speech/.

Turner, Stansfield. 1991. "To a New World Order." *Christian Science Monitor*, October 30. https://www.csmonitor.com/1991/1030/30181.html.

"2020 Country Reports on Human Rights Practices." 2021. United States Department of State. March 30. https://www.state.gov/reports/2020-country-reports-on-human-rights-practices/.

"UN Security Council Resolution 242." 1967. https://peacemaker.un.org/sites/peacemaker.un.org/files/SCRes242%281967%29.pdf.

Vitalis, Robert. 2021. *America's Kingdom: Mythmaking on the Saudi Oil Frontier*. Stanford, CA: Stanford University Press.

Wall Street Journal. 2002. "How to Liberate Iraq." October 8, sec. Opinion. https://www.wsj.com/articles/SB1034036495773276720.

Walt, Stephen. 2018. *The Hell of Good Intentions: America's Foreign Policy Elite and the Decline of U.S. Primacy*. New York: Farrar, Straus & Giroux.

Walt, Stephen M. 2018. "The World Wants You to Think Like a Realist." *Foreign Policy*, May 30. https://foreignpolicy.com/2018/05/30/the-world-wants-you-to-think-like-a-realist/.

Waltz, Kenneth N. 1979. *Theory of International Politics*. New York: McGraw Hill.

Waltz, Kenneth N. 1981. "The Spread of Nuclear Weapons: More May Be Better." *The Adelphi Papers* 21 (171). https://doi.org/10.1080/05679328108457394.

Waltz, Kenneth. 2001. *Man, the State, and War: A Theoretical Analysis. Topical Studies in International Relations.* New York: Columbia University Press.

Washington Post. 2022. "The Post Endorses Glenn Ivey for Maryland's 4th District Democratic Primary," May 24. https://www.washingtonpost.com/opinions/2022/05/24/glenn-ivey-maryland-4th-district-primary-endorsement-2022/.

Waterbury, John. 2013. "The Political Economy of Climate Change in the Arab Region." The Arab Human Development Report Research Paper Series. United Nations Development Programme. http://citeseerx.ist.psu.edu/viewdoc/download?doi=10.1.1.363.5511&rep=rep1&type=pdf.

Weiss, Michael. 2012. "Break the Stalemate! A Blueprint for a Military Intervention in Syria." *The New Republic*, February 9. https://newrepublic.com/article/100599/syrian-intervention-humanitarian-alawite-assad-crisis.

Weiss, Michael. 2012. "Threat of Force Would Work." *New York Times*, March 30. https://www.nytimes.com/roomfordebate/2012/03/26/stopping-assad-saving-syria/threat-of-force-would-work.

Wertheim, Stephen. 2019. "The Only Way to End 'Endless War.'" *New York Times*, September 14, sec. Opinion. https://www.nytimes.com/2019/09/14/opinion/sunday/endless-war-america.html.

"West Bank." 2022. In *The World Factbook.* Central Intelligence Agency. https://www.cia.gov/the-world-factbook/countries/west-bank/.

Wezeman, Pieter D., Alexandra Kuimova, and Siemon T. Wezeman. 2022. "Trends in International Arms Transfers, 2021." Stockholm: SIPRI.

Wilford, Hugh. 2017. *America's Great Game.* New York: Basic Books.

World Islamic Front Statement Urging Jihad against Jews and Crusaders. 1998. Accessed April 6, 2022. https://irp.fas.org/world/para/docs/980223-fatwa.htm.

"Worldwide Manpower Distribution by Geographical Area." 1990. United States Department of Defense Directorate for Information Operations and Reports. June 30, 1990. (AD-A228 509).

Yergin, Daniel. 2009. *The Prize: The Epic Quest for Oil, Money, and Power.* New York: Simon & Schuster.

Young, Karen. 2022. "How Russia's Invasion of Ukraine Will Impact Energy Markets." *Al-Monitor*, February 28. https://www.al-monitor.com/originals/2022/02/how-russias-invasion-ukraine-will-impact-energy-markets.

Zakaria, Fareed. 2003. "It's Time to Talk to the World." *Newsweek*, January 26. https://www.newsweek.com/its-time-talk-world-135205.

Zaken, Danny. 2021. "Qatar, Israel Reach Agreement on Diamond Trade." *Al-Monitor*, December 15. https://www.al-monitor.com/originals/2021/12/qatar-israel-reach-agreement-diamond-trade.

Zaken, Danny. 2022. "Israelis Begin Doing Deals in Saudi Arabia." *Al-Monitor*, June 2. https://www.al-monitor.com/originals/2022/06/israelis-begin-doing-deals-saudi-arabia.

Index

For the benefit of digital users, indexed terms that span two pages (e.g., 52–53) may, on occasion, appear on only one of those pages.

Abbas, Mahmoud, 56–58, 101
Abdalla, Abdulkhaleq, 114
Abraham Accords (2020), 52, 53, 101–2
Abu Nidal Organization, 81
Afghanistan, 10–11, 27
al-Assad, Bashar, 3–4, 118–19
Almarzoqi, Mansour, 113–14
American Airborne Warning and Control
    Systems, 111
American Israel Public Affairs Committee
    (AIPAC), 61, 62–63
Anglo-Iranian Oil Company (AIOC), 19,
    20
Anglo-Persian Oil Company, 19
antiwar demonstrations, 15
Arabian American Oil Company
    (Aramco), 18–19
Arab-Israeli peace attempt, 30–31
Arab Peace Initiative (2001), 52
Arab Spring, 89–90, 116
Arafat, Yasir, 70
Arms Export Control Act, 48
Arrow anti-ballistic missile system, 48
authoritarianism, 4, 8–10, 34, 35, 71–73,
    75–76, 85–86, 89, 91, 109, 124–25,
    129

al-Baghdadi, Abu Bakr, 2–3, 137
Baker, James, 65
Balfour Declaration (1917), 39–40, 57
Bardarash Refugee Camp, 1–6, 13–14
Belafonte, Harry, 15
Belt and Road Initiative (China), 150
Ben Ali, Zine al Abidine, 89
Ben-Gurion, David, 54
Biden, Joe
    China and, 150–53

inauguration, 10
Israeli-Palestinian conflict and, 132–34
Joint Comprehensive Plan of Action
    and, 116–17, 124
Saudi Arabia and, 7, 114–15
against terrorism, 136–37, 139
US-Middle East policy, 112, 124–25,
    127, 132–34, 136–40, 150–53, 156
Binational Science Foundation (BSF),
    49–50
bin Laden, Osama, 59–60, 136
bin Salman, Mohammed, 114–15, 117–18,
    152–53
bin Zayed, Abu Dhabi Mohammed, 119
Bissell, George, 16
Blinken, Antony, 5
Boot, Max, 79–80
Bouazizi, Mohamed, 89
Boycott, Divestment, and Sanctions (BDS)
    movement, 54
Browne, Jackson, 15
Build Back Better World, 150–51, 153
Bureau of Near Eastern Affairs, 83
Bush, George H. W.
    attempts to contain Hussein, Saddam,
        73–75
    Iran and, 91
    Saudi Arabia and, 15, 29–30
    US global order and, 65, 67–68, 69–70
    US-Middle East policy, 15, 29–30,
        61–62, 65
Bush, George W.
    Israeli-Palestinian conflict and, 82–87
    US democratic transformation goals,
        76–82
    US global order and, 82–87
    US-Middle East policy, 48

Bush, Jeb, 97–98
Bush v. Gore (2000), 93

California Arabian Standard Oil
    Company, 18
Carter, Jimmy, 26, 27
Carter Doctrine, 27–28, 29, 32, 99, 102–3
Center for Climate and Security, 144–45
Center for International Policy, 106–7
Central Command (CENTCOM), 29, 31–32
Chalabi, Ahmed, 74–75
China
    Belt and Road Initiative, 150
    Biden, Joe and, 150–53
    Egypt and, 120
    impact on US-Middle East policy,
        147–53
    Iran and, 149
    Saudi Arabia and, 119, 148–49, 152–53
    Trump, Donald and, 150
Chinese Communist Party, 120
civil rights movement, 93
civil-society groups, 85–86
Clarke, Richard, 79–80
climate crisis, 143–47
Clinton, Bill
    attempts to contain Hussein, Saddam,
        74–76
    Declaration of Principles and, 70–71
    domestic policy and, 69–70
    dual containment of Iraq and Iran,
        30–31
    election win, 68
    human rights and, 69–70
    peace talks, 70
    US democratic transformation goals,
        73–76
    USISTC and, 50–51
    US-Middle East policy, 5, 8
Clinton, Hillary, 96
Cold War, 4–5, 10–11
Coolidge, Calvin, 17
coup d'état, 20, 23, 115–16, 118–19
COVID-19 pandemic, 130, 147
Cruz, Ted, 121–22

David's Sling, 48
Declaration of Principles (1993), 70–71

*Democracy: Stories from the Long Road to
    Freedom* (Rice), 81–82
Democratic Front for the Liberation of
    Palestine, 81
Democratic Republic of Yemen, 20–21
Dhahran airfield project, 18–19
Dhofar Rebellion, 22–23
al-Dura, Mohanned, 82–83

Earnest Will naval escort, 29
economic shock therapy, 68
Edwards, Donna, 62–63
Egypt
    China and, 120
    climate crisis and, 146
    human rights and, 109–10, 120
    Israeli-British-French action against, 41
    liberal democracies and, 69
    Muslim Brotherhood, 115–16
    Obama, Barack and, 88–89, 92–93
    US relations, 34–35, 115
Egypt-Israel peace, 35
Eisenhower, Dwight D., 39–41
energy security, 12, 32–36
environmental concerns, 143–47
Erdoğan, Recep Tayyip, 115–16, 118–19
Eshkol, Levi, 44
ethno-nationalism, 68–69
ethno-religious nationalism, 68–69
extremism, 2–3, 5, 10, 26, 59–60, 72, 76–
    77, 88, 115–16, 118–19, 126, 135–38

al-Faisal, Turki, 113
Foreign Affairs, 107
Fourth Geneva Convention (1949), 55–56
Freedom Agenda (2003), 10, 85–86,
    151–52

General Electric (GE), 67
General Security Service, 59
Generation X, 67
Germany, 16, 18
global war on terror, 3–4, 105, 108–9, 136
Gorbachev, Mikhail, 69–70
Graham, Lindsey, 121–22
Grand Ethiopian Renaissance Dam
    (GERD), 146
Grand Mosque seizure (1979), 26

Green Zone, 2, 99
Gulf Cooperation Council, 150–51

Haftar, Khalifa, 119
Hamas, 57–58, 86–87, 131–35
Harriman, Averell, 21
Hezbollah, 132, 135
Hizballah, 121–22
Holocaust, 39–40, 45, 89
Houthis, 113–14
Hull, Cordell, 18
human rights
    Biden, Joe and, 7
    Clinton, Bill and, 69–70
    Egypt and, 109–10, 120
    Israel and, 54
    protection of, 109–10, 124–25, 152–53
    as threat to power, 121
    US indifference to, 34–35
    violations of, 57, 124, 128, 154
Hussein, Saddam
    Bush, George H. W. and, 73–75
    Clinton, Bill and, 74–76
    invasion of Kuwait, 29–32, 111, 112
    Iran and, 28
    Palestinian support by, 81
    US attempts to contain, 2–3, 73–76
    weapons of mass destruction and, 9

imperial Japan, 18
Indyk, Martin, 30–31, 71
Institute for Policy Studies, 106–7
International Atomic Energy Agency,
    92–93, 142
International Security, 107
Iran
    Bush, George H. W. and, 91
    China and, 149
    climate crisis, 143–44
    Clinton, Bill and, 30–31
    Hussein, Saddam and, 28
    Iraq invasion of, 28–29
    Islamic Republic of Iran, 25–26
    Joint Comprehensive Plan of Action,
        9–10, 92–96, 102, 116–17, 139–40
    Nixon Doctrine and, 22–23
    nuclear weapons proliferation risk,
        140–42

Obama, Barack and, 9–10, 61–62,
    91–92, 95
oil discovery in, 19–20
Trump, Donald and, 98–101
US-Iran relations, 91
US oil security and, 9–10, 32–36
Iran Air Flight 655 attack, 36
Iran hostage crisis (1979), 26
Iran-Iraq War, 36
Iraq
    Bardarash Refugee Camp, 1–6, 13–14
    climate crisis, 143–44
    Clinton, Bill and, 30–31
    invasion of Iran, 28–29
    invasion of Kuwait, 29–32
    Iran-Iraq War, 36
    Obama, Barack and, 104
    Operation Iraqi Freedom, 15, 81, 85,
        110
    Trump, Donald and, 96–102
    US invasion of, 2–3
    US oil security and, 32–36
    withdrawal from Kuwait, 15
Iraqi National Congress (INC), 74–76
Iraq Liberation Act (1998), 75–76
Iraq Petroleum Corporation, 17
Iron Dome, 48–49
Islamic Republic of Iran, 25–26. *See also*
    Iran
Islamic Resistance Movement, 57
Islamic Revolutionary Guard Corps, 99,
    100
Islamic State (ISIS), 1–3, 96–97, 118–19,
    136, 137, 167n.22
Israel
    action against Egypt, 41
    American commitment to, 47–52
    Arab-Israeli peace attempt, 30–31
    Declaration of Principles, 70–71
    early years, 39–41
    economic development, 49–52
    Egypt-Israel peace, 35
    as global power, 52–55
    impact of Zionism, 55–64
    Johnson administration and, 44–45
    Kennedy administration and, 41–44,
        63–64
    Nixon administration and, 45–47

Israel (*cont.*)
    Obama, Barack and, 88–96
    political turbulence, 37–39
    Second Intifada, 8–9, 58–59, 72–73, 81,
        82–83
    State of Israel, 37–38, 43, 132, 164n.67
    threats to security, 4–5
    Trump, Donald and, 53
    US democratic transformation goals for,
        8–9, 73–76
    US energy security and, 12
    Yom Kippur War, 23–24
Israel Defense Forces (IDF), 44–45, 46
Israel-Hamas war (2023), 58–59
Israeli Defense Forces, 23
Israeli-Palestinian conflict
    Biden, Joe and, 132–34
    Bush, George W. and, 82–87
    climate crisis and, 145–46
    Trump, Donald and, 101–2
    US and, 8–9, 82–87, 131–35
Israel lobby, 61–62
Ivey, Glenn, 62–63

jihadists, 59–60, 135
Johnson, Lyndon B., 21, 44–45
al-Jabouri, Khaled Ayyad Ahmad, 137
Joint Comprehensive Plan of Action
        (JCPOA), 9–10, 92–96, 102, 116–17,
        139–40
Jordan, 55–56
J Street, 62–63

Karine A, 83
Kataib Hizbollah, 100
Kennedy, John F., 34, 41–44, 63–64, 142
Khamenie, Ayatollah Ali, 91
Khatami, Mohamed, 91
Khomeini, Ayatollah Ruhollah, 25–26, 29
Kim Jong-un, 98
Kinzinger, Adam, 121–22
Kissinger, Henry, vi, 23, 143
Koch, Charles, 107–8
Kurds/Kurdish State, 1–3, 73, 74–75, 95,
        118
Kuwait
    Iraq invasion of, 29–32
    Iraq withdrawal from, 15

Soviet Union and, 28–29
US oil security and, 32–36

Lake, Anthony A., 70–71
Lavrov, Sergey, 154
Leaf, Barbara, 124–25
leaflet vandalism, 132–33
Libertarians, 107–8
Libya, 90–91
limited-access agreements, 21–22
Lipton, David, 68

Madrid Peace Conference, 69–70
Marshall Plan, 19
Massie, Thomas, 133–34
McCarthy, Kevin, 121–22
McGurk, Brett, 124–25
Mearsheimer, John, 111
Meir, Golda, 43, 46
Mineral Leasing Act (1920), 17
Missile Technology Control Regime
        (MTCR), 142
Mossadegh, Mohammed, 20
Mother Jones, 106–7
Mubarak, Hosni, 35, 85–86, 89
al-Muhandis, Abul Mahdi, 100
Muslim Brotherhood, 92–93, 115–16
Myers, Richard B., 79–80

nakba, 55–56
Nasser, Gamal Abdel, 34, 41, 117–18, 135
Nation, 106–7
National Security Council, 83
Naval Vessels Transfer Act (2008), 47–48
Nazi Germany, 18
neocolonialism, 7–8
Neorealists, 107
Netanyahu, Benjamin, 72
New York Times Magazine, 94
Nixon, Richard M., 23–24, 43, 45–47
Nixon Doctrine, 21–23
non-proliferation goals, 139–43

Obama, Barack
    Egypt and, 88–89, 92–93
    Iran and, 9–10, 61–62, 91–92, 95
    Iraq and, 104
    Israel and, 88–96

Joint Comprehensive Plan of Action
    and, 9–10, 92–96, 102, 116–17
Palestine and, 88–96
Saudi Arabia and, 88–89
Syria and, 90–91
Syrian uprising and, 4, 116
against terrorism, 136, 138
Turkey and, 88–89
US-Middle East policy, 88–96, 102–3
withdrawal from Iraq, 104
offshore balancing, 110–11, 159n.45
oil embargo (1973), 24–25
oil resources
    Allied agreement over, 17–18
    dual containment of Iraq and Iran,
        30–32
    energy security and, 12, 32–36
    Nixon Doctrine and, 21–23
    oil embargo, 24–25
    US dependence on, 16–21
    US-Middle East policy, 15–16
    Western Europe reliance on, 19
    Yom Kippur War, 23–24
OPEC+, 114, 121, 154–55
Open Radio Access Network (ORAN),
    151–52
Operation Desert Storm/Desert Shield, 29,
    31–33, 35, 73
Operation Iraqi Freedom, 15, 81, 85, 110
Operation Prime Chance, 29
Organization of Petroleum Exporting
    Countries (OPEC), 23–24

Pahlavi, Mohamed Reza, 19, 158n.18
Pahlavi, Reza Shah, 19, 22–23
Pakistan, 143
Palestine. See also Israeli-Palestinian conflict
    Balfour Declaration, 39–40, 57
    Declaration of Principles, 70–71
    Hussein, Saddam support to, 81
    impact of Zionism, 55–64
    nakba, 55–56
    Obama, Barack and, 88–96
    Second Intifada, 8–9, 58–59, 72–73, 81,
        82–83
    UN Resolution 181 partitioning, 37–38
    US democratic transformation goals
        for, 73–76

Palestine Liberation Organization
    (PLO), 43
Palestinian Authority (PA), 58, 83, 86–87
Palestinian Liberation Organization
    (PLO), 70
Palestinian refugees, 56–57, 69
Paul, Rand, 104
People's Protection Units (YPG), 2–3
Peres, Shimon, 70
peshmerga. See Kurds/Kurdish State
Popular Front for the Liberation of
    Palestine, 81
Popular Mobilization Units, 2
Powell, Colin, 83
Progressives, 107–8
Project for the Next American Century
    (PNAC), 74
public-opinion polling in Middle East,
    162–63n.45
Putin, Vladimir, 112, 117–21, 153–54

al-Qaddafi, Muammar, 87, 89, 90–91
al-Qaeda, 59, 76–80
qualitative military edge (QME), 46–48
Quincy Institute for Responsible
    Statecraft, 107–8

Rabin, Yitzhak, 50–51, 70, 72
Reagan, Ronald, 48
Reagan Corollary, 28, 29, 32, 99, 102–3
Red Line Agreement (1928), 17–18
Reiner, Rob, 15
retrenchment efforts, 105–11
Rice, Condoleezza, 78–79, 81–82, 83
Rogin, Josh, 121
Rumsfeld, Donald, 79–80
Rusk, Dean, 21
Russia. See also Soviet Union
    impact on US-Middle East policy,
        147–55
    intervention in Syria, 118
    invasion of Ukraine, 7, 112–13, 115,
        130, 147, 154–55
    Putin, Vladimir, 112, 117–21, 153–54

Sachs, Jeffrey, 68
el-Sadat, Anwar, 35, 60
Saleh, Ali Abdallah, 89

Sarandon, Susan, 15
Al Saud, Abdallah bin Abdulaziz, 82–83
Al Saud, Abdulaziz bin Abdulrahman, 18
Al Saud, Faisal bin Adbulaziz, 25
Saudi Arabia
  Biden, Joe and, 7, 114–15
  Bush, George H. W. and, 15, 29–30
  China and, 119, 148–49, 152–53
  Dhahran airfield project, 18–19
  Grand Mosque seizure, 26
  Nixon Doctrine and, 22–23
  nuclear weapons proliferation risk,
    142–43
  Obama, Barack and, 88–89
  Standard Oil Company and, 18
  Trump, Donald and, 99
  US oil security and, 32–36
  US relations with, 23–25
  in Yemen, 35–36
  Yom Kippur War, 23–24
Saudi Arabian National Guard, 26
Schlesinger, James, 23
Schwarzkopf, Norman, 65
Scowcroft, Brent, 65
Second Intifada (early 2000s), 8–9, 58–59,
    72–73, 81, 82–83
September 11, 2001 attacks, 76
Shabak, 59
Sharon, Ariel, 72–73, 83
Shihabi, Ali, 114–15
al-Sisi, Abdel Fatah, 119
Soleimani, Qassem, 100–1
Soros, George, 107–8
Soviet–Afghan War, 27
Soviet Union
  collapse of, 10–11, 67
  Kuwait and, 28–29
  US containment of, 4–5
  US relations with, 19
Standard Oil Company, 18
State of Israel, 37–38, 43, 132, 164n.67. See
    also Israel
Strategic Defense Initiative (SDI), 48
Suez Canal, 17, 21, 23
Syria, 3–4, 90–91, 116
Syrian Democratic Forces, 2–3

Taliban, 116

terrorism
  Biden, Joe against, 136–37, 139
  global war on terror, 3–4, 105, 108–9,
    136
  Obama, Barack against, 136, 138
  Trump, Donald against, 136, 138
  US-Middle East policy against, 135–39
Treaty on the Non-Proliferation of Nuclear
    Weapons (NPT) (1968), 142
Tripartite Agreement (1950), 40, 42
Truman, Harry S., 39–40
Trump, Donald
  China and, 150
  Iran and, 98–101
  Iraq and, 96–102
  Israel and, 53
  Israeli-Palestinian conflict and, 101–2
  Joint Comprehensive Plan of Action
    and, 9–10, 116–17, 139–40
  racism of, 96–97
  Saudi Arabia and, 99
  against terrorism, 136, 138
  US-Middle East policy, 1–2, 96–103,
    105–7, 116
Tunisia, 89
Turkey, 2–3, 88–89, 120
Turkish airstrikes, 1, 3–4
Tutu, Desmond, 15

U-boats, 16
Ukraine, Russia's invasion of, 7, 112–13,
    115, 130, 147, 154–55
UN Educational, Social, and Cultural
    Organization, 53–54
UN General Assembly, 53–54
UN Human Rights Council, 53–54
United Nations High Commissioner for
    Refugees (UNHCR), 1
UN Resolution 181 partitioning Palestine,
    37–38
UN Security Council, 45
UN Special Commission on Palestine
    (UNSCOP), 159–60n.2
US global order
  Bush, George H. W. and, 65, 67–68,
    69–70
  Bush, George W. and, 82–87
  democratic transformation goals, 68–82

introduction to, 65–66
Israeli-Palestinian conflict and, 82–87
US invasion of Iraq (2003), 2–3
US-Iran relations, 91
US-Israel Binational Research
    Development Foundation (BIRD),
    50, 51
US-Israel Free Trade Agreement (FTA), 51
US-Israel Science and Technology
    Commission (USISTC), 50–51
US-Middle East policy
    Biden, Joe, 112, 124–25, 127, 132–34,
        136–40, 150–53, 156
    Bush, George H. W., 15, 29–30, 61–62, 65
    Bush, George W., 48
    chances for success, 6–7
    China's impact on, 147–53
    climate crisis and, 143–47
    Clinton, Bill, 5, 8
    future of, 11–14, 124–27, 129–55
    global war on terror, 3–4, 105, 108–9,
        136
    idealist impulse, 7–11
    introduction to, 2–3, 4
    non-proliferation goals, 139–43
    Obama, Barack, 88–96, 102–3
    offshore balancing, 110–11, 159n.45
    prime directive and, 129–55
    reduction efforts, 105–11
    retrenchment efforts, 105–11
    Russia's impact on, 147–55
    success and failure of, 127–29

against terrorism, 135–39
transformative agenda, 5
Trump, Donald, 1–2, 96–103, 105–7
waveform metaphor for, 155–56
withdrawal efforts, 105–11
US trade policy, 108

Wagner Group, 119
Walt, Stephen, 111
Warren, Elizabeth, 134
Washington Post, 121, 152–53
weapons of mass destruction, 9, 30–31, 74,
    80–81, 87, 126
Weinberger, Caspar, 28–29
Wilson, Harold, 21
Wolfowitz, Paul, 79–80
World Bank, 58
World Conference Against Racism, Racial
    Discrimination, Xenophobia and
    Related Intolerance, 53–54
World War I, 16–17
World War II, 18

Xi Jinping, 119

Yemen, 35–36
Yom Kippur War, 23–24, 46–47

al-Zawahiri, Ayman, 137
Zionism, 55–64
Zionist Organization of America (ZOA),
    42–43